JOHN FREETH

JOHN FREETH
1792

JOHN FREETH
(1731–1808)

*Political ballad-writer
and innkeeper*

JOHN HORDEN

LEOPARD'S HEAD PRESS

1993

Leopard's Head Press Ltd.,
2a Polstead Road,
Oxford OX2 6TN

© John Horden 1993

ISBN 0 904920 19 4

*The publication of this volume
has been assisted by a grant from the
Marc Fitch Fund,
which is gratefully acknowledged.*

British Library Cataloguing in Publication Data
CIP data for this book is available on request from
the British Library

Printed in Great Britain by Antony Rowe Ltd,
Bumper's Farm, Chippenham,
Wiltshire SN14 6QA

PREFACE

John Freeth was landlord of a celebrated tavern that became the meeting place of Birmingham radicals, and the ballads he nightly sang to his patrons were strongly weighted with social and political comment. Much about him epitomizes provincial opinion in late-Georgian England. For that alone (and he has other claims to attention) Freeth merits wider recognition. The purpose of this study is both to offer an introduction to his career and to provide a full analytical bibliography of all that he is known to have written. This is, therefore, not to be taken as an edition of his songs with the usual apparatus of introduction and notes. Rather, the Biographical Essay, Iconography, Bibliography, and Indexes are the substance of the book; to them, by way of example and no more, is appended an unannotated reading version of fifty of Freeth's characteristic songs and other pieces.

The Essay and the Iconography together provide the most extensive account of Freeth yet published, and it is hoped that they – perhaps aided by a sampling of the selected pieces – will adequately delineate him in his time and place. In the Bibliography Freeth's publications are analysed and the location of examples given, while the Indexes record the contents of each songster, identify all compositions by title and first line, and list the tunes to which Freeth set the words of his surviving compositions. Anyone seeking information about Freeth's life and work ought to be able to find here either that information itself or the point of departure for the next step in the enquiry.

ACKNOWLEDGEMENTS

My interest in Freeth and his contemporaries is of long standing, and my consequent indebtedness for scholarly assistance is proportionately large. Acknowledgement to individual scholars and collectors for particular help, and to various institutions for permission to use material in their custody, has generally been made in the text. But I would particularly like to record my appreciation of the many kindnesses that I have received over the years from the officers and staff of the Birmingham Reference Library, and of the City Museum and Art Gallery, Birmingham. As a small tribute to her memory I beg to mention my happy recollections of the late Dorothy McCulla of the Reference Library who so many times came to my aid.

The President and Committee of the Birmingham Book Club have treated my enquiries with the greatest courtesy and helpfulness. The University of Birmingham generously permits me to publish here for the first time six songs from Freeth's holograph manuscript of his *Modern Songs*, 1782 (BX5149.B2), as well to cite the manuscript in other contexts.

Mrs W. B. Stephens, beside initially typing all of Freeth's songs in each of their several versions (more than six hundred pieces all told), has also typed everything else found here, sometimes more than once. My colleague Dr Douglas Mack undertook the intricate business of computer-setting the entire bibliography. Miss Yvonne McClymont keyed the selection of songs, which Mr Martin Gray, also a colleague, then encoded. The Hon. Adrian Bullock has expedited virtually every aspect of production in its later stages. And Mr Roy Stephens, of the Leopard's Head Press, has proved himself an exemplary publisher. I am most sincerely grateful for all this assistance.

John Horden
University of Stirling

CONTENTS

List of illustrations   xiii
Abbreviations   xv

BIOGRAPHICAL ESSAY
   John Freeth: the Birmingham Poet   I

NOTES   35

ICONOGRAPHY
   Oils (Nos I–V)   47
   Pastels (Nos VI–VII)   49
   Engravings (Nos VIII–IX)   50
   Token coin (No. X)   51
   Waxwork (No. XI)   51
   Other attributions (Nos XII–XIII)   53

BIBLIOGRAPHY
   EPHEMERA
   Songs in newspapers (Nos 1–12)   55
   Broadside (No. 13)   58
   BOOKS AND PAMPHLETS
   The Political Songster, 1766, 1771, 1784, 1786,
      1790, 1798, (Nos 14–25)   59
   Inland Navigation, an Ode, 1769 (Nos 26–27)   66
   Wilkes's Enlargement, an Ode, 1770 (No. 28)   67
   The Warwickshire Medley [1780] (Nos 29–30)   67
   Modern Songs, 1782 (Nos 31–32)   69
   A Touch on the Times, 1783, 1803 (Nos 33–34)   70
   A Collection of New Songs, 1793 (No. 35)   71
   The Annual Political Songster, 1794 (No. 36)   72
   New Ballads, 1805 (No. 37)   73
   Complete Collection of Songs [1822] (No. 38)   74
   INVITATION CARDS
   1770–1803 (Nos 39–95)   74
   MANUSCRIPT
   [1782] (No. 96)   87

CONTENTS

LINES ATTRIBUTED TO FREETH
  (Nos 97–98)   88

INDEXES
  Table of Contents of Songsters   90
  Index of Song Titles   93
  Index of First Lines   108
  Index of Tunes   122

SONGS
  A dialogue [1766]   130
  Hospitality [1766]   131
  Inland navigation [1766]   133
  Taxation [1766]   135
  Wilkes's enlargement, an ode [1771]   136
  The French tonsor [1771]   139
  The jovial cocker [1771]   141
  The Royal commodore [1771]   143
  Bunker Hill; or, the soldier's lamentation [1780]   145
  Liberty's call [1780]   147
  Skipwith, Holte, and independency [1780]   148
  The pride of Worcester: on Sir Watkin Lewes's
    arrival [1780]   149
  British volunteers [MS 1782]   150
  On the glorious success of the English privateers
    [MS 1782]   151
  On the threaten'd invasion at the breaking out of
    the Spanish war [MS 1782]   152
  Scale of talent, a political cantata [MS 1782]   153
  The players' march: on information being laid for
    performing [MS 1782]   155
  The tripe eaters [MS 1782]   156
  The volunteers [MS 1782]   158
  Admiral Parker's engagement with the Dutch
    fleet [1782]   159
  Birmingham ale tasters [1782]   160
  Britain's glory [1782]   161
  Lord G. Gordon's procession [1782]   162
  Prescott's breeches; or, the old soldier's voyage to
    America [1782]   163

CONTENTS

The cottager's complaint: on the intended bill for
enclosing Sutton Coldfield [1782]   165
Britannia triumphant: on the glorious victory of
April 12, 1782 [1783]   166
The female canvasser: on the Westminster election
[1783]   167
The new window tax [1783]   169
Whipcord; or, the walking stationers [1784]   171
On Blanchard's aerial voyage to the Continent, a
balloon song [1785?]   173
Billy's quite too young [1786]   174
A strolling ballad-singer's ramble to London [1790]   175
Blood Royal [1790]   179
Botany Bay [1790]   180
John Wesley's prophesy [1790]   181
Song on the Regency Bill [1790]   183
The Birmingham overseers [1790]   184
The coach drivers; or, Billy's not too young [1790]   187
The diversion of quoits playing [1790]   188
Lord Macartney's embassy to China, a
Warwickshire ballad [1793]   191
Patentee pads [1793]   192
Alarms of war in the Spring of 1794 [1798]   194
More guineas, and less paper credit [1798]   196
On Admiral Nelson's victory: Britannia
triumphant [1798]   197
On the uncommon dearness of corn [1798]   198
The tars of old England. (Written on the day the
news came of Lord Howe's victory.) [1798]   200
Bull-baiting [1803]   201
Peace and plenty [1803]   202
Bonaparte's coronation [1805]   203
The piebald coalition [1805]   204

LIST OF ILLUSTRATIONS

(With the exception of the frontispiece, illustrations appear between pp. 48–49.)

(A roman numeral appearing in parentheses after the entry for an illustration in this list refers to the number in the iconography, where full details about that illustration may be found.)

John Freeth in 1792. (**VI**) (*frontispiece*)

1. John Freeth, probably aged 59. (**I**)

2. Members of the Jacobin Club in 1792. (**II**)

3. John Freeth. (**III**)

4. John Freeth (possibly by his friend James Bisset). (**IV**)

5/6. Engraved portrait frontispieces and letterpress title-pages of *The Political Songster* (1786) and *A Touch on the Times* (1803). (**VIII** and **IX**)

7. Freeth's Coffee-House.

8. Token coin as used in Freeth's Coffee-House. (**X**)

9. Freeth's invitation cards.

10. Freeth's invitation cards (continued).

11. Freeth's invitation cards (continued).

12. Manuscript of *Modern Songs* (1782).

Plan of Birmingham 1731, by William Westley. (*end-papers*)

Commemorative plaque near the former site in Birmingham of Freeth's Coffee-House. (*back panel of the dust jacket*)

ACKNOWLEDGEMENTS

The publishers would like to thank the following for permission to reproduce the illustrations:

Birmingham Museums and Art Gallery: 1, 2, 3, 4, 7

Birmingham Reference Library, Local Studies Department: 5, 6, 10, 11

The Keeper, Department of Coins and Medals, The British Museum: 8

The President and Committee of the Birmingham Book Club: 9

University of Birmingham: 12

The Birmingham Post: for the illustration of the commemorative plaque, which appears on the back panel of the dust jacket.

ABBREVIATIONS

Aris	*Aris's Birmingham Gazette*
BBkC	Birmingham Book Club
Bibliography	Bibliography of Freeth's songsters, invitation cards, and other works (arabic numerals), pp. 55–88
BirmUL	Birmingham University Library
BL	British Library (Reference Division)
BMAG	City of Birmingham Museums and Art Gallery
BRL	Birmingham Reference Library
BTHRC	British Transport Historical Records Collection, Public Record Office, London
Gaskell	Philip Gaskell, *John Baskerville: a Bibliography*, 1959
Harding	W.H.N. Harding bequest, Bodleian Library, Oxford
Hill	Joseph Hill, *The Book Makers of Old Birmingham*, 1907
Iconography	Iconography of Freeth (roman numerals), pp. 47–53
Jennings	H.J. Jennings, '"Poet" Freeth', *The Birmingham Examiner*, I, 1876, pp. 68–78
Johnson	John Johnson Collection, Bodleian Library, Oxford
Langford	J.A. Langford, *A Century of Birmingham Life* (second edition; 2 vols), 1870–71
Making of Birmingham	Robert K. Dent, *The Making of Birmingham*, 1894
Memoir	*Memoir of James Bisset written by himself*, ed. T.B. Dudley, 1904
Money	John Money, *Experience and Identity: Birmingham and the West Midlands 1760–1800*, 1977

ABBREVIATIONS

MSS Songs	James Bisset, Original MSS Songs (in Bisset's autograph), c.1805, BRL, press-mark: 184534
Old and New Birmingham	Robert K. Dent, *Old and New Birmingham* (3 vols), 1879–80
PL	Priestley Library within The Birmingham and Midland Institute (formerly The Birmingham Library)
PRO	Public Record Office, London
Reminiscences	James Bisset, *Reminiscences of James Bisset* (in Bisset's autograph), [c.1828–32], BRL, press-mark: 263924
Straus-Dent	Ralph Straus and Robert K. Dent, *John Baskerville*, 1907. (Numerals refer to examples of Baskerville's type-ornaments illustrated in Plate No. XIV)
Swinney	*Swinney's Birmingham and Stafford Chronicle*
Thieme-Becker	Conrad Ulrich Thieme and Felix Becker, *Allgemeines Lexicon der bildenden Künstler*, 1948–51
Timmins	Samuel Timmins, *The Buildings of Birmingham Past and Present*, 1866
Tomey	B. Vaughan Tomey, *The Birmingham Book Club* [c.1926] (typescript), BRL, press-mark: 441622
ULC	University Library, Cambridge
Vernal	'Joshua Vernal' in 'Memorabilia', *The Birmingham Journal*, 4 June 1856, p. 2

BIOGRAPHICAL ESSAY

John Freeth: the Birmingham Poet

John Freeth, who sometimes called himself 'John Free', must have been a notable figure in the Birmingham of his day – the Birmingham, that is, of the closing decades of the eighteenth century: the city of Boulton, Paul, and Watt, of Priestley and Baskerville, of the Lunar Society and the Bean Club. For forty years or more Freeth was landlord of a well-known tavern and coffee-house, much frequented by visitors to the town as well as by inhabitants, and the resort of locally prominent men. Here he nightly entertained the assembled company with songs of his own composition set to popular tunes. 'My hobby-horse and practice for thirty years past', he wrote in 1790, 'have been, to write songs upon the occurrence of remarkable events, and nature having supplied me with a voice somewhat suitable to my stile of composition, to sing them also, while their subjects were fresh upon every man's mind'.[1] Freeth gratefully acknowledged that this custom had been profitable to him, and that it had crowded his house with patrons in the evenings, and led him to friendships he might not otherwise have experienced. It also earned him the familiar style of 'Poet Freeth',[2] and secured his recommendation to posterity as 'the Birmingham Poet',[3] rather than by name.

Toward the end of his career Freeth described himself as 'a veteran in the class of political-ballad street-scribblers'.[4] As a final estimate this is too modest. More than a dozen collections of his songs were published during his lifetime, Baskerville being among the printers. Every indication is that they were all successful, and some of them were favourably noticed in the critical reviews. One of his songs, 'Britain's glory', achieved a wellnigh national popularity. Furthermore, Freeth issued printed invitations to his tavern written in verse, and with these he seems to have originated an unusual, if not unique, kind of trade-card. As for the man himself, it is clear that he was most highly regarded. Some measure of his standing is the number of times – unusually large in the eighteenth century for one who was a publican – that he sat for his portrait.[5] Five oil paintings (two of them at least by artists of repute) and two pastels are extant, and there is record of another portrait being paid for by subscription. Also (as William Godwin was to mention in a letter to Mary Wollstonecraft Godwin), Freeth had once been depicted in wax, probably by George Bullock.[6]

Yet his name is not to be found in the more authoritative reference books, and the few existing accounts of his work in histories of Birmingham are neither comprehensive nor always scholarly in intention. Although Freeth's career offers significant insights into the radical politics, and provincial social customs, of the period, recent specialist studies have found no occasion to explore it thoroughly.[7]

*   *   *

John Freeth, the son of Charles Freeth and his wife Mary, was born in Birmingham in 1731.[8] At this time Charles Freeth kept the Bell Tavern in Philip Street, Birmingham. By 1736 he had moved to Bell Street, where he became landlord of the Leicester Arms. This was the tavern, standing on the corner of Bell Street and Lease Lane, which was to become so well known as Freeth's Coffee-House during the years his son John presided there.[9]

Charles Freeth died before the end of 1765, by which time the Leicester Arms had passed to his widow. By 1768, perhaps at the death of his mother, John Freeth had become landlord of the Leicester Arms.[10] So he remained until his death in 1808.

Little is known of John Freeth's early years. It is believed that he was apprenticed to a brass-founder in Park Street, Birmingham, where Timothy Smith, later a prominent manufacturer in the town, was a fellow apprentice.[11]

One of Freeth's songs, which relates the adventures of a ballad-singer in making the journey from Birmingham to London on foot, may describe an episode in his own career.[12] According to the song the ballad-singer left Birmingham on 1 April 1763. He supported himself on the way in traditional fashion by singing in the streets:

> At *Coventry*, I stopp'd to see
> If anything was wanting,
> From pocket lodge, pull'd out my *fodge*
> And straight'way fell to chanting.

The 'fodge' (or bundle of wares) no doubt consisted largely of copies of songs to be offered for sale. Freeth frequently wrote 'in character', and his use of the first person is generally not to be strictly interpreted. But this song, which he afterwards revised, could be based on personal experience. Thus, it may be that the description of himself as a 'street-scribbler' is to be taken literally, and that he once plied the trade of itinerant writer and singer of street-ballads before he succeeded his mother at the Leicester Arms.

The following month, May 1763, Freeth advertised his services as a teacher of 'the Science or Doctrine of Geography, with the Knowledge and Use of the Celestial and Terrestrial Globes'.[13] He volunteered to wait upon any gentleman 'at his own Dwelling, in or near the Town, that is provided with proper Materials'. Possibly Freeth, like many another, was doing no more than seize an opportunity provided by the growing vogue for self-improvement and especially for scientific instruction.[14] He thereby reveals something of his own standard of education, however acquired.

In this advertisement Freeth gives his address as Park Street, but he did not, it seems, become a householder until 1765.[15] Yet within two years he was so well established there in his literary activities that it was these by which he was to be publicly identified, even before he became an innkeeper. In Sketchley's *Birmingham, Wolverhampton and Walsall Directory* for 1767, John Freeth, listed among the town's 'Miscellaneous

Tradesmen' is described as 'Poet, Park-street' – an occupation unique even in the multiplicity of Birmingham trades.

Where and when John Freeth married is not known.[16] But his wife's name was Sarah, she was five years his junior, having been born in 1736, and she predeceased him by ten months in November 1807.[17] In later years Freeth more than once mentioned the nine children of his household.[18] Only eight are named in his Will:[19] his son John, who was to be the sole executor, and his daughters Sarah Wyer and Ann Fox, and Elizabeth, Theodosia, Jane,[20] Martha, and Frances Freeth. After the death of her father Elizabeth Freeth was landlord of Freeth's Coffee-House for many years.[21]

*   *   *

Freeth apparently began to write ballads and sing them in public about 1760.[22] It seems that the earliest of his signed publications to survive is a song, 'On a late verdict', found in *Aris's Birmingham Gazette* for 18 July 1763. The song applauds the freeing of John Wilkes, arrested after the publication of the notorious *The North Briton*, No. 45. Several other compositions by Freeth were later published in *Aris's Birmingham Gazette* and in another local paper, *Swinney's Birmingham and Stafford Chronicle*, but, unlike some of these, 'On a late verdict' was not reprinted in any of his collections of songs.

Freeth's first book, *The Political Songster*, 1766, was a modest volume of less than forty pages, costing 6d, and containing twenty-three of his pieces.[23] There are no illustrations and no music, but nearly every song is accompanied by the title of the tune to which it should be sung. It is a typical songster[24] of the period, though better printed than most.

Over the following thirty-nine years Freeth was to publish, in a similar style, another twelve different collections of his songs: *The Political Songster*, 1771, 1784, 1786, 1790, 1798, *The Warwickshire Medley*, [1780], *Modern Songs*, 1782, *A Touch on the Times*, 1783, 1803, *A Collection of New Songs*, 1793, *The Annual Political Songster*, 1794, and *New Ballads*, 1805. Some of these were reissued with additional leaves, *The Political Songster*,

1790, in particular, being substantially and variously augmented. Copies of nearly all Freeth's books are now extremely rare.

In addition to thirteen songsters Freeth also published two shorter, though very characteristic, pieces of work: *Inland Navigation, an Ode*, 1769, and *Wilkes's Enlargement, an Ode*, 1770.

Inland Navigation, an attractively printed quarto pamphlet, includes the 'ode' of the title, and three songs, 'Birmingham lads', 'The artists' jubilee', and 'On the first arrival of the barges with coals', all celebrating the opening of the Birmingham canal. The 'ode' is some 170 lines in length, and is divided into several parts, with recitative, airs, and choruses. Unlike the songs it does not seem designed to be sung to a tavern audience. *Inland Navigation* is 'humbly inscribed to the inhabitants of Birmingham and the proprietors of the canal', and Freeth avows his purpose to be 'nothing more than a Compliment of Joy to the Inhabitants'. The 'ode' was, therefore, probably written only for publication to mark the occasion. A revised version, with the title 'Birmingham navigation, an ode', was included in the second edition of *The Political Songster* in 1771.

Unfortunately, no copy of *Wilkes's Enlargement, an Ode*, 1770, is known. An Advertisement in *Aris's Birmingham Gazette*, 16 April 1770, announced its publication, price 6d, 'at twelve o'clock to-morrow'. It was subsequently printed in *The Political Songster*, 1771, though the text, like that of *Inland Navigation*, may have first been revised. An earlier advertisement notes that with *Wilkes's Enlargement* is 'an occasional Song, in lieu of the old K.'s Ghost, which is deemed unsafe'. It is not wholly clear how this reference to the ghost of, presumably, George II is to be interpreted, but a song 'The Old King's ghost', in which some allusions might have been politically inopportune in April 1770, was also to be found in *The Political Songster*, 1771. As with the previous 'ode', Freeth's intention appears to have been to commemorate an event – here John Wilkes's release from prison – in print only.

Initially *Wilkes's Enlargement* was to have appeared on 18

April, but during the previous week publication was advanced by twenty-four hours,[25] no doubt so that it should coincide with Wilkes's release a day earlier than had originally been expected. Certainly Freeth took some pains to introduce this work to the public. The announcement of publication concludes: 'An entertainment will be provided by the Author on Wednesday the 18th, who is fitting up a commodious Room for the Reception of those Friends of the Cause that think proper to attend. – Dinner to be ready at One o'Clock'.

*　　　　*　　　　*

The 'remarkable events' which moved Freeth to comment in song were usually feats of war, national emergencies, affairs of state, and important political occasions. Songs such as 'Bunker Hill, or the soldier's lamentation', 'Langara's defeat or the British flag triumphant', 'Song for the British tars, on the sailing of Lord Howe's fleet', and songs on the Budget, the India Bill, elections, and the activities of Ministers and Parliament – these represent Freeth at his weightiest. But to such serious topics he added a substantial leavening of songs – complimentary, facetious, and good-humouredly satirical – on more trivial matters: on pugilism and the manufacture of shoe buckles, on the Duke of Rutland's birthday and the jocular boiling of a vintner's wig, on ale-tasting, bull-baiting, and the cock-fight, and on all types of sport from quoits and fishing to fives and hunting. He often sang, too, of his beloved Birmingham. As he admitted:

> My sentiments are frank and free
> I love my native town.

With fervour he proclaimed its peacefulness and prosperity, the skill of its tradesmen, and the superiority of its ale. Appropriately, it is one of Freeth's songs of Birmingham that may most conveniently be taken here (on account of its untypical brevity) to illustrate his work:

Birmingham Recruits

FIFE and DRUM afford enjoyment,
And what trade so brisk appears;

As that spirited employment,
  Beating up for VOLUNTEERS.

Mark those youths parading yonder,
  Scarcely one turn'd sixteen years;
Cursing fate because they're under,
  Standard proof for VOLUNTEERS.

LADS as tight as coat can cover,
  BIRMINGHAM for service rears;
Not a Town from TWEED to DOVER,
  Sends the King more VOLUNTEERS.

Scorning in the cause to waver,
  Sworn to go where glory steers;
FORTUNE will for ever favour,
  All true-hearted VOLUNTEERS.[26]

In its pride, high spirits, simple diction, and stirring lilt, 'Birmingham Recruits' displays the characteristics of nearly all of Freeth's best songs.

Neither the murders, rapes, and gallows tales nor the romantic fables traditionally cherished by street-ballad writers seem to have held any attraction for Freeth. The topics which did engage his pen with more urgency than most were political ones.

The three hundred and ninety or so compositions that Freeth saw fit to preserve in his songsters are presumably only a fraction of the total number that he sang in his Coffee-House in more than forty years of entertaining customers. Unfortunately, it is impossible to estimate whether the political ballads that do survive are truly representative of their kind. It seems quite likely that events which demanded his speedy attention could often have led only to songs that he did not think worth preserving. Indeed, in the preface to his *Warwickshire Medley*, [1780], Freeth apologized for the imperfections of some of the songs included, and asked the reader to remember that they 'were written during the heat and hurry of contested elections' when the 'clamours of party zeal' allowed him insufficient time to arrange his thoughts properly. Freeth's rejection of some songs because of their indifferent quality may partially account for the many curious omissions that become apparent when the affairs on which his comments survive are compared with those that surely excited him. For instance, in a preface dated 1793, he deplores the fact that:

> Detested anarchy still reigns
> On Gallia's desolated plains,
> Where on a sea of troubles tost!
> Both King and Queen their lives have lost.
> What horrid scenes! from shore to shore,
> The country has been drench'd with gore,
> And still to keep the current flowing,
> The GUILLOTINE is daily going.[27]

Yet no song has survived that is wholly devoted to any of the events of the Terror in France, although there are a few passing references to some of them. Similarly, with affairs at home; Freeth sang of riots in both Birmingham and Dudley, but he takes only an oblique glance at the later, notorious, Birmingham riots of 1791. In these riots there was widespread damage to property, and Joseph Priestley lost both his house and laboratory, together with his accumulated scientific papers. Freeth's Coffee-House, well within the area of destruction, may have been secured with bolted door and shuttered windows at the time. But it seems improbable that Freeth would have had no explicit comment to make when the immediate danger was passed.

Freeth's political sympathies were unremarkable: he firmly supported Whig opposition to the ministry of Lord North, he watched the events leading to the War of American Independence with growing concern and scarcely diminishing sympathy for the colonists, he repudiated the Fox-North coalition, and he expressed increasing disillusionment with William Pitt the Younger and the acts of his government. But to threats of French aggression he unfailingly responded in terms that were vigorously patriotic. The tone of his voice was often bitter, but when he sang of events like the transportation of convicts to Botany Bay or a proposal for the enclosure of Sutton Coldfield his irony and sarcasm never obscured his humanity. He seldom missed an opportunity of linking an event to the fundamentals of life, such as the cost

8

of food, and especially the price of a loaf, the oppression of taxes, and the development of trade; it is characteristic of Freeth that he should conclude a lighthearted account of Blanchard's balloon ascent with a toast to commerce and the wish that an English balloon might carry the first pattern-card to the moon.

Freeth was to express regret that he had been obliged to write of so many 'temporary and local' subjects. 'I now lament', he observed, 'I did not go more upon general topics'.[28] The songs he has preserved about local elections assume more often than not the complexion of a temperate rallying cry rather than that of a polemic. The three elections fought at Worcester in 1773 and 1774 by Sir Watkin Lewes have been described as 'one of the major efforts made in the provinces by the Wilkite radicals'.[29] Yet nothing of the turbulence of those campaigns is reflected in Freeth's songs at the time, as may be seen in the concluding stanza of a ballad soliciting voters on Lewes's behalf:

> The patriot who makes bribing aldermen tremble,
> By all honest Englishmen reverenc'd shall be;
> Reward real merit, together assemble,
> In choosing Sir Watkin we prove ourselves free.

Freeth came to view political wranglings with a smile and indifference, or so he professed in 1790, 'being fully convinced that the contest of most politicians is only for power and for favours'.[30] Yet all the evidence points to his deeply committed and lifelong interest in political affairs. It has been authoritatively remarked that the 'history of popular political consciousness in Birminham, especially during the years of the American revolution, is in good part the history of the Leicester Arms'.[31] Freeth wrote of events with indignation, rough good humour, and a turn of phrase that would have made his songs very effective at the time. It is not without justification that a contemporary described him as being one of the best political ballad-writers and election poets in the kingdom.[32]

*   *   *

Many of Freeth's songs must have been published initially on slips, song-sheets, and broadsides, and in garlands and chapbooks. Such ephemera do not commonly survive, and only a few examples have so far been traced. Eleven of his compositions are first found in *Aris's Birmingham Gazette* between 1763 and 1795.[33] Otherwise the earliest version of each of Freeth's compositions that can be dated is that found in his books and pamphlets.

The majority of Freeth's songs appear in more than one of his songsters. Only *Modern Songs*, 1782, the appropriately named *Collection of New Songs*, 1793, and *The Political Songster*, 1798, (in addition to his first book, *The Political Songster*, 1766) contained an entirely fresh selection. But in most of the other songsters the proportion of songs that had been included in Freeth's earlier books is surprisingly large. For instance, to take three songsters of which only one edition is known: of the eighty-five pieces in the first issue of *The Warwickshire Medley* [1780], thirty-one had already been published; and of the thirty-two pieces in the first issue of *Modern Songs*, 1782, twenty-three were printed in later collections, while *A Collection of New Songs*, 1793, though containing only nine songs, lent five of them to a subsequent collection.

The frequent inclusion of old songs in new songsters is no doubt explained by public demand, and Freeth's consequent need to keep the most individually popular of his songs in print. Many of them appeared over a considerable number of years in each new songster he produced. *Modern Songs*, 1782, for example, has a song about the engagement fought by Admiral Sir Hyde Parker with the Dutch fleet off the Dogger Bank in 1781. It was then included in five of the six songsters Freeth published during the next twelve years before appearing finally in a *A Touch on the Times*, 1803. For historical reasons, and because of its patriotic sentiments and stirring air, a song such as this has some lasting appeal. But Freeth often reprinted pieces of small merit and no special interest long after they had lost any topicality – the quality he particularly sought. Probably he was always more concerned to assemble enough songs to constitute a new songster than to choose his material with discrimination. The survival of one of his manuscripts permits a glimpse of him engaged in the task of selection. It shows him on that occasion, at least, to have been a painstaking editor.

*   *   *

The manuscript,[34] now in Birmingham University Library, formerly belonged to the Birmingham Library which acquired it in 1808, the year of Freeth's death.[35] The date of acquisition must be treated with reservation since the Accessions Book of the Library, in which it was entered, was not begun until some years later. The Birmingham Library, one of the oldest private subscription libraries, had originated in 1779, but its early minutes are now lost. It is thought that many of the members of the Birmingham Book Club[36] were associated with the formation of the Library,[37] although Freeth himself did not become a member of the Club until later. Possibly it was through the interest of other members that his manuscript was secured for the Library. In 1955 the Birmingham Library was amalgamated with the Birmingham and Midland Institute, and from there the manuscript was purchased for the University during 1974-1975. Nothing else is known of its provenance, nor does the manuscript itself offer any positive proof that it is in Freeth's hand. But this is clearly the printer's copy for *Modern Songs*, 1782, and it seems certain from the alterations and corrections that whoever compiled it was also the author of the songs. The writing is well formed, bold, and clear, and the spelling is consistent and uneccentric. In no way does the manuscript suggest an author deficient in education.[38]

Originally it contained thirty-six songs. At different times, however, as is shown by the renumbering of the songs, five of them were cancelled.[39] This was probably only because there was too much material, and not on account of any objections to these particular songs. The choice of what to exclude may have been difficult, for the quality of the cancelled songs is not appreciably worse than that of the remainder of the collection. Only one of the five songs was afterwards included in any of Freeth's other songsters.[40]

At a later stage, perhaps while the manuscript was at the

printer's, the decision was taken to omit two more songs[41] and in their place to put three others, together rather longer and of greater moment: 'Taxation: or, the courtier's creed', 'Navigation', and 'The Georges: on Lord Sackville's promotion'. Like four of the five songs cancelled earlier, these two do not appear elsewhere in Freeth's published works.

The manuscript is a 'clean' one, and the printer has commonly followed the author's intentions in the use of two sizes of capitals and other accidentals. The printed text, however, does show some departures from the manuscript. One six-line stanza is omitted, some small corrections have not been carried out, and there are a number of other minor differences. But nothing is incompatible with these changes having been approved by the author while the work was in proof, especially as he was also the publisher.

The most important feature of the manuscript is the way in which the printer has marked it to indicate the text of each printed sheet. As it was initially printed (that is, without a later additional leaf) *Modern Songs*, 1782, has the signatures A^4 $B-F^6$. Preliminaries are printed on A1-4, and the text proper begins on B1r. None of the preliminaries is included in the manuscript. Since the beginning of printed half-sheet B coincides with the beginning of the manuscript no printer's copy mark is called for there, and none has been added. But the printer has indicated the first line of text of each of the other four half-sheets by noting against it the signature and the pagination found on the corresponding page of the printed book, thus: 'C13', 'D25', 'E37', and 'F P49'.

Until the end of the previous century printers seem to have marked their copy by pages, commonly indicating the first line of text with the signature letter and the number of the page within its gathering – 'D6', for example, being a reference to page D3v. Freeth's manuscript provides additional evidence that by the eighteenth century this long-established custom had been superseded by the practice of indicating only each sheet, and employing the signature letter and the page number of the printed book to show where its text began. (This was the method also used in the printer's copy of a famous book published some three years after

Modern Songs – Boswell's *Journal of a Tour to the Hebrides*, 1785.)[42]

Modern Songs, 1782, is without press-figures, and there seem no obvious conclusions to be drawn about the practice obtaining in this particular printing-house (which appears to have been that of Pearson and Rollason).[43] Nevertheless, besides introducing Freeth's hand, the manuscript is a welcome new example of eighteenth-century printer's copy.

*   *   *

Freeth is not named in his first book, *The Political Songster*, 1766, and he is identified as the author of *A Touch on the Times*, 1803, by a portrait frontispiece and his signature on a preface. All his other books have his name - either as 'Freeth', or in its alternative form of 'Free' - on the title-page. In the 1771 edition of *The Political Songster* Freeth used the curious style of 'J. Free' for the first time. He seems then to have adopted it, at least for public use, for a period of exactly fifteen years.

From 1771 to 1785 all Freeth's works that have so far come to light which bear more than his initials were, with one exception, published under the pseudonym of 'Free'. The single exception known is an invitation card dated 28 November 1771, which is signed in Freeth's usual manner. Otherwise, for these years, his surname appears as 'Free' on the title-pages of five different songsters and their various re-issues[44] (that is, from the 1771 edition of *The Political Songster* to the edition of 1784), on his invitation cards, (fifteen different examples surviving from the period),[45] and with those compositions published in newspapers.[46] Similarly the only one of Freeth's signed prefaces belonging to those years which has a name instead of initials, the preface to *The Warwickshire Medley* [1780], is also subscribed 'J. Free'. Whatever Freeth's original purpose in adopting a pseudonym, he cannot have long expected to conceal his identity. The name 'J. Free', or 'John Free', eventually became associated with him publicly, not only as his *nom de plume*, but also with him in his occupation of innkeeper.

In advertising the amenities of his Coffee-House in 1772 he

names himself normally as John Freeth,[47] but two years later, the identification with 'Free' was made in the local press. On 3 August 1774 an epilogue, written by Freeth, was spoken before a theatre audience in Birmingham.[48] It concludes with the exhortation: 'Call at his House, you'll find ROAST BEEF to-morrow'. Yet despite this obvious advertisement for Freeth's Coffee-House *Aris's Birmingham Gazette* of 8 August, and *Swinney's Birmingham and Stafford Chronicle* of three days later,[49] which both carry reports of the occasion and publish the text of the epilogue, name the author as 'Mr. Free'.

In the same year, 1774, 'Free's Coffee-House in Bell-street' was announced as the venue for political meetings.[50] Freeth refers to his House simply as 'J. Free's' on his invitation card of 12 June 1776,[51] and the same style is used in William Hutton's *History of Birmingham*, 1781. Also, on 2 August 1784, *Aris's Birmingham Gazette*, reporting Thanksgiving Day celebrations, noticed that a numerous company had been entertained by 'that well-known songster of the times J. Free'.[52]

In the extant Birmingham directories[53] for this period, 1771 to 1785, Freeth's name is always given in its original form, and there is no reference to him as 'J. Free'. But in 1785 there appeared for the first time the name of John Free, a victualler, of Newton Street.[54] He was still at this address in 1808, when Freeth died. Perhaps it was this man's taking up trade in Birmingham which caused Freeth to abandon his alias.

Freeth, probably a Radical, undoubtedly of liberal opinions, and certainly a Nonconformist, constantly addressed himself to 'the sons of freedom' and 'the lovers of freedom', and described himself as 'the Bard of Freedom'.[55] Also, he more than once expressed his admiration for a passage 'free and easy through life'. Presumably the name 'Free' was intended only as a punning allusion to his convictions and tastes.

*   *   *

The standard of printing in Freeth's books is well above average for work of this nature. Neither *The Political Songster*,

1766, nor *Inland Navigation*, 1769, carries a printer's name (though the latter has the imprint 'Birmingham'), and about the printing of *Wilkes's Enlargement*, 1770, nothing is known. But all the other books are the work of well-known Birmingham printers.

Although they have various imprints, the majority of Freeth's books come from the same printing-house. This was part of the important printing, publishing, and bookselling business in High Street, Birmingham, which had been founded by Thomas Aris in 1741, and where *Aris's Birmingham Gazette* was printed for more than a century.[56]

After Thomas Aris's retirement at the end of 1760 control of the press passed to the partnership of Richard Pearson and Samuel Aris (the nephew of Thomas Aris).[57] From 1768, when Pearson died, the business was conducted by Ann Pearson, Richard's widow, and by Samuel Aris. Samuel Aris died in January 1775, and Ann Pearson was eventually joined in partnership by James Rollason. It is Pearson and Rollason who are named as the printers of *The Warwickshire Medley* [1780], the first of Freeth's songsters to come from their press. They also appear to have been responsible for the printing of *Modern Songs*, 1782, *A Touch on the Times*, 1783, and *The Political Songster*, 1784 and 1786. In these the typography is characteristic of Pearson and Rollason's work, and although the imprint names them specifically only as booksellers it is possibly intended to identify them also as the printers.[58]

Ann Pearson and James Rollason were followed in 1789, the year of Rollason's death, by Thomas Pearson, who printed *The Political Songster*, 1790, and *The Annual Political Songster*, 1794. During 1798 the name of Thomas Pearson was replaced in the imprint of the house by that of Thomas Aris Pearson,[59] printer of the 1798 edition of *The Political Songster* and of Freeth's invitation card of 27 November 1799.[60]

When Thomas Aris Pearson died in December 1801 the business was conducted for some time on behalf of his executors by Jonathan Knott. During this period Knott printed *A Touch on the Times*, 1803. Knott was already in partnership with Robert Lloyd, in charge of bookselling at the premises in High Street, when, in January 1804, they became sole proprietors of the entire business. Knott and Lloyd appear as the printers of Freeth's last songster, *New Ballads*, 1805.

The most distinguished printer employed by Freeth was John Baskerville, who printed *The Political Songster*, 1771. His type was also used in printing some of Freeth's invitation cards and three of them are decorated with frames of Baskerville type-ornaments.[61] These cards were probably the work of Myles Swinney, another Birmingham printer and a much undervalued craftsman, whose imprint is found on three other cards.[62] After Baskerville's death, Swinney, who was also a type-founder, had acquired some of his matrices.[63]

Among Freeth's other printers, Baskerville type was also used by Pearson and Rollason and by Thomas Chapman, who printed a *A Collection of New Songs*, 1793.[64] However, it is difficult to be certain whether they used any of it in working for Freeth. As with much Birmingham printing of the period the general influence of Baskerville can readily be detected in the typography of Freeth's books.

*   *   *

No publisher is named in *A Collection of New Songs*, 1793, but in all his other books Freeth is identified as publisher, either by name or as the author. In undertaking the expense of publishing his own songs, Freeth's declared purpose was to earn money rather than to seek recognition. 'Contracted Circumstances', he wrote in 1771, 'or the Hope of acquiring Fame, are Motives that often induce a Person to commence Author, whose Abilities are inadequate to the Task; that the former happens to be my Case, is what I am not ashamed to own'.[65] These were sentiments he was frequently to repeat, and it seems clear that Freeth was never affluent.

Records of transactions by which his finances might be judged are few. In 1770, the year after he 'humbly inscribed' his *Inland Navigation* in part to the proprietors of the new Birmingham canal, his name is found among the Company's shareholders.[66] Shares were then £140 each, no one being permitted to hold more than ten. Originally Freeth had one share, but by 1771 he had acquired another, though he seems to have disposed of both in the summer of 1772.[67] This was unfortunate, for large dividends were soon being paid,[68] and in 1782 it was claimed that a share was sold for as much as £420,[69] while by 1792 their price had reached £1170 each.[70] Freeth's caustic observation that some had become 'Navigation mad' must have seemed singularly apt at that time.

In 1774 Freeth applied to the actor-manager of the new theatre (afterwards the Theatre Royal) which had just been built in New Street, Birmingham, for one night's performance to be devoted to his benefit. This request was granted, and in the epilogue which Freeth wrote to express his thanks, and which was spoken for him to the audience, he described himself as being then 'in needy Plight'.[71] An occasion such as this is probably not to be taken as testimony to Freeth's standing in the community since Richard Yates and his company at the New Street Theatre were noted for their charity performances, and a correspondent of Thomas Aris, writing four years later, refers to the actors' 'having done all in their power to alleviate the Distresses of some Individuals in this Town, by giving them Benefits'.[72]

Freeth was named as an agent of the Liverpool Fire Office in 1791.[73] Whether his earnings in this capacity were other than negligible is doubtful.

The probate of his Will shows his estate to have been valued at less than £1500 in 1808. By how much £1500 exceeded the worth of his possessions is not clear, but Freeth, though obviously poor, did not die in unrelieved poverty.

Freeth's difficulties were not uncommon. They arose because the needs of his family outgrew the resources of the business on which he depended for his livelihood. In introducing The Warwickshire Medley [1780], he referred to the 'increasing necessities' of those for whom it was his 'indispensable duty' to provide, but for which he found his 'common business in life . . . altogether insufficient'. Some two years later he returned to this theme, expressing himself more precisely:

> . . . each day, when children nine,
> In perfect health sit down to dine –
> Think not, the whole can be maintain'd
> By what is from the ale-score gain'd.[74]

The money brought him by his songs was, it seems, essential. Even on one of his invitation cards he did not refrain from making this clear:

> I'll live well this Year, if a Bankrupt the next,
> And that, or sing Ballads, will sure by my Lot,
> For the Profits on Ale-selling scarce boil the Pot.[75]

Nevertheless, the following year, he has to admit that:

> Profits on BEER and BALLADS too,
> In these hard times will barely do.[76]

There is a tradition that it was really Mrs Freeth and her daughters who conducted Freeth's Coffee-House. Freeth himself, it is said, never performed any of the routine domestic duties of an innkeeper, but devoted himself solely to being agreeable to his customers. Apparently Mrs Freeth and the daughters were in the habit of retiring early each night at a fixed hour, having drawn such ale as was likely to be required. If more were needed, a customer had to go to the cellar to fetch it, Freeth never doing so.[77] If he gave so little attention to the supervision of his house is it surprising that he was in financial difficulties?

A contemporary recalled of Freeth:

> In Winter, by a blazing fire,
> He smokes his yard of clay;
> In Summer, on the bowling green,
> He slips his time away.[78]

An unconsidered description, perhaps, but one which gives some confirmation to the suspicion that Freeth was indolent and with no taste for the exigencies of trade.

Freeth's troubles were complicated by failing health. In 1782 he made the first, perhaps not wholly serious, reference to his

> . . . having worn, beyond a doubt,
> His constitution almost out.[79]

Yet he was then only fifty-one. That he became prematurely aged seems to be confirmed by the portrait frontispiece published four years later in *The Political Songster*, 1786.[80] By

1790 he was excusing himself from further writing: 'the old and favourite trade of *ballad-making* is almost over with me'. The reason he gives is that a 'complaint in my head, to which I am daily subject, prevents me pursuing that business in the manner I have hitherto done'.[81] He was, however, still able to sing, and he expressed the hope that his best endeavours in singing his old compositions would satisfy his customers.

However severe Freeth's affliction[82] it did not, in the end, prevent his publishing many more songs. Indeed, two out of his four wholly new collections of songs were published after this date. As late as 1802 it was observed of Freeth that 'many strangers make a point of visiting this sprightly *septuagenarian*, whose voice is a little affected by years, but whose easy poetry trickles almost as freely from his pen as ever'.[83] Thirteen years from the time he first mentioned his ailment, Freeth, writing his last preface, still complained of weakness. Now, however, he attributed it to the toil of '*thirty-six* years hard service in the humble station of a publican'.[84]

In the first songster he introduced Freeth protested his lack of ability. In his last preface he similarly declared, at the age of seventy-two, that even in 'the best of his days' he was not by nature fitted to the task of composition. In the intervening years he so strenuously makes the same apology – even offering his 'station in life, and small knowledge of Literature'[85] as an excuse for his deficiencies – that it must be allowed some weight. Perhaps it was because he always found the task of writing uncommonly arduous, as much as on account of his failing health, that he frequently expressed the wish to have finished with it.

It was always Freeth's aim to sing of the news while it was still fresh. (The title-page of *Modern Songs*, 1782, it may be noticed, proclaims that the songs it contains were 'written on the immediate arrival of the accounts of the different events'.) He tells us of himself that he,

> . . . when good News is brought to town,
> Immediately to work sits down,
> And business fairly to go through,
> Write SONGS, finds TUNES, and SINGS them too.[86]

Having to compose with such urgency could have been very wearisome. Nevertheless, this description does suggest that, rather than suffering the poet's creative pangs, he enjoyed something of the journalist's facility.

Freeth undoubtedly achieved success in what he more than once calls 'the trade of ballad-making'. A close acquaintance described him as

> . . . a Poet that's very well known
> By High and by Low – and by Travellers all
> Who composing and Singing New Songs of his own
> Induces them oft at his House for to call.[87]

But in publishing his songs Freeth was aware that he faced a particular hazard. 'In regard to making Songs appear to Advantage, the Difference between reading, and singing, is so remarkably great, that I should not expect any Encouragement . . . if I had not a flattering Hope of having many Times pleasured my Friends by the latter . . . '.[88] Yet the demand for his songsters was enduring. In 1803 he claimed that it was only 'the repeated solicitations for copies of various Songs' that had induced him (and not for the last time, as it proved) to come forward with a new songster. Otherwise, he declared, 'he would not have risked the sale of another *twelve-penny Touch on the Times*'. [89] His public was a wide one, and included 'travellers in the mercantile line from every county, who pay me such frequent and friendly visits, for copies of my songs'.[90] Without success, and the encouragement he drew from it, Freeth observed in 1790, he would probably not have written a tenth of the songs (some one hundred and fifty) contained in *The Political Songster* of that year.

*   *   *

Reviewers noticed Freeth's songsters kindly, if uncritically. Typical of their judgements was the comment 'that though his expressions are sometimes coarse, his observations are often shrewd, and that he possesses a happy knack at versification . . . we like his humour'.[91] One critic ranked him with 'Taylor the water-poet, and Ned Ward of facetious memory'.[92] But three years later this estimate was revised. 'We formerly compared him with Taylor, the noted water-poet, of the last age: but we begin to think better of him; – for, although he may not possess the learning of the famous Tom. Brown, nor perhaps quite so brisk and constant a flow of wit, yet his compositions are not, on the whole, inferior to those of Brown in regard to ease and harmony; and they may justly boast a greater degree of chastity'.[93] The quality in which he was held to be superior to Brown no doubt gave special pleasure to Freeth, of whom obituarists declared 'his morals were unsullied'.

Freeth was encouraged in his work by what he describes as 'the partiality of friends'. Yet he also enjoyed distinguished patronage. Though aware that it might be said he was moved by vanity, he could not forbear to claim that he had 'met with attention and respect from personages of the first rank in life', and in particular from the Duke of Norfolk, the Earl of Harborough ('The Hospitable Peer of Stapleford'), and Earl Stanhope. These dignitaries were among the subscribers to *The Political Songster*, 1790.

The list of subscribers found with some issues[94] of the book provides the only factual evidence of the size of any edition Freeth published. In all, 516 copies at 3s 6d each were bespoken by 396 subscribers. Their names include those of several notable members of the aristocracy and gentry; the Earl of Exeter, Lord Sherard, and Sir John Dashwood, as well as the three noblemen already mentioned, being among them. None of these gentlemen, it may be noticed, requested more than one copy. The most substantial purchaser was a Mr Tankard of Birmingham,[95] who bought twenty copies, though nineteen others took up to a dozen each.

Most of the subscribers resided in Birmingham and its environs, but others were from towns as far afield as Chester, Lincoln, Manchester, Sheffield, Spalding, Bristol and London. It should be remarked that only one of Freeth's songsters, *The Annual Political Songster*, 1794, carries the name of a London bookseller, that of R. Baldwin of Pater Noster Row.

*   *   *

One of Freeth's songs was a marked success. This was

'Britain's glory', a patriotic song of forty-eight lines. It is a competent piece of work, though of no great distinction, and its quality is well exemplified by the first two stanzas, and one of its two choruses:

> Come ye lads who wish to shine
>   Bright in future story,
> Haste to arms and form the line
>   That leads to martial glory.
>
> Britain, when the LION's rous'd,
>   And her FLAG is rearing,
> Always finds her sons dispos'd
>   To drub the foe that's daring.

> *Chorus*
> Charge the MUSQUET, point the LANCE,
>   Brave the worst of dangers;
> Tell the blustering sons of France
>   That we to fear are strangers.

These sentiments so well reflect the feeling of the times – and were to become so increasingly apt – that the continuing popularity of the song is not surprising.

The earliest of Freeth's songsters to include 'Britain's glory' was *Modern Songs*, 1782. With a new title, 'Recruiting song: on the commencement of hostilities with the French', it was later to appear in *A Touch on the Times*, 1783 and *The Political Songster*, 1784 and 1790. But others besides Freeth had published this song of his. Wanting contrary evidence, his authorship must be allowed since he implicitly claimed it, and since the song is included in his manuscript. It had been printed in perhaps a dozen different songsters earlier than *Modern Songs*. Under several titles and in a variety of forms it is to be found subsequently in many songsters and collections, on slips and broadsides, and in garlands and chapbooks. It was also adapted and parodied. For instance, *Paddy's Resource, or the Harp of Erin*, published in Dublin about 1830, includes an adaptation in which the first stanza is as Freeth wrote it, but which continues as a plea for Irish freedom. Also, among the addresses and songs relating to an election in Exeter in 1818 there is a song, 'Come ye lads who wish to share', which is an obvious parody.

Presumably Freeth had initially published 'Britain's glory' in some ephemeral form, of which no copy has come to light. It must have attracted considerable attention for so many others to have included it in their own collections and songsters. The earliest of these were *The Vocal Magazine* and *The Charms of Chearfulness*, both published in 1778. The following year the song was reprinted in *The Scots Nightingale*, and the year after in both *The Scots Vocal Magazine* and *Bull-Finch*. In 1781 it was included in at least six more different songsters, and in the following year in four others, as well as in Freeth's *Modern Songs*. Over the next few years it appeared in yet another half-dozen collections. 'Britain's glory' could still be found in a song-book as late as 1816.

In Freeth's *Modern Songs*, 1782, 'Britain's glory' is to be sung to the well-known tune 'Come then all ye social powers'. But it had earlier been given an original musical setting by Henry Heron, and had been included, with this music, in his *Choice Collection of Songs . . . Sung at Vauxhall Gardens*, 1779. About this time it was also published with yet a third different musical setting.

There is no indication that any other song by Freeth achieved a similar success. It is interesting that many of the songsters containing 'Britain's glory' were published in Scotland and the north of England, only about half of them appearing in London and in the South.

*   *   *

The 'profits on beer' may have been insufficient for the needs of Freeth and his family, but there can be no doubt that the Coffee-House was well-attended and respectable. James Bisset, a distinguished figure in Birmingham, who knew it intimately, mentioned that 'convivial parties used often to meet at "the Poet Freeth's" '.[96] And more than twenty years after Freeth's death one writer recalled that during the 'Poet's' lifetime, 'no tavern in the town was held in higher repute or better frequented',[97] while another was to remark that 'some of the most respectable men in Birmingham frequented his house'.[98] The identity of some of Freeth's patrons is well known.

Among the regular visitors to his Coffee-House was a group
of men, all locally prominent, known as 'The Jacobin Club'.
In 1790 the 'Club' commissioned an artist 'to take off their
likenesses in a social group'.[99] The artist was Johann
Eckstein, a German painter who spent much of his working
life in London. He depicted a party of twelve sociably at table,
some sitting, others standing, a tankard, glasses and clay pipes
before them. The work took two years to complete.[100] For
this Eckstein's fee was forty-eight guineas.[101]

The picture is a notable one, perhaps most valuable for its
portraiture of individuals. Bisset, one of the group, declared
that the portraits 'are all striking likenesses',[102] each one being
'executed with great exactness'.[103] The sitters are James
Murray, a linen draper and a member of the Antiquarian
Society of Scotland; John Wilkes, a cheese factor, who held a
commission in the militia; Richard Webster, brass-founder;
Jeremiah Vaux, a distinguished surgeon; John Collard, hatter
and tailor, and the author of works on logic; John Miles,
patent lamp manufacturer; Samuel Toy, steel toy manufacturer, and afterwards landlord of the Mitre Inn; James
Bisset, connoisseur, publisher, writer of verse, and author of
the *Magnificent Directory*, 1800; Joseph Fearon, tin merchant
and a constable of the town for many years; James Sketchley,
publisher and auctioneer, prominent in Freemasonry; and
Joseph Blunt, brazier. With them, presumably as one of their
number, though possibly by courtesy as their 'host', was John
Freeth, characteristically depicted wearing a cocked-hat, with
a long clay pipe to his lips.[104]

The picture was held by the group on the tontine
principle,[105] the survivor among them becoming its eventual
owner. As it had originally been painted especially to hang in
Freeth's Coffee-House,[106] they decided that it should remain
there until it was finally claimed. By 1829, according to the
writer of an obituary of Jeremiah Vaux, the surgeon, 'many
thousands of visitors' had been attracted to Freeth's by a wish
to see the painting, 'as the generality of the gentlemen whose
portraits were drawn were well-known, being rather of
eccentric habits . . . '.[107] The survivor of the group proved to
be James Bisset who became owner of the picture in March

1832 on the death of the cheese factor, Wilkes.[108]

Among the Tory wits of the day this group was ironically known as the 'Twelve Apostles'. Yet a distinguished Birmingham citizen and antiquary of note, Samuel Timmins, has since taken the activities of the 'Twelve Apostles' very seriously indeed. Of these 'Celebrities', as Eckstein depicted them, he wrote that they were

> . . . highly esteemed and applauded by a very large number of their fellow Citizens and Countrymen for the political opinions peculiar to their body, and which were strongly opposed to the views advocated by the numerous and wealthy Tory Party of the day.
>
> When it is taken into consideration that the nightly debates and the clever productions of these Worthies gave birth to and assisted in diffusing those great and glorious principles which in after years resulted in the passing of the Reform Bill, the Catholic Emancipation Bill, together with other progressive measures, and mainly contributed towards infusing into the hearts of '*the people*' those sentiments of Liberalism and Loyalty which experience has proved to have been productive of highly beneficial effects - taking these and similar facts into consideration, the . . . [picture] may almost be looked upon as possessing a national as well as local interest . . . [109]

Those of Freeth's customers seeking political news found their needs well served. In 1772 Freeth advertised under the heading 'Politics' in *Aris's Birmingham Gazette* for subscribers to the use of his newspapers, stating that he was also able to provide 'Political Literature on the most reasonable Terms'. He added that 'the London Papers have been regularly filed for upwards of thirty-seven Years'; that is, since his father first became landlord of the Leicester Arms.[110]

Indeed, Freeth's Coffee-House was a recognised meeting place for those of liberal political views. The supporters of the Tory party gathered at The Minerva tavern in Peck Lane, kept by Joe Lyndon. Considerable ill-feeling existed between the habitués of the two houses, and in The Minerva a notice was displayed over the fireplace proclaiming 'No Jacobin Admitted Here'. The notice is said to have been the consequence of a brawl involving James Bisset. About 1790,

JOHN FREETH

when party feeling was particularly strong, a defiant message
was sent to Freeth to the effect that none of his friends would
dare to show his face in The Minerva. The challenge was
accepted by Bisset. While there, he behaved with perfect
indifference to all the petty annoyances and insulting remarks
addressed indirectly at him. But when someone blew smoke in
his face Bisset responded to this direct affront by felling the
offender. A general mêlée ensued, and Bisset was ejected only
after damage amounting to some £5 had been done. He was
forced to pay for this after being sued in the Court of
Requests.[111]

A visit to the meeting of a political club held at Freeth's,
perhaps a meeting of the Jacobin Club, has been described by
the friend of a member. When he expressed a wish to be
present he was told that because of the law relating to political
societies the Club had the rule that anyone might attend its
meetings. But he was warned that he must judge for himself
whether the visit would be of interest. Accordingly he was
introduced at the next meeting. 'The room in which they met
was in an out of the way part of the house, and about 16 feet
by 14 feet in size; every member had his pipe, not a word was
said during the time I was there, but such a smoke was made
by these jolly gentlemen that I was very soon fairly smoked
out'. His friend explained that this was the way in which all
strangers were treated.[112] The visit took place about 1826,
some eighteen years after Freeth's death, though at a time
when his daughter was still landlord.

Another group which met regularly at Freeth's for many
years was a book society which still flourishes today as the
Birmingham Book Club. Membership was limited to twenty-
four, meetings were held on alternate Wednesdays (with a
forfeit for absence), and there was also an annual dinner. At
this yearly meeting, books purchased during the previous
twelve months were sold by auction to the members.

The earliest records in the archives of the Birmingham
Book Club belong to 1816.[113] But these include lists of
members for 1775, 1786, 1796, (each containing twenty-four
names), and 1806 (with twenty-five names). Another list notes
the names of twenty-seven 'intermediate' members, apparently

26

belonging to the Club only between those years.

Earlier records were extant at the end of the nineteenth century. A historian of the Club has noted that Minutes of meetings held at Freeth's in 1775 indicate that some members had then belonged to it for thirty years.[114] The Club's foundation ought probably to be dated about 1745.[115]

John Freeth's name is in the list of members for 1796 and in 1806. Another John Freeth, presumably 'Poet Freeth's' son, was later a member, but he resigned on 10 September 1832. His reason is perhaps revealed by an entry in the Minutes Book dated 15 August of the same year. This records that because Freeth's Coffee-House had closed[116] members had met at the White Horse Tavern in Congreve Street, and that it had been resolved by a considerable majority to hold future meetings there.

An early date when the Club was already meeting at Freeth's is suggested by the list of subscribers to Wellins Calcott's *Thoughts, Moral and Divine*, 1758. This includes 'The Reading Society at Mr. Freeth's Coffee-House, Bell Street, Birmingham'. If the reference is to the society which became the Birmingham Book Club[117] then it seems Freeth's Coffee-House must have entertained its members over a period of at least seventy-four years. Thus, not only John Freeth, but both his father before him and his daughter after him also played host to the Club.[118]

As well as those who met for political discussion, as members of clubs, or in mere conviviality, some repaired to Freeth's Coffee-House to deal with affairs of a different order. It is an indication of the respectability of Freeth's that the trustees of the Old Meeting House, the nonconformist chapel situated nearby, used it for meetings.[119]

*   *   *

The most interesting evidence of the hospitality offered at Freeth's Coffee-House is provided by the printed invitation cards it was his practice to issue. Of these, fifty-six different examples, dating from 1770 to 1803, have fortunately survived.[120]

The cards are printed, most of them competently, on one

side only[121] of medium-quality white card. Their average size is approximately that of the modern playing-card, though a few are appreciably larger. With the exception of one invitation, which is entirely in prose,[122] all of them have between eight and twenty-two lines of verse by Freeth. Nearly all the invitations begin formally with the word 'Sir', and each one is dated and (apart from one in the third person) signed, either with Freeth's initials, his pseudonym, or his name.[123] Though lacking many of the details commonly given in soliciting custom, these cards provide an apparently unique version of the trade-card. On fourteen cards the name of the person for whom the invitation was intended is written on the blank verso.[124] In several instances the handwriting resembles Freeth's.

In extending his invitation Freeth usually mentions some affair of the day, either making a general observation on, say, the price of bread or the state of trade, or noticing a particular event, such as the trial of Warren Hastings, a speech by Lord Thurlow at the Lord Mayor's banquet, or the victories of Nelson and Howe:

On the First Day of June, gallant HOWE – right and tight,
Whom many had frequently swore ne'er would fight,
The GALLIC CHIEF met, a proud hour to dispute,
And gave him HAWKE-like an old English salute.[125]

On occasion Freeth's comments clearly indicate his current political views. With his invitation of 15 June 1775, he firmly supports the cause of the Whigs in Britain and the colonists in America:

And foremost for FREEDOM may EFFINGHAM stand,
Not forgetting Lord GRANBY a SAVILLE and BURKE
Our good friends at BOSTON and those at NEW YORK.

Similarly, the lines devoted to wishing success to William Pochin in a Leicestershire election in 1774 suggest how the Dissenting interest in politics may then have been viewed in Birmingham. Sometimes events provided Freeth with an extended metaphor, as when he referred to a celebrated encounter in the prize-ring at Banbury:[126]

> My CONTEST, which full thirty minutes will hold,
> I hope, to attend you will feel yourself bold;
> BOTTLE-HOLDERS and SECONDS I've always at hand,
> To answer whilst combating ev'ry command.[127]

He assures his guests that

> No *blood* will be spilt, tho' the *claret* may run

and concludes by reminding them that the dinner he offers is

> For the *stomach* much better than BANBURY THUMPS.

Similarly, with the invitation of 11 June 1777 he drew his metaphor from the stage and from Birmingham theatrical events, while for that of 6 June 1798 he borrowed the terminology of the duel.

Most of Freeth's invitations conclude with a resounding toast, such as:

> Then let this be the toast on the present occasion,
> Long life to the KING – to the PRINCE Reformation.[128]

And on 28 November 1798:

> One Toast let me offer whilst wetting
> Our PIPES in our SNUG LITTLE ISLE,
> 'All true British Hearts – not forgetting
> Brave NELSON, the LORD of the NILE'.[129]

Not all Freeth's toasts were loyal or patriotic. Several reflect the difficulties of trade and the hardness of the times in which he lived. There were, for instance, many in 1800 who would have echoed his wish that 'soon through the land may be found'

> 'Twelve Ounces of Bread for one Penny,
> And good Beef at Four-pence per Pound'.[130]

Sometimes Freeth's sentiments were more personal, as when his toast was

> 'That our Children may make the best Use of their Days'.[131]

That the cards were precisely dated can, at times, add significant weight to remarks made almost in passing. After a happy sojourn in Cheltenham in the summer of 1788, George

III was greatly restored in health and was enjoying wide popular respect. His health broke down again in the Autumn, by mid-November it was causing acute anxiety, and on 26 November matters were critical. In an invitation of that same day Freeth's frustration over reform was given ascerbic expression:

> For the *Sins* of the People, I'm sorry to find,
> The KING should be punish'd in Body or Mind,
> If he waits a REFORM in their Lives being made,
> 'Twill be a long Time ere he's well I'm afraid.

Two other invitations, at the time of the short-lived Peace of Amiens, provide momentary reflections of provincial opinion: that of 25 February 1802 expresses something of the wary optimism felt shortly before the signing of the Treaty, while the other, dated the following 25 January, when the renewal of war seemed inevitable, reflects the pessimism created by Napoleon's restless ambition:

> By woeful experience, since England well knows
> That Europe but seldom finds general repose.

Invitations often include an indication of the fare provided:

> I therefore to please,
> Shall have GEESE and GREEN-PEAS,
> With BEEF and PLUMB-PUDDING to boot.[132]

Freeth offered only a few simple, traditional, dishes – roast beef, goose, and duck, with green peas (sometimes difficult to obtain) being regarded as a delicacy – and he observed the old custom of commencing the meal with pudding. On feast days, it seems, proceedings might be long continued. Two cards, each bearing an invitation for 1.30 p.m., refer to spending a 'winterly evening'[133] and to the 'Evening's Regale'.[134]

A number of cards seem to be designed only as advertisement of the meal that the casual visitor to Freeth's Coffee-House would be able to obtain on a certain day. But others, all of which are headed 'Society Feast' or 'Annual Feast', are obviously intended to remind members of various societies of particular engagements.

One of the societies to whose members these cards were

sent was the early Birmingham Book Club. There is a card announcing their annual feast for 1795,[135] and another for each year from 1799 to 1803.[136] All are issued for the month of January, and all specifically mention the usual sale of books. Some of the other cards, similarly announcing a feast, but without any reference to a book auction, may also have served to summon the Club's members. But these cards seem too numerous for them all to have been for that purpose; there are three cards for 1796, announcing feasts in February, June, and November. Regrettably, the other societies to which they refer are now impossible to identify with any certainty. One of them was, perhaps, the Jacobin Club. It is difficult to believe that its members were not accustomed, on occasion, to holding a Club feast at Freeth's. Another society appears to have been an association of local tradesmen. One of Freeth's songs (first found in *A Touch on the Times*, 1783) is a 'Birmingham Tradesmen's Society song', and on an invitation card of 23 November 1785 his lines commence:

> FRIDAY next is festive Day,
> Why should Tradesmen not be gay?[137]

On one occasion, at least, the host was not even nominally Freeth. A card issued on 2 December 1794,[138] though having the usual passage of verse over Freeth's initials, extends an invitation to sup at Freeth's, and is signed 'Smith, Son, & Smith'. (This is the only card to bear an invitation to supper, instead of dinner). The hosts were, no doubt, the firm of Timothy Smith, Son and Smith, merchants, of Bartholomew Street, Birmingham,[139] whose senior partner was either Freeth's reputed sometime fellow apprentice,[140] or else his son. To whom would a company of merchants most likely offer hospitality if not their own employees or members of some trade association?

It seems clear that over the years there were a number of societies or associations[141] – political, educational, industrial, and social – some of them of long standing, which 'the charter of old to keep up' (as their host has it), dined regularly at Freeth's Coffee-House.

*   *   *

Freeth's was an engaging personality. He seems to have been a convivial, friendly, upright, simple man, sturdily sincere and oddly talented. His greatest joy in life, or so he frequently stated, was an evening spent with his friends, his pipe, and his 'cheering cup'.

> My pipe, my bottle, and my friend,
> Amidst the bustle of the age,
> My constant evening hours engage.[142]

That his company was much sought by strangers, and that the number of his acquaintances was large, is partly explained by the attitude he expressed in the lines:

> Then give me the man that is honest and free,
> I care not how rugged his feathers may be.[143]

A frequent companion of Freeth described him as 'good man and very jolly'.[144] His portraits — tinctured by continuing illness — rather suggest someone naturally melancholy and thoughtful, becoming dour in middle age, and irascible when old. Another contemporary, whose sentiments were to be echoed many times, declared that Freeth was 'respectable for his probity'.[145] Even a local 'rival-poet' could write of him:

> What Magic sweet Simplicity displays,
> Thy Manners, FREETH, are artless as thy Lays:
> Averse to Satire, Enemy to Strife,
> No Rancour stains thy Paper or thy Life.
> All Friends to native Wit, and social Glee,
> Shall charge a sparkling Glass, and fill a pipe to thee.[146]

There can be no doubt that Freeth was particularly admired for the honesty of his character and the quality of his friendship.

An eloquent tribute to the regard in which he was held was a subscription for the painting of his portrait. The picture was apparently displayed in the Coffee-House with the inscription:

> By Gen'rous Subscription this Piece was placed here;
> Had the Bard Gave the order himself,
> The World at the Picture not only would stare,
> But ask how he came by the Pelf.[147]

Freeth had few authentic claims to the style of 'poet', though he undoubtedly possessed a flair for writing verse. Some of his songs are the merest doggerel, and not many of them have any poetic expression or feeling. But the majority show that he could command an arresting turn of phrase, make a point effectively, and criticise without offensiveness. His best songs are spirited and stirring.

Freeth's prowess as a ballad-writer must have been exaggerated by the surroundings in which he sang. Before a tavern audience – no doubt sociably uncritical – and with topical news to impart, possessing a fine voice and with a well-known tune enhancing his words, Freeth probably enjoyed a success far greater than the literary merit of his songs warranted. Neverthless, it is valuable that such a substantial body of ephemeral work has survived, and that so much, comparatively, can be learned of its author. To the historian of Birmingham, to the student of ballad literature and of popular opinion, and to the bibliographer, Freeth's songsters and invitation cards offer material of some importance and no small interest.

*   *   *

Freeth's wife, Sarah, died on 25 November 1807. Ten days afterwards, on 5 December, Freeth made his Will, dividing his estate equally among eight children.[148] His signature suggests a man who is either ailing, or old and frail. He survived less than another year.

Freeth died on Thursday, 29 September 1808, in his seventy-eighth year. *Aris's Birmingham Gazette*[149] recorded the passing of 'Mr. John Freeth, of this town, commonly called the Poet Freeth, a facetious bard of nature', in terms which are immediately recognisable:

> His morals were unsullied, and his manners unaffected. Formed to enliven the social circle, possessing wit without acrimony, and independence of mind without pride, he was beloved by his friends, courted by strangers, and respected by all. The harmless, yet pointed sallies of his muse, will be remembered with pleasing pain by thousands who admired his talents and revere his virtues.

33

On 3 October 1808 Freeth's body was interred in the burial ground of the Old Meeting House.[150] This was not to be its final abode. The enlargement of New Street railway station necessitated the closing and ultimately the disappearance of the burial ground. As a result, in 1882 all the remains were taken for re-interment in the new City of Birmingham Cemetery at Witton. It is recorded, by an old friend of Freeth's son John, that Freeth's coffin was opened at this time, and that 'the face was almost as fresh, and quite as perfect, as on the day of the old man's interment seventy-four years before . . . '.[151] Yet in a letter published in the *Daily Gazette*, John Rabone of Handsworth challenges the accuracy of this statement, and recalls that when he visited the burial ground during the exhumations he was told that in 'the case of poet Freeth there was no coffin – it had all rotted away – the remains were all abroad, and were put into a shell and taken to the cemetery at Witton'.[152] As well as the bodies, tombstones and monuments were also transferred. The new graves lie within an enclosed space marked by a large granite obelisk erected by the London and North Western Railway Company. There the bodies of John Freeth and his wife still share the same grave. On the tombstone an epitaph, said to have been written by Freeth himself, commemorates him with an accuracy rare in memorial valedictions:

Free and easy through Life 'twas his wish to proceed,
Good men he revered be whatever their Creed:
His pride was a sociable evening to spend,
For no man lov'd better his Pipe and his Friend.

NOTES

1. *The Political Songster*, 1790, p. [iii].

2. cf. Freeth's obituary, quoted p. 33 and references in *Aris* and by William Godwin (Iconography No. XI), James Bisset (p. 23 and n. 106) and on a Broadside of 1832 (Bibliography No. 13). There is a copy of Freeth's *Annual Political Songster*, 1794, inscribed as 'the gift of poet Freeth' (*v.* Bibliography No. 36n.), and in 1829 he was remembered as having been 'known by the name of "Poet Freeth"' (*Gentleman's Magazine*, XCIX, pt I, 1829, p. 281).

3. A title also used by Freeth himself; *v.* the token coin bearing his portrait with the inscription 'THE BIRMINGHAM POET' (Iconography No. X). Plate 8. Morfitt (q.v. n.32) refers to Freeth in his letter as 'the Birmingham bard'.

4. Letterpress title-page and upper wrapper of *A Touch on the Times*, 1803 (Bibliography No. 34).

5. *v.* Iconography, pp. 47-53.

6. Iconography No. XI.

7. The most extensive recent use of Freeth and his work is that made by Money; but also see John Brewer, *Party Ideology and Popular Politics at the Accession of George III*, 1976, Peter Clark, *The English Alehouse: a social history, 1200-1831*, 1983, Roy Palmer, *The Sound of History: songs and social comment*, 1988, and Eric Hopkins, *Birmingham: the first manufacturing town in the world, 1760-1840*, 1989.

8. The registers of the Old Meeting House, where Freeth and members of his family worshipped and were buried (*v.* p. 34), do not contain entries of births before 1774. There is no record of Freeth's baptism in his parish church of St Martin's (though it would be convenient to identify him with the 'John', whose father is unnamed, who was baptized there on 26 October 1731). In a preface dated 28 June 1803 (in his *Touch on the Times*, 1803) Freeth

refers to himself as then being seventy-two years of age, and his obituarists, the entry of his burial in the Old Meeting House register, and the inscription on his tombstone, all agree that he was seventy-seven years of age when he died in September 1808.

9. Bell Street and Lease Lane disappeared with the construction of the Bull Ring shopping centre (formally opened in 1964).

There is an illustration of the Coffee-House in *Making of Birmingham* (p. 154) and an interesting large watercolour by Paul Braddon (1864-1938), a local artist, gives a better impression of the building as it must have looked in Freeth's time (BMAG: F825'75). Plate 7.

10. Charles Freeth's name last appears in the Birmingham Levy Book (Middle Town Quarter; BRL, press-mark: 244561) as a householder in Bell Street in 1764. His wife, named as 'widow Freeth', succeeded him, making the payments for 1765 and the two following years, and John Freeth's name is found from 1768 onward. In 1803 Freeth referred to himself as a publican of thirty-six years' experience, having commenced, that is, in 1767 (*v. A Touch on the Times*, 1803, p. [3]). His obituarists describe him in 1808 as having been proprietor of Freeth's Coffee-House for forty-eight years (or since 1760). This is almost certainly wrong. But 1760 was the year that he seems to have begun his career as a writer and singer of ballads (*v.* n.22) and the obituarists no doubt confused the two vocations which Freeth for so long conducted as one.

11. *Warwickshire Apprentices and their Masters, 1710-1760*, ed K. J. Smith (Dugdale Soc. Publ., XXIX) 1975, does not confirm this; *v.* also p. 31.

12. 'A ballad-singer's ramble to London', *The Political Songster*, 1771, pp. 36-41; *v.* pp. 175-79 *infra*.

13. *Aris*, 9 May 1763.

14. cf. 'The Necessity of the Knowledge of the use of the Globes, Sphere, and Orrery, for an easy Conception and due Understanding of the first Principles of Geography, Astronomy, Dialling, Navigation, Chronology, and other liberal Sciences, is known to every one; and is of the first Consideration among those Qualities required for forming the Scholar and the Gentleman', Benjamin Martin, *The Description and Use of Both the Globes, the Armillary Sphere, and Orrery*, 1762, p. iii.

15. Birmingham Levy Book (Digbeth Quarter); BRL, press-mark: 244505.

16. On 17 October 1753 a John Freeth married Anne Edwards at St

NOTES

Martin's, Birmingham, but unless Freeth was married twice this is not he. The members of the Freeth family in all its branches who resided in Birmingham during the 'Poet's' lifetime were numerous, and many of the men were called 'John'. For instance, to take but two examples near the extremes of Freeth's career as a publican, Sketchley and Adam's *Tradesman's True Guide and Directory*, 1770, lists three John Freeths; a cutler and engraver, a maltster and dealer in cast-iron goods, and the 'Poet'. Similarly, in 1808 three men of this name were noted in *The New Triennial Directory of Birmingham*: a silver caster, a wood-turner, and again the 'Poet'. Comparable examples may be found at almost any time during the intervening years.

17. ' . . . Sarah wife of John Freeth who departed this life Novr 25th 1807 Aged 71 years . . . ' (from the inscription on Freeth's tombstone).

18. According to Timmins, Langford, and other writers on Birmingham, Freeth had a family of two sons and eight daughters at the time of his death.

19. q.v. pp. 17, 33.

20. Jane Freeth was still alive in 1855 when she was mentioned in the Will made by her brother John on 28 January of that year. She is probably the 'Miss Freeth' referred to in an inscription found in a copy of Freeth's *New Ballads*, 1805 (*v.* Bibliography No. 37n.) and is thus shown to have been living in 1858.

21. *v.* n.116.

22. He refers to himself as having been writing songs 'more than twenty years' in *Modern Songs*, 1782 (p. vi), 'more than twice twelve years' in *A Touch on the Times*, 1783 (p. vi) and *The Political Songster*, 1784 (p. [iii]) and 1786 (p. vii), and 'for thirty years past' in *The Political Songster*, 1790 (p. [iii]). The earliest of his songs to bear a date of composition is 'The Warwickshire Militia. Written in the Year 1761' (*The Political Songster*, 1771, pp. 57-58).

23. One piece consists of a group of four songs. It was not unusual for Freeth to offer two or more songs under one title, for a composition to have several parts (as in his 'odes', 'cantatas', and medleys), or for a song virtually to be divided into sections through having various passages set to different airs. He seems to have regarded each kind of composition as a single unit, both in performing and in printing. Only when an actual count is involved has a distinction been made between a 'piece' or 'composition' of more than one part, and a single 'song'. Otherwise, for convenience

the word 'song' has been used to embrace any composition designed to be sung which Freeth treated as a unit.

24. The term 'songster' here designates a collection of songs in which the words are given but not the music.

25. *v.* Bibliography No. 28n.

26. *The Political Songster*, 1790, p. 38*. A longer version of this song, containing one additional stanza, had previously appeared in *Modern Songs*, 1782, where it was set to the tune of 'Jolly Mortals'. No air is specified in *The Political Songster*.

27. *The Annual Political Songster*, 1794, p. viii.

28. *The Political Songster*, 1790, p. [iii].

29. Money, p. 105.

30. *The Political Songster*, 1790, p. iv.

31. Money, p. 103.

32. In 1802 John Freeth was said to be 'venerable for his years, respectable for his probity, and distinguished by home-spun wit and good-humoured satire. He is one of the best political ballad writers and election poets in the kingdom' (letter from J. Morfitt, dated from Birmingham 24 December 1802, quoted by S. J. Pratt, *Harvest Home*, 1805, I, p. 274). I am indebted to Mr John Marks for kindly tracing the source of this extract for me.

33. Bibliography Nos 1-5, 7-12.

34. *v.* Bibliography No. 96 for a description. Plate 12.

35. I am indebted to Mrs S. M. T. Stone, formerly the Librarian, and to the Committee of the Birmingham Library (now the Priestley Library within The Birmingham and Midland Institute) for their kindness in allowing me access to the records of the Library.

36. q.v. pp. 26-27.

37. Langford, I, p. 58.

38. The Birmingham Reference Library has two books suggesting a measure of classical education which bear the ownership marks of a John Freeth. These are a copy of Elisha Coles's *Dictionary, English-Latin and Latin-English*, 1755, with the inscription, *inter alia*, 'John Freeth His Book Sep^t 25th 1789', and of the 1784 edition of Michael Maittaire's *Caesar* inscribed 'John Freeth 1788'. Both inscriptions are in a formal hand difficult to identify. The dates, when Freeth was at least fifty-seven years of age, suggest that the books belonged either to his son or to one of his numerous kinsmen (*v.* n.16).

I am indebted to Miss D. M. Norris, formerly of the Birmingham Reference Library, for drawing my attention to these two books.

NOTES

39. i.e. 'On the glorious success of the English privateers'; 'On the threaten'd invasion at [the] breaking out of the Spanish war'; 'Scale of talent: a political cantata'; 'The tripe eaters'; 'The players' march: on information being laid for performing'; *v.* pp. 151-57 *infra.*

40. A slightly different version of 'Scale of talent: a political cantata' was later published in *The Political Songster*, 1790 (Bibliography Nos 20-24), with the title of 'Burgoyne's defeat on the plains of Saratoga'. Another example of Freeth's re-use of material may be seen here in 'Britannia triumphant' (pp. 166-67) and 'On Admiral Nelson's victory' (pp. 197-98).

41. i.e. 'British volunteers'; 'The volunteers'; *v.* pp. 150-51, 158 *infra.*

42. cf. Frederick A. Pottle, 'Printer's Copy in the Eighteenth Century', *The Papers of the Bibliographical Society of America*, 27, 1933, pp. 65-73, and Wytze Gs Hellinga, *Copy and Print in the Netherlands*, 1962, pp. 95-109.

43. q.v. p. 15.

44. Bibliography Nos 15-17, 29-33.

45. Bibliography Nos 41-55.

46. Bibliography Nos 5-7.

47. *Aris*, 3 February; *v.* also p. 25.

48. *v.* p. 17.

49. Bibliography Nos 5-6.

50. *Aris*, 3 and 10 October.

51. Bibliography No. 44.

52. Bibliography No. 7.

53. *v.* Benjamin Walker, 'Birmingham Directories', *Birmingham Archaeological Society Transactions*, LVIII, 1937, pp. 1-36.

54. *v.* Pye's *New Directory for the Town of Birmingham*, 1785, p. 27.

55. Freeth's token coin has on its reverse the lines: BRITONS BEHOLD | THE BARD OF FREEDOM | PLAIN & BOLD | WHO SINGS AS DRUIDS | SUNG OF OLD (Iconography No. X).

56. *v.* Hill, pp. 51, 53, 96-97.

57. The changes of partnership in the business, and the family relationships of the persons concerned, are obscure. Some of the details given by Hill (pp. 96-97) are wrong. Evidence for the statements made in this and the two following paragraphs is to be found in the changing imprint of *Aris's Birmingham Gazette*, and in the obituary notices of the various partners and their kin (*Aris*: 6

July 1761, 30 May 1768, 9 January 1775, 6 April 1789, 14 December 1801, 21 February 1820).

58. From 13 February 1775 until 19 May 1783 *Aris's Birmingham Gazette* had the imprint 'A. Pearson and Co'. From the issue of 26 May 1783 onwards the imprint was changed to show the names of Pearson and Rollason.

59. *v.* Bibliography No. 25n.

60. Bibliography No. 86.

61. Bibliography Nos 43, 46, 47.

62. Bibliography Nos 52, 57, 58.

63. cf. Straus-Dent, p. 90n., and Hill, p. 63.

64. *v.* Straus-Dent, pp. 90-91, 128.

65. *The Political Songster*, 1771, p. [3].

66. Freeth's son John became an employee of this Company in 1790, and spent the whole of his working life in its service, eventually becoming Clerk (i.e. chief executive officer of the Company). He was initially articled as a 'writing clerk' for six years from 25 March 1790 with a commencing annual salary of £10 rising to £20 in his sixth year of employment. On 25 March 1796 he was appointed a 'Compting-House Clerk' for five years, his salary beginning at £60 per annum and rising by yearly increments of £10 to a maximum of £100. He resigned from the Company's service on 7 November 1842 giving ill health as his reason, and, praised for his 'long, valuable and faithful service', was awarded a 'retiring Annuity' of £375 for life. He made his Will on 28 January 1855 (BMAG, *v.* Iconography No. VI).

67. According to Robert K. Dent (*Old and New Birmingham*, I, p. 149) a list of shareholders issued on 30 March 1770 shows Freeth to be the holder of one share. His name does not appear on the original subscription deed of 12 June 1767 (BTHRC SUB 2/1), or in the Act of 1768. The earliest records of the Company to mention Freeth are the Minutes of the General Assembly of 27 September 1771 and 27 March 1772 (at both of which meetings he was present in person) and these register his holding as two shares (BTHRC, *General Assembly Minutes Book*, BCN.1.41) But in the Minutes of the Assembly held on 25 September 1772, and on subsequent occasions, Freeth does not appear as a shareholder.

The records of the Company, originally 'The Company of Proprietors of the Birmingham Canal Navigation', held by the Registrar of Companies (File No. C.9) begin no earlier than 1 January 1889.

68. *v.* H. R. Hodgkinson, 'Notes on the History of Midland Waterways', *Birmingham Archaeological Society Transactions*, XXXIX, 1913, p. 77; cf. John Phillips, *The General History of Inland Navigation* (4th edn), 1803, p. 258.

69. *v.* *Further remarks on the printed case of the Proprietors of the Birmingham Canal*, 1782. This is one of several pamphlets issued during a public controversy over the conduct of the canal company's affairs. In 1783 the proprietors were accused of, among other things, 'Breach of Faith, Want of Public Spirit, Oppression, Folly, and Injustice' (*The Conduct of the Birmingham Canal Company towards Individuals, and the Public fairly stated*, 1783).

70. W. Hutton, *History of Birmingham* (3rd edn), 1795, p. 402. The price of a share in 1782 is here given as about £370. The figure of £420 quoted above was no doubt exceptional.

71. cf. Bibliography No. 5, and *The Warwickshire Medley* [1780], pp. 135-36.

72. Quoted in *Old and New Birmingham*, II, p. 260.

73. Pye's *Birmingham Directory for 1791*, p. 28.

74. *Modern Songs*, 1782, p. viii.

75. 27 November 1782 (No. 50).

76. *The Political Songster*, 1790, Preface (dated 1783), p. xvi.

77. cf. Jennings, p. 72.

78. *v.* Vernal.

79. *Modern Songs*, 1782, p. vi.

80. Iconography No. VIII. Plate 5.

81. *The Political Songster*, 1790, p. vi.

82. I am indebted to Dr J. W. A. Moxon for the suggestion that Freeth's description of his complaint and the nature of the changes in his appearance over the years are compatible with his being a victim of Paget's Disease.

83. *v.* J. Morfitt, letter of 24 December 1802 (*v.* n.32).

84. *A Touch on the Times*, 1803, p. [3].

85. *Inland Navigation*, 1769, p. [3].

86. *A Touch on the Times*, 1783, p. vii.

87. MSS Songs, p. 35.

88. *The Political Songster*, 1771, p. 4.

89. *A Touch on the Times*, 1803, p. [3].

90. *The Political Songster*, 1790, p. iv.

91. *The Critical Review*, 58, 1784, p. 73.

92. *The Monthly Review*, IV (N.S.), 1791, p. 470.

93. *The Monthly Review*, XIV (N.S.), 1794, pp. 348-49.

94. Bibliography Nos 23-24.

95. Perhaps John Tankard, a Factor, of New Street (*v.* Pye's *Birmingham Directory for 1791*, p. 73).

96. *Memoir*, p. 79.

97. *Gentleman's Magazine*, XCIX, pt I, 1829, p. 281.

98. [William West], *Fifty Years' Recollections of an Old Bookseller*, 1835, p. 55.

99. *Memoir*, p. 76.

100. According to Bisset it was commissioned in 1790 (*Memoir*, p. 76) and painted during 1791-2 (*Reminiscences*, p. 108). A contemporary inscription on the back of the picture (given in full, Iconography No. II) dates it 1792. Plate 2.

101. *Reminiscences*, p. 108. In the *Memoir*, which is posthumously edited from Bisset's papers and may not be reliable, the amount is given (p. 76) as thirty guineas. But four guineas from each of the twelve sitters seems the more probable fee.

102. MSS Songs, p. 34.

103. *Reminiscences*, p. 108.

104. There survives what is apparently a preliminary study for this portrait of Freeth, taken from life (Iconography No. VI). Frontispiece.

105. cf. the inscription on the back of the picture (*v.* n.100) and *Reminiscences*, p. 108.

106. ' . . . painted for a public Tavern called The Poet Freeths' (*Reminiscences*, p. 108).

107. *Gentleman's Magazine*, XCIX, pt I, 1829, p. 281.

108. *Memoir*, p. 43.

109. Timmins, Key to Eckstein painting.

110. *Aris*, 3 February. This provision of newspapers would seem to be an early example of a facility that was much valued by working men who frequented coffee-houses. See, for example, Thomas Carter's appreciative remarks, with reference to the years 1815 and after, in *Memoirs of a Working Man*, 1845, pp. 186-87; Carter, interestingly, also became a member of a book club.

Money interprets the advertisement as stating that Freeth 'received regular personal reports of speeches and votes in Parliament' (p.

NOTES

103). This reading seems difficult to justify. But Dr Money's conjecture that, if such a claim were genuine, it may reveal an association between Freeth and John Almon should be noted. Almon was one of the best-known newspaper men of the day and a leading supporter of John Wilkes.

111. Eliezer Edwards, *The Old Taverns of Birmingham*, 1879, p. 12. The same story, which was told to him by an eyewitness, is related by Samuel Timmins (Key to Eckstein painting), but he makes no reference to the challenge, and though mentioning the notice, does not describe it as a result of the affray.

112. *v.* Vernal.

113. I am very much indebted to Mr Eric Dinwiddie, formerly Honorary Treasurer and Librarian of the Birmingham Book Club, to its present Honorary Secretary, Mr P. I. Addison, and to its members for their kindness in allowing me access to the Club's records.

114. Tomey.

115. Tomey takes the Eckstein painting to depict the members of the Birmingham Book Club. His view is accepted by Paul Kaufman in his article 'English Book Clubs and their Role in Social History' (*Libri*, 14, 1964, pp. 1-31; reprinted in Dr Kaufman's *Libraries and their Users*, 1969). Yet there appears to be no evidence for the identification. With the exception of Freeth's the name of none of the 'Twelve Apostles' is found in the Book Club's existing records. Also their numbers would represent only half the membership of the Book Club. Furthermore, as has been noticed, James Bisset, one of those who actually commissioned the painting, describes the sitters as 'a party of gentlemen who were in the habit of frequenting a tavern in Bell Street, called "Freeth's Coffee-House"' and who wished the artist 'to take off their likenesses in a social group' (*Memoir*, p. 76). It seems improbable that he would thus describe exactly half the members of a club that had been established for some forty-five years, and which had then been formally meeting and dining at Freeth's for at least fifteen years.

116. Elizabeth Freeth, the 'Poet's' daughter, was still landlord in 1830 (*v.* William West, *History, Topography and Directory of Warwickshire*, 1830, pp. 335, 463). Perhaps she died or retired two years later.

117. The identification is accepted in *VCH Warwickshire*, VII,1964, p. 211. There may have been other similar societies in Birmingham at the time, as there certainly were by 1781 (though not noted by

Kaufman, *Libraries and their Users* (*v.* n.115). The list of subscribers for William Hutton's *History of Birmingham*, 1781, includes the book societies at the Swan Inn, the Red Lion, and the Chain in Bull Street, as well as at 'J. Free's'.

118. An indication of the charges made for the Club's annual dinner (though not during Freeth's lifetime) is given by a Minute of 31 December 1823. It was then resolved that the house should charge the Club 3s 6d per head, which was to include 'the usual drinking' until the cloth was removed, and that twenty-four such payments (i.e. one from each member) should be guaranteed annually. Furthermore 24s should be allowed for punch, 24s for the annual use of the room, and 12s for servants, making an annual total due to the house of £7 4s 0d. Every member was required to pay 6s whether present or not. At this meeting the dinner hour was fixed at 4 p.m.

119. Old Meeting House, *Register of Resolutions of the General Assembly of the Subscribers*, 1771-1791, pp. 72, 74, 75, 77 (BRL, press-mark: 641586). Payment is also recorded of 'Mr. Freeth's Accnt' of £2 on 1 October 1794, and of £1 10s 8d on the following 3 November (*Subscribers*, 1792-1794, fol. 48; BRL, press-mark: 641587).

120. For a census of these cards *v.* pp. 74-87.

121. The card of 28 November 1771 (Bibliography No. 40) is apparently printed on the back of half a playing-card. Its verso shows part of one of the suit of clubs.

122. Bibliography No. 44 (12 June 1776).

123. One card also has another signatory; *v.* p. 31.

124. In each instance a member of the well-known Birmingham family of Colmore.

125. Bibliography No. 72 (18 June 1794).

126. Also the subject of Freeth's 'The pugilists; or, Banbury thumps', *The Political Songster*, 1790, pp. 163-64.

127. Bibliography No. 64 (25 November 1789).

128. Bibliography No. 58 (6 June 1787).

129. Bibliography No. 84.

130. Bibliography No. 88 (24 November).

131. Bibliography No. 61 (10 June 1788).

132. Bibliography No. 54 (8 June 1785).

133. Bibliography No. 73 (26 November 1794).

134. Bibliography No. 57 (22 November 1786).

NOTES

135. Bibliography No. 75 (21 January).

136. Bibliography Nos 85, 87, 89, 93, 95.

137. Bibliography No. 55.

138. Bibliography No. 74.

139. cf. Pye's *Birmingham Directory for 1791*, p. 69, and for 1797, p. 66. The modern descendants of this company were Messrs Chamberlain and Hookham of New Bartholomew Street. The Company became dormant on 1 April 1971, and although not currently trading it is still registered.

140. q.v. pp. 2-3 *supra*.

141. For conjectural identifications *v*. Money, pp. 98ff.

Concerning another aspect of Freeth's affiliations, Dr Money, emphasising the significance of Freemasonry in Birmingham at the time, assumes, as others have done, that he was a member of St Paul's Lodge, No. 43. The only evidence cited by Dr Money (p. 137) for John Freeth's having been a Freemason is derived from B. H. Joseph and J. H. Boocock's *Early Records of St Paul's Lodge, No. 43, 1764 to 1863* (n.d.) (BRL, 184100). But the 'Bro. Freeth' noticed there was Samuel Freeth, a distinguished member of that Lodge.

I am indebted to Mr Edward S. Jacobs, a Past Master of St Paul's Lodge, for kindly having the Lodge's minutes searched on my behalf and for his assurance that they do not contain any mention of John Freeth (only of Samuel Freeth) and that there is no record of John Freeth's ever having been a member.

142. *The Annual Political Songster*, 1794, p. [iii].

143. 'The foibles of dress' in *The Political Songster*, 1766, p. 22.

144. *v*. Vernal.

145. Morfitt, letter of 24 December 1802 (*v*. n.32).

146. 'Lines addressed to Poet Freeth' by 'No Matter Who', *Aris's Birmingham Gazette*, 29 December 1788. 'No Matter Who' was Joseph Weston (*v*. *Poems by Mrs. Pickering*, 1794, pp. 14-15 second count).

Similar sentiments were also expressed by the unidentified 'G. D.', apparently a contemporary of Freeth, who wrote:

> To all mankind at large, Freeth acts the brother,
> Enjoys his glass, yet shares it with another.
> Never, in vain, to him did mis'ry pray,
> To sooth it's cares and wipe it's tears away;
> Free as the air, his gen'rous hand bestows
> The needful balm that gives the mind repose;

> And genuine sympathy his breast inspires
> With love sincere and undiminished fires,
> Such as might dignify the highest birth,
> And give a taste of paradise on earth.

(Autograph MS, from the Kempson estate; BMAG, *v.* Iconography No. VI).

147. cf. Langford, II, pp. 277-78, and Jennings, p. 70.

148. Proved at Lichfield 7 February 1809 (now in the City Museum and Public Library, Lichfield).

149. 3 October 1808. This notice was copied in almost identical terms, with one short omission, in *The Gentleman's Magazine*, October 1808 (LXXVIII, pt II, p. 955).

150. *Register of Burials, 1807-47* (PRO, R.G. 4/1431). Most of the interments at this time were in the new burial ground of the Old Meeting House. But Freeth was presumably buried in his wife's grave since his name follows hers on the original tomb-stone. The position of the grave is shown on a map of the burial ground as it was in 1881 which is found in Catherine Hutton Beale's *Memorials of the Old Meeting House and Burial Ground*, 1882. A facsimile (though with some inaccuracies) of Freeth's tombstone is also given (No. 161).

151. C. M. Ingleby, *Shakespeare's Bones*, 1883, p. 32.

152. 7 September 1883.

ICONOGRAPHY

Iconography of Freeth

I. Portrait, oil on wood panel, oval, 28.6 × 24.1 cms, by James Millar (c. 1735-1805). Plate 1.

Short half-length to right, eyes looking at the spectator; probably aged 59 though appearing older; wearing cocked-hat, coat unbuttoned, loosely tied neckcloth (in which is a small ornamental pin), and waistcoat unfastened on the chest; the right hand (ring on little finger) holds a walking-stick with a bird's-head handle.

Inscribed on back of frame (? in artist's handwriting) 'Mr. John Freeth, the Poet'. A portrait by Millar of an unnamed sitter was exhibited at the Royal Academy in 1790 (Exhibition Catalogue, p. 8, No. 180), and its subject has been identified by Algernon Graves as 'Mr J. Frith' (*The Royal Academy of Arts*, vol. 5, 1906, p. 248). The compiler of the *City of Birmingham Art Gallery Catalogue of Paintings*, 1930, accepts that it was probably this picture of Freeth that was shown in 1790.

BMAG (144' 22)

II. Members of the Jacobin Club (now usually called 'John Freeth and his Circle'), oil on canvas, 111.8 × 163.8 cms, by Johann Eckstein (ob. c. 1802). Plate 2.

Freeth, (aged about 61) is shown seated at table, third figure from the left, with the eleven companions named below, some standing, others sitting.

Freeth is half-length to right, the eyes cast down; the left hand holding the head of a walking-stick also supports a long clay pipe to the mouth, the right hand is thrust into the front of the waistcoat; dress as in No. I, except that the waistcoat is fastened up to the neck, the neckcloth is neater, and no pin can be seen.

On the back of the picture is a panel inscribed in a contemporary hand:

'This picture is the common property of the twelve following gentlemen represented on the reverse, to be disposed of at all times as a majority of them shall think proper, and to be the sole property of the survivor.-

James Sketchly	Joseph Fearon
John Freeth	Jeremia Vaux
John Miles	Sameul Toy [sic]
James Murray	John Collard
Joseph Blunt	James Bisset
Richd Webster	John Wilkes

The picture painted by John Eckstein 1792'.

For further details *v.* pp. 24-25 *supra.*

BMAG (6' 09)

III. Portrait, oil on canvas, 74.0 × 61.0 cms, English School, 18th century. (Once conjectured to be the work of James Millar; *v.* No. IX.) Plate 3.

Half-length seated to right, the left arm supported by the back of the chair; the left hand holds a long clay pipe, the right hand is thrust into the front of the waistcoat; dress as in No. I except that the waistcoat is fastened on the chest, though with two middle buttons undone, the neckcloth is neater and no pin can be seen. Before him on a table are an ink-well holding a quill pen, and a single sheet of manuscript.

No. IX appears to have been derived from this portrait.

BMAG (2567' 85)

1. John Freeth, probably aged 59.

2. Members of the Jacobin Club in 1792.
Freeth, with a long clay pipe to his lips, is third from the left.

3. John Freeth.

4. John Freeth
(possibly by his friend
James Bisset).

THE

POLITICAL SONGSTER;

OR, A

TOUCH ON THE TIMES,

ON

VARIOUS SUBJECTS,

ADAPTED TO COMMON TUNES.

THE FOURTH EDITION.

BY JOHN FREETH.

BIRMINGHAM,
PRINTED FOR THE AUTHOR,
AND SOLD BY PEARSON AND ROLLASON.
MDCCLXXXVI.

A

TOUCH ON THE TIMES;

BEING

A COLLECTION OF

NEW SONGS

TO OLD TUNES,

INCLUDING SOME FEW WHICH HAVE APPEARED
IN FORMER EDITIONS.

BY A VETERAN

In the Class of Political Ballad Street Scribblers,

Who, when good News is brought to Town,
Immediately to Work fits down,
And Business fairly to go through,
Writes Songs, finds Tunes, and sings them too.

Birmingham,
PRINTED FOR THE AUTHOR,
AT THE OFFICE OF THE EXECUTORS OF T. A. PEARSON,
AND SOLD BY KNOTT & LLOYD.
1803.

5 and 6. Engraved portrait frontispieces and letterpress title-pages of
The Political Songster (1786) and *A Touch on the Times* (1803).

7. Freeth's Coffee-House, from a watercolour
by Paul Braddon (1864–1938).

8. Token coin as used
in Freeth's Coffee-House.

SOCIETY FEAST,

AND

Sale of Books,

on
FRIDAY NEXT.

☞ Dinner at Half paſt One o'Clock.

Sir,

AS Food much in vogue, for the keen craving
    Mind,
The PRINTS though we daily peruſe ;
Till Peace is obtain'd, we may read ourſelves
    blind,
Before we find SPECIAL good NEWS.

The DUTCH, DAM'D or UNDAM'D, their ALL
    have at ſtake,
I pity our brave BRITISH BAND ;
And ſoon, both for Trade and Humanity's ſake,
May the OLIVE BRANCH gladden the Land.

             J. Freeth.

Birmingham, Jan. 21, 1795.

Annual Feaſt, and Sale of Books,

ON FRIDAY NEXT.

DINNER AT TWO o'CLOCK.

SIR,

IN theſe plentiful days,
  If the heart is at eaſe,
And you've got a few minutes to ſpare,
  With a friend and a cup,
  Keep the old cuſtom up,
And be happy o'er good Engliſh fare.

Be the times bad or good,
  If its now underſtood,
That the CENTURY ends with this year,
  May the next we begin,
  Be with PEACE uſher'd in,
And its Bleſſings diffus'd far and near.

By reading we find,
  Conſtant food for the mind,
But as WAR we have cauſe to deplore ;
  As a TOAST whilſt I live,
  Free and fondly I'll give,
"GOOD FELLOWSHIP all the World o'er."

Birmingham, Jan. 23, 1799.   *J. F.*

Annual Feaſt and Sale of Books—on Friday next.

DINNER AT TWO O'CLOCK.

Reſpecting mankind's old habitual fare,
  Whatever new modes are invented :
If WHITE BREAD I can't for my table prepare,
  I truſt you'll with BROWN be contented.

For ſupport, on a generous public much lies,
  Wholeſome Soup many keeps from ſtarvation ;
Good Ale very ſcarce is, and Chriſtmas Mince-pies,
  It ſeems are almoſt out of faſhion.

On Ruſſia, ſince England has got a ſtrong claim,
  JOHN BULL—as to there a ſhort dance is ;
May ſerve the magnanimous PAUL much the ſame
  As the French ſerve the Emperor FRANCIS.

Although common food is uncommonly dear,
  Endeavour to make the heart gay ;
And let at the Board over plain Engliſh cheer,
  BETTER TIMES be the Toaſt of the Day.

Birmingham, Jan. 27, 1801.   J. FREETH.

SOCIETY FEAST,

And Sale of Books, on Friday next.

DINNER AT TWO O'CLOCK.

SIR,

THO' much *blood* and treaſure the war must have cost,
Bloody angry are they who their *places* have loſt ;
And tho' thrown aſide is the ſword and the gun,
As a war upon paper is ſtill going on,
What a happineſs 'twill to poſterity be,
If our ſons, and our ſons ſons, no other war ſee!

By woeful experience, ſince England well knows
That Europe but ſeldom finds general repoſe ;
Let the Toaſt of the Day—wiſhing Trade may increaſe,
Be "FRIENDSHIP & ADDINGTON, PLENTY & PEACE."

            J. FREETH.

Birm. Jan. 25, 1803.

9. Freeth's invitation cards.

SIR.

AS few when the Season its kindness displays,
But love to partake of young Ducks and green peas,
And as in the Town there is known to be plenty,
To-morrow I purpose to cater for twenty,
Pudding time is at One — to the Custom adhere,
For the Summons must please that invites to good Cheer:
In the TOASTS of the Day as a friend to the Land,
And foften oft for FREEDOM may EFFINGHAM stand,
Not forgetting Lord GRANBY a SAVILLE and BURKE
Our good friends at BOSTON and those at NEW YORK.

J. FREE.

Birmingham; June, 15th 1775.

SIR.

WHILST some to the Throne are ADDRESSES conveying,
For Slaughter and Slavery servilely praying,
And false as their Language is fulsome pretend,
They'll hazard their Lives, and their Fortunes they'll spend;
Accept from a Lover of peace this PETITION,
To festive enjoyment the Card of Admission:
Next FRIDAY I purpose to garnish my Board,
For Feasting I always to fighting preferr'd.
As friends to Conciliat'ry Measures are those,
Who wish well to COMMERCE and FREEDOM espouse,
May those who oppose 'em and more Blood would spill,
Be forc'd into Service, and mount BUNKER's HILL.

J. FREE.

November 21st. 1775.

SIR,

FRIDAY next being FEAST DAY,
the Favour of your Company is
humbly requested to DINE at J. FREE's,
at ONE o'Clock.

JUNE 12, 1776.

SIR.   November, 25, 1778.

THO' as bad as Times are. 'tis a folly to grieve,
For Murmuring cannot Misfortunes retrieve;
Resolv'd in my mind that dull care shall be drown'd,
With plenty next FRIDAY my Board will be crown'd,
Good Cheer few despise. and as Life's but a span,
Attend to the Summons, and come if you can.
Old ENGLAND's run hard. for its rather too much.
To be bully'd by FRENCHMEN. and mob'd by the DUTCH;
But let through the Land unanimity reign.
And BRITONS shall still be the Lords of the Main;
For CHARTRES since KEPPEL disfigur'd his CREST
Thinks Danger is near if he peeps out of BREST.

J. FREE.

---

10. Freeth's invitation cards (*continued*).

SOCIETY FEAST.

SIR,

FRIDAY next, if you've nothing material on Hand,
Let the plentiful Board your Attention command;
The Limb of a Goose, on a Plate of Green Peas,
I make not a Doubt, will the Appetite please:
Look sharp for a While, and, if one will not do,
Disdain to be sparing—make certain of two.

As to Matters of State, strange as may be the Rout!
Not much does it matter who's IN or who's OUT:
As GOVERNMENT WHEELS I can only compare
To *Birmingham Streets*—always wanting Repair;
For when LEVIES run high, and are chearfully paid,
Ducks and *Drakes* of the Cash, are too frequently made.

May the Youth at the Helm, whom the People admire,
Inherit those Virtues which dwelt in his Sire!
And a Bumper be given—That Wrangling may cease,
Less TAXES, more TRADE—and with all the World PEACE!

Birmingham, *June 9th* 1784.   J. FREE.

Swinney, Letter Founder and Printer.

SOCIETY FEAST.

SIR,

FRIDAY next is festive Day,
Why should Tradesmen not be gay?
Though our Burthens still are sore,
Sorrow drown—the worst is o'er;—
Cheer the Heart, and Mirth enjoy,
The Times *will mend—I'll tell you why.*

Thurlow, at the Lord Mayor's Feast,
Seated as a welcome Guest,
And getting groggy—by the Bye—
Told the Cits, (I hope no Lie),
An odious Tax might be repeal'd,
And Substitution still with-held:—
He told it with a merry Look,
The Scowl had then his Brow forsook.—
Such News, what Pleasure to reveal?
Hang the Man who stole his Seal!

The TIMES *will mend, there's not a Doubt,*
For PITT has worn the BUDGET out.

Birmingham,   J. FREE.
23d Nov. 1785.

SOCIETY FEAST.

SIR,   Dinner at Half after One.

THE Gloom of November is apt, People say,
   On the Spirits of Englishmen always to prey;
But if to be chearful the Heart is inclin'd,
On FRIDAY, I trust, you'll no Gloominess find;
For, temper'd with Prudence, an Evening's Regale,
The Mind that is social, to please cannot fail.

COMMERCIAL ARRANGEMENTS give general Joy!
The Prospect is pleasing—keep sacred the TIE:
May Kingdom 'gainst Kingdom no more live in Spite,
For both 'twere much better to TRADE than to FIGHT!
We'll drink to each other, nor longer seem strange,
Old STINGO for CLARET we'll freely exchange.

The Season is chequer'd, and Wonder excites!
And so does the Talk of PEG NICHOLSON'S KNIGHTS!
The Plan throughout LIFE is—of LIFE make the most,
Let that be observ'd—and let this be the TOAST—
" Keep WAR at a Distance—with WRANGLERS away;
" Disturbers of Peace send to BOTANY BAY."

Birmingham, *Nov.* 22, 1786.   J. FREETH.

M. Swinney, Printer.

SOCIETY FEAST.

SIR,

      YOUR Company is desired at J. FREETH's, on FRIDAY next.

         ☞ DINNER at TWO o'Clock.

MY House has been thoroughly warm'd, never fear,
   And Doctors—if right I remember,
Prescribe for their Patients a Drop of good Cheer,
   In the dull foggy Month of November.

Trade will soon come about—nay, there seems little Doubt,
   Town and Country good Orders will find;
And before Christmas Day—to compleat Matters—may
   The DEFINITIVE TREATY be sign'd.

BIRMINGHAM, NOVEMBER 24, 1801.   J. FREETH.

11. Freeth's invitation cards (*continued*).

12. Manuscript of *Modern Songs* (1782) in Freeth's handwriting, showing the printer's marking-up by signature and page.

IV. Portrait, oil on canvas, 30.5 × 25.4 cms, (? by James Bisset). Plate 4.

Half-length seated to left, eyes looking at the spectator, otherwise as in No. VII, from which it is apparently derived.

Inscribed on back of canvas: 'THE POET FREETH'.

This may be the painting attributed to Bisset described below, *v*. No. XII.

BMAG (P. 39′ 64)

V. Portrait, oil on canvas, 75.3 × 63.3 cms, British School, 19th century copy after 18th century original.

Short half-length seated to right, eyes cast down, the left arm supported by the back of the chair; the left hand holds what is perhaps a white handkerchief or napkin, the right hand is not seen. Dress as in No. II.

Inscribed in chalk on verso: 347-41.

BMAG (3191′ 85)

VI. Portrait, pastel, oval, 30.5 × 24.1 cms, 18th century (? by Johann Eckstein). Frontispiece.

This appears to be a preliminary study for No. II.

The picture formerly belonged to the late Miss Ethel Mary Kempson (ob. 1965) of Birmingham, who claimed to be a descendant of Freeth.

In a codicil to his Will dated 28 January 1855 (the date also of the Will) John Freeth jun. (q.v. n.66), the son of 'Poet' Freeth, made special provision for putting into a trade Edward and Frederick Kempson, sons of one Charlotte Kempson (BMAG, acquired in 1965; neither inventory number nor press-mark is available; believed now to be in BMAG Local History Department but cannot be found). Miss Ethel Mary Kempson, whose father's name was Edward, appears to have been related to these protégés of John Freeth, jun.

Coll. Horden.

VII. Portrait, pastel, 24.8 × 22.9 cms, British School, 18th century.

Three-quarter length seated to left; probably aged 70 or more; dress as in No. I except that no buttons are visible, the neck-cloth is neater and no pin can be seen, and the shirt is revealed through the cuff-vent of the left sleeve; the right hand holds a long clay pipe, the left a slip of paper.

BMAG (242' 32)

VIII. Portrait, engraving (plate-mark: 12.7 × 8.9 cms; engraving: 11.7 × 7.4 cms). Plate 5.

Half-length to left, hatless, within an ornamental oval frame. Inscribed [*upon a ribbon beneath the portrait:*] JOHN FREETH | [*beneath the ribbon:*] Writes Songs finds tunes, | & Sings them too. [*at the foot of the plate:*] *Matt.ʷ Haughton, fculpsit.* | *Birmingham, Printed by E.Ralph Nᵒ 9 Bell Street.* (verso: blank) Matthew Haughton was presumably the son of Moses Haughton (1734-1804) (q.v. Thieme-Becker).

Elizabeth Ralph, a near neighbour of Freeth in Bell Street, is described in the *New Directory for the Town of Birmingham*, 1785 (p. 62), as a 'Copper-plate Printer, Bookbinder, and Victualler'. She was, no doubt, the successor of Barnaby Ralph, the bookbinder, of Bell Street.

Found in Freeth's *Political Songster*, 1786 (Bibliography Nos 18-19).

IX. Portrait, stipple-engraving, oval (plate-mark: 14.9 × (?)10.3 cms; engraving: 13.3 × 9.5 cms). Plate 6.

Half-length seated to right, hands clasped, the left arm supported by the back of the chair; dress as in No. I, except that only the top two buttons of the waistcoat are undone, the neckcloth is neater and no pin can be seen. Before Freeth on the table are an ink-well holding two quill pens, and an open book. Inscribed, immediately below the oval [*to the left:*] *Miller delin* [*to the right:*] *Martin Sculp* | [*at the foot of the plate:*]

ICONOGRAPHY

JOHN FREETH, | Publish'd Ap.^{l} 22.^{d} 1788 as the Act directs, by | PEARSON & ROLLASON *Birmingham*. (verso: blank)

Apparently derived from No. III.

'Miller' is unidentified, but possibly James Millar (q.v. No. I) is meant. He was not unfamiliar with drawing for an engraver, having, for instance, designed the engraved front-ispiece (and perhaps some of the other copperplates) for an edition of Josephus's works published in 1770 by Christopher Earl of Birmingham. If this portrait is the work of James Millar then it may be that No. III should also be attributed to him.

The engraver was presumably F. B. Martin (q.v. Thieme-Becker).

Found in Freeth's *Political Songster*, 1790 (Bibliography Nos 20-24) and his *Touch on the Times*, 1803 (Bibliography No. 34).

X. Token coin, struck in copper and brass. Plate 8.

Bust to right, body three-quarters, face in profile. Dress similar to Nos. I-IV. Inscribed [*encircling the bust:*] THE BIRMINGHAM POET [*on the reverse:*] BRITONS BEHOLD | THE BARD OF FREEDOM | PLAIN & BOLD | WHO SINGS AS DRUIDS | SUNG OF OLD [*on the edge:*] MANUFACTURED BY W.LUTWYCHE BIRMINGHAM

cf. R. Dalton and S. H. Hamer, *The Provincial Token Coinage of the 18th. Century*, pt IX, 1915, p. 263 (No. 30); for an account of the use of such coins *v.* Peter Mathias, 'The people's money in the eighteenth century', in *The Transformation of England: Essays in the Economic and Social History of England in the Eighteenth Century*, 1979, pp. 190-208.

There is an example, in copper, in the BM Department of Coins and Medals: T 6338.

XI. Portrait relief (?), wax, by George Bullock.

An exhibition of wax figures presented by a Mrs Bullock was

widely advertised in Birmingham from 1794 onward. On 29
May 1797 *Aris's Birmingham Gazette* reported that 'Mrs
Bullock and Son' had been modelling new figures for the
exhibition including likenesses of the 'Prince and Princess of
Wirtemberg, and of the Poet Freete'. William Godwin,
visiting Birmingham just over a week later, saw a handbill to
the same effect. He wrote to Mary Wollstonecraft Godwin on
7 June 1797:

> '. . . I amused myself [while spending two hours in Birmingham
> the previous day] with enquiring the meaning of a hand-bill,
> respecting a wax-work exhibition, containing among others,
> lively & accurate likenesses of the Prince & Princess of
> Wirtemberg, & poet Freeth. As I had never heard of poet Freeth,
> my curiosity was excited. We found that he was an ale-house
> keeper of Birmingham, the author of a considerable number of
> democratical squibs. If we return by Birmingham, I promise
> myself to pay him a visit . . .'

(Abinger Collection of Shelley Papers: Bodleian, MS Film 61
(129). Cf. Ralph M. Wardle (ed.), *Godwin & Mary: Letters of
William Godwin and Mary Wollstonecraft*, 1967, p. 86. I am
indebted to the Lord Abinger for permission to refer to the
original.)

A few months after Godwin's visit to Birmingham another
traveller, again only passing through the town, also noticed
the exhibition. This was one 'J. P. L.' from whom a letter was
published in *Aris's Birmingham Gazette*, 27 November 1797,
praising the work of a young modeller at whose shop in Bull
Street he had seen, among other works of art, 'an exhibition
of Wax Figures, in such perfection as we have never seen in
London'. The young modeller was George Bullock, at this
time apparently only fourteen or fifteen years of age, who was
in partnership with his mother at No. 29 Bull Street. He was
to go on to have a brilliant career as a modeller, sculptor, and
cabinet-maker. His genius has only recently been fully
acknowledged, and his reputation is still growing (*v. George
Bullock: Cabinet-maker*, introd. Clive Wainwright, 1988). In her
advertisement of 1794 Mrs Bullock describes the figures of the
exhibition as being 'all of the full size of life', but there is no

indication later of the nature of Freeth's likeness. Most of Bullock's surviving works as a sculptor are substantial busts. The only known example of his work in wax, which is dated 1801, is a portrait relief (25.5 × 19.0 cms) of Henry Blundell of Ince (*v. Bullock*, p. 129).

If extant, location unknown.

XII. Portrait, oil, 25.4 × 20.3 cms, by James Bisset (1760-1832).

'It represents him [i.e. Freeth] with the large hat of the period, with a pipe in one hand and a spill in the other, and possibly about 60 years of age' (Jennings, p. 70). Though the dimensions which Jennings gives are not exactly right, the picture he describes may be No. IV. Otherwise, if extant, location unknown.

XIII. Portrait, with the lines:

> By Gen'rous Subscription this Piece was placed here;
> Had the Bard Gave the order himself,
> The World at the Picture not only would stare,
> But ask how he came by the Pelf.

The picture has been variously described as representing Freeth as a comparatively young man, having in his hands a scroll upon which these lines are written, or, alternatively as depicting him holding a copy of *Lloyd's Evening Post*, with the lines of verse beneath the picture (cf. Langford, II, pp. 277-78, and Jennings p. 70).

If extant, location unknown.

BIBLIOGRAPHY

In passages of quasi-facsimile transcription the distinction between the plain and swash forms of italic capitals represents their use in the originals. There is one exception. In No. 16 correct transcription calls for the swash form of the letter 'Z', but unfortunately this is not available in the fount of type used here (but see No. 16n.).

EPHEMERA

SONGS IN NEWSPAPERS

Copies of *Aris's Birmingham Gazette* cited here are to be found in BRL; but *v.* No. 6. Transcriptions are given in quasi-facsimile (Nos 1-12) chiefly because of the possibility that cards or slips may have been printed from the same type-setting. Also cf. Nos 5 and 6. Where the first word of the text is shown as being in two sizes of capitals, it is to be assumed that the first letter is a drop initial indenting the second line of text (with the exception of Nos 10 and 12, where the initial capital is on the base line).

1. *Aris*, 18 July 1763] *On a late* VERDICT. Tune, The Lillies of France. | [*18 ll. beginning:*] SINCE Freedom each pow'rful Opponent repels, | [*last line:*] *Whilſt Shouts from the Weſt make the vaulted Sky ring.* | [*to the left:*] BIRMINGHAM. [*to the right:*] J.F.

2. *Aris*, 31 October 1763] BIRMINGHAM BEER. A NEW SONG. | *To the Tune of* Ye Prigs who are troubled with Confcience's Qualms. | [*32 ll. beginning:*] YE Mortals who never in all your wild Trips, | [*last line:*] If only to taſte of fam'd *Birmingham Beer!* | [*to the right:*] J.F.

Note: Later reprinted in Nos 20-24, and No. 34.

3. *Aris*, 20 March 1769] *On the* BILL *depending for removing* PUBLIC | NUISANCES. | EPIGRAM. | [*8 ll. beginning:*] WONDER not that this Contention, | [*last line:*] And ev'ry Day are ſeen above. [*to the right:*] J.F.

4. *Aris,* 4 June 1770] *Written extempore, on hearing that Mr.* Skipwith, *Member* | *for the County of Warwick, was remarkably active in prevent-* | *ing the* Exportation *of* Wheat, *by oppoſing the Motion in the* | Houſe *of* Commons, &c. | [*24 ll. beginning:*] In nervous — animated — Lays, | [*last line:*] In Spite of Lordly Power.

Note: Later reprinted in Nos 29 and 30.

5. *Aris,* 8 August 1774] EPILOGUE written by Mr.FREE, for his Benefit, and ſpo- | ken on Wedneſday Evening laſt, by Mr. PENN, with great | Judgment and Propriety to a very crouded and reſpectable | Audience at the New Theatre in this Town. | [*36 ll. beginning:*] In Times of old it often has been ſaid, | [*last line:*] Call at his Houſe, you'll find Roast Beef to-morrow.

Note: Later reprinted in Nos 29 and 30 (*v.* also No. 6).

6. *Swinney,* 11 August 1774] [*As in No. 5 except:*] ... and | ſpoken ... with | great judgment and propriety ... reſpecta- | ble audience ... | ... times ... | ... houſe ...

Notes: I have been unable to seè a copy of *Swinney's Birmingham and Stafford Chronicle* for Thursday 11 August 1774. But a newspaper cutting carrying a report of the occasion which is found pasted on a leaf at the front of the BRL copy of Freeth's *Warwickshire Medley,* [1780] (press-mark: 57527; Bibliography ·No. 29) may be identified from the typography and from parts of advertisements as coming from an issue of this paper for that date.

Also *v.* No. 5n.

7. *Aris,* 2 August 1784] *The following, amongſt other ſongs upon the occaſion,* | *was ſung before a numerous company on the Thankſ-* | *giving day, by that well-known ſongſter of the* | *times* J.Free ... [*16 ll. beginning:*] SONS of Trade for mirth prepare, | [*last line:*] "Of a bad bargain make the beſt." | Tune — *Come ye party jangling ſwains.* | [*24 ll. beginning:*] Now no more to distant lands | [*last line:*] Trade and Peace with all the world.

Notes: It was not unusual for Freeth to divide a song into several parts, each to be sung to a different tune (*v.* n.23). Sometimes, as with the first part here, he does not specify tunes for all the parts.

A slightly different version of this composition had previously appeared in 1783 as part of an 'Ode: written and sung on the evening of the Thanksgiving Day for a general peace' (No. 33), and was later included in *The Political Songster*, 1790 (Nos 20-24). There, in each instance, the first part is to be sung to the tune of 'Drink and set your hearts at rest'.

The report in *Aris's Birmingham Gazette* of these Thanksgiving Day celebrations also notes that 'at the same time many constitutional toasts were given in honour of the day, by that ingenious mechanic of whom it has been so justly said he . . .

> "Makes a song and forms a buckle,
> Whilst a pipe's between his lips."'

These two lines are from a song by Freeth called 'Tutania Buckles' in Nos 20-24 and No. 33, and 'Tutania' in No. 32 (where one stanza of four lines is omitted). The 'ingenious mechanic', whose manufacture of 'the metal called Tutania' these lines commemorate, was William Tutin of Birmingham. He was described at that time as a 'manufacturer of fine white Tutania, Yellow, and Pinchbeck Buckles, Tutania Spoons, Coach Furniture, &c' (Charles Pye, *New Directory for the Town of Birmingham*, 1785, p. 77).

8. *Aris*, 15 November 1784] *On a benefaction of Five Hundred Pounds being pre-* | *ſented to the General Hoſpital by a Lady unknown.* | [*8 ll. beginning:*] Of Ruffel, though much has been ſaid, | [*last line:*] The eſſence of charity dwells. [*to the right:*] F.

9. *Aris*, 9 October 1786] FREEDOM's FAIR GROUND: | *A* SONG *on the* TREATY *of* COMMERCE. | Tune — "Lillies of France." | [*24 ll. beginning:*] YE Friends to Fair Freedom, and Sons of True-worth, | [*last line:*] Its equal is not in the WORLD to be found. | [*to the right:*] BIRMINGHAM.

Note: Later revised and reprinted in Nos 20-24.

10. *Aris*, 7 April 1788] *On the death of the truly facetious Mr.* Job Hart. | [*12 ll. beginning:*] DEATH who to all muſt give the fatal ſtroke, | [*last line:*] For ready WIT, he has not left his FELLOW. F.

Note: Later reprinted in Nos 23 and 24.

11. *Aris,* 1 August 1791] SONG, *on obtaining the*
BIRMINGHAM *and* | WORCESTER CANAL BILL. | [*32
ll. beginning:*] COME, now begin delving, the Bill is obtain'd, |
[*last line:*] "Health, plenty, and peace, Navigation and Trade." |
[*to the left:*] *The Seat of the Arts, July* 5, 1791. [*to the right:*] J.F.
Note: Later reprinted in No. 36.

12. *Aris,* 7 September 1795] *On the uncommon* RISE *and* FALL *in the
Price of Bread.* | [*4 ll. beginning:*] SPECULATION much varied 'twixt
June and *September,* | [*last line:*] So fudden a rife, and fo rapid a
fall. | [*to the right:*] F.

BROADSIDE

13. [*Heading:*] Job Nott, in Worcester.
[*At foot:*] TYMBS AND DEIGHTON, PRINTERS,
JOURNAL OFFICE, WORCESTER.
42.5 × 34.3 cms. Printed in three columns, verso blank. Signed
'JOB NOTT.' and dated 'Worcester, | Nov. 30th. 1832.'.
Includes: THE LOYAL SONG | WHICH POET FREETH
WROTE FOR OLD JOB NOTT. [*36 ll., in nine quatrains,
beginning:*] When party feuds and crafty wiles, [*last line:*] By
wholesome laws protected. [*chorus, tenth quatrain, beginning:*] Then
let us join with spirits bold, [*last line:*] Our GLORIOUS
CONSTITUTION.

Notes: Nott's text (third column) has a reference to 'the old Poet,
FREETH that lived in Constitution Hall, the pink of loyalty'.

Freeth's song draws substantially upon the versions of 'Love
and Unanimity' found in Bibliography Nos 35, 36, and 34, one of
which is quoted in *The Life of Job Nott ... as written by himself,*
1793, pp. 24-25.

'Job Nott' was the pseudonym of Theodore Price (*v.* Samuel
Halkett and John Laing, *Dictionary of Anonymous and Pseudonymous
English Literature,* IX, 1962, p. 179).

The price is given as 1d each, or 3s 6d for fifty copies, and 6s
for one hundred, to be obtained of Mr William Close, at the
Albion Printing Office, 49 Broad Street.

Copy: Formerly in the collection of Mr John Marks, location
now unknown.

BOOKS AND PAMPHLETS

A few entries include transcriptions of the letterpress on wrappers, but as wrappers are to be met so infrequently it has seemed most convenient here (Nos 14-37) to record their survival rather than notice their absence. It is to be assumed, therefore, that wrappers, plain or with letterpress, are found only in those copies where their presence is noted in the list of locations.

Only when an uncut copy is available has an attempt been made to indicate the size of the sheet of paper by name. Elsewhere the measurements (in cms) given in the collations are those of the leaf of the tallest copy examined.

Any composition containing more than one part which Freeth appears to have treated as a unit (*v.* n.23) has here (Nos 14-37) been counted as a single piece for the purpose of enumeration.

Locations do not record any copy in private ownership unless no other copy is known.

The Political Songster

14. THE | POLITICAL | SONGSTER. | CALCULATED | For the PRESENT YEAR. | [*double rule*] | [*cluster of four foliar type-orns*] | [*double rule*] | PRINTED for the AUTHOR, | M DCC LXVI. | [*within square brackets:*] *PRICE SIX-PENCE.*

HT] [*double row of type-orns*] | A | COLLECTION | OF | SONGS, *&c.* | [*row of type-orns*]

Collation: (17.1 × 9.6) 12°: A-C⁶ (-C6) D² [$3 (-C3 D2) signed]: 19 leaves, pp. [1-3] 4-34 37-40 (= 38)

Contents: p. [1]: title-page. [2]: blank. [3]: text (21 pieces). On 34: <? 'FINIS.'>. 37: text (2 pieces). On 40: 'FINIS.'.

RT] A COLLECTION OF SONGS, &c. [SONGS. (? broken comma, or full point) A4v A6v B4v; RT in larger type, approx. small pica, on sheet D, on other sheets approx. long primer]

CW] A6v II. B2v A [As] B6v V. D1v With

Copy: BRL (257599 + cutting of No. 2 on free leaf at back)

15. THE | POLITICAL SONGSTER; | ADDRESSED TO THE | SONS of FREEDOM, | AND | LOVERS of HUMOUR, | By *J.FREE.* | *[rule]* | *BIRMINGHAM:* | Printed for the AUTHOR, by J.BASKERVILLE, | and Sold by S.ARIS, and M.SWINNEY. | MDCCLXXI.

HT] *[row of type-orns, Straus-Dent 2 and 6]* | THE | POLITICAL SONGSTER. | *[parallel rule]*

Collation: (20.6 × 12.6) 8°: A^2 B-P⁴ [\$2 (-F2 K2 M2) signed], 58 leaves, pp. [1-3] 4 [1] 2-100 [101] 102-106 [107] 108-112

Contents: p. [1]: title-page. [2]: blank. [3]: 'To the PUBLIC.'. On 4: '*J.F.*'. [1]: HT and text (47 pieces, numbered 'I' to 'XLV', with 'XXVII' omitted, followed by three unnumbered pieces). [101]: '*WILKES*'s ENLARGEMENT, | AN | ODE.' (full point misaligned) and text (2 pieces, unnumbered). [107]: 'BIRMINGHAM NAVIGATION. | AN | ODE.' ('ODE.' full point misaligned) and text (1 piece, unnumbered). On 112: '*FINIS.*'.

RT] The *POLITICAL* | *SONGSTER.* [*SONGSTER* (no point) E4r G4r I1r L4r N2r; broken *T* E2r; *SONGSTER* omitted O3r; The *POLITICAL,* &c. P1v P4v; (?) *POLiTICAL* (numeral) M3v; *in some copies:* POLCTICAL B4v]

CW] F4v 'Mongſt [The] ("Mongſt' is the first word of the second stanza on G1r) G4r Fo [For] G3v H1v I3v K4r (no CW) O4v INLAND [*The*]

Gaskell No. 42.

Copy: BRL (81720, wrappers, though cut and bound)

16. Another issue, as in No. 15 except that here P4 (pp. 111-12) is followed by:

χ^1, 1 leaf, pp. 113-14 (p. 113: '*BELZEBUB*'s TOUR to *LEICESTER.*' 1 piece)

Gaskell No. 42.

Notes: Apparently this leaf was also printed by Baskerville.

In the song title noted as being on p.113 the word '*BELZEBUB*' should be represented here with the letter '*Z*' in swash form; but see the rubric to 'Bibliography' p. 55.

Copy: Bodleian (280 i. 141)

17. THE | POLITICAL SONGSTER; | OR, A | TOUCH ON THE TIMES, | ON | VARIOUS SUBJECTS, | ADAPTED TO COMMON TUNES, | THE THIRD EDITION. | By JOHN FREE. | BIRMINGHAM, | PRINTED FOR THE AUTHOR: | AND SOLD BY PEARSON AND ROLLASON. | MDCCLXXXIV.

HT] A | COLLECTION | OF | NEW SONGS.

Collation: (16.6 × 9.8) 12°: A⁴ B-F⁶ ˣG⁶ χ¹ G² [$3 (-G2) signed], 43 leaves, pp. [i-iii] iv-viii [1] 2-60 *61 62-72 ²63-4 ³61-3 [64] (=78)

Contents: p. [i]: title-page. [ii]: 'CONTENTS.'. [iii]: 'THE | PREFACE.'. [1]: HT and text (38 pieces). On ³63: 'THE END.'. [64]: blank

RT] [none; page number (arabic numerals, no full point, within square brackets) in centre of headline; *61, with asterisk]

CW] B6v (no CW) C6v He D6v CHORUS. E4r WHIP-[WHIPCORD] F6v Tʜᴇ G6v Tʜᴇ

PF] B1v: 1; E6v G3v: 2; A1v C6v D6r F3v: 3

Price: 1s (Preface and reviews).

Reviewed: Monthly Review, LXXI, 1784, p. 386; *Critical Review*, 58, 1784, p. 73.

Notes: This book was apparently issued in at least one earlier state than is described here. As it was initially printed it has the collation A⁴ B-F⁶ G², and the table of contents confirms that in this form it was complete. A single unsigned leaf (*χ¹) with the pagination *59-*60, containing only the song 'The female canvasser: on the Westminster election', was subsequently inserted after F6 (p. 60). At this time, it seems, an errata slip listing errors on D6ʳ⁻ᵛ, *χ1v, and G1r was also printed and in the BRL copy it is attached to the foot of G2r. Presumably the book was issued in this state, if not in the earlier one.

In a later state the single leaf *χ¹ was replaced by a gathering ˣG⁶ with the pagination *61 62-72. The first leaf of the gathering, ˣG1ʳ⁻ᵛ, contains a revised version of 'The female canvasser'. This song refers to the notorious activities of Georgiana, Duchess of Devonshire, during the Westminster election of 1784. It was the revised version that was afterwards reprinted in *The Political Songster*, 1790 (Nos 20-24).

The BRL copy (57554) has both $*\chi^1$ and $^X G^6$.

As described here (No. 17) the book includes a single leaf (χ^1). One of the songs from this leaf, 'On Blanchard's aerial voyage to the Continent', has an allusion to 'the year eight-five'. It may thus be that the addition of the leaf represents yet another and even later state than that described immediately above (i.e. A^2 B-F^6 $^X G^6$ G^2).

$^X G^6$ and χ^1 are from the same setting of type as in No. 33.

Re printers *v*. No. 31n.

Copy: BRL (57554)

18. THE | POLITICAL SONGSTER; | OR, A | TOUCH ON THE TIMES, | ON | VARIOUS SUBJECTS, | ADAPTED TO COMMON TUNES. | THE FOURTH EDITION. | By JOHN FREETH. | BIRMINGHAM, | PRINTED FOR THE AUTHOR: | AND SOLD BY PEARSON AND ROLLASON. | MDCCLXXXVI.

HT] A | COLLECTION | OF | NEW SONGS. | [*short spread rule*]

Collation: (17.2 × 10.8) 12°: A^4 B-F^6 G^2 H^2 [\$3 (-A3 G2 H2) signed], 38 leaves, pp. [i-iv] v-viii [1] 2-68; frontispiece

Contents: frontispiece, Iconography No. VIII. p. [i]: title-page. [ii]: 'CONTENTS.'. [iii]: 'THE | PREFACE.'. [1]: HT and text (33 pieces). On 68: 'THE END.'.

RT] [none; page number (arabic numerals, no full point, within square brackets) in centre of headline; 64, second bracket missing]

CW] A4v A COL- [see HT] B6v But C4v C6v (no CW) D6v A ftrange F6v Duty G1v G2v (no CW)

PF] A4r B3v C2v D4v E1v F6r: 3

Price: 1s (Preface).

Note: Re printers *v*. No. 31n.

Copy: BRL (57532)

19. Another issue, as in No. 18 except that here H2 (pp. 67-68) is followed by:

H^6, 6 leaves, pp. 69-80 (6 pieces; first piece (p. 69): 'The PRINCE IN FITZ')

PF] H1v: 4

Copy: Johnson (wrappers); copy now missing.

20. THE | POLITICAL SONGSTER | OR, A | *TOUCH ON THE TIMES*, | ON | VARIOUS SUBJECTS, | AND ADAPTED TO COMMON TUNES, | [*rule*] | THE SIXTH EDITION, WITH ADDITIONS. | [*rule*] | By JOHN FREETH. | [*short double line*] | BIRMINGHAM, | *PRINTED BY THOMAS PEARSON*, | FOR THE AUTHOR, | AND SOLD BY ALL THE BOOKSELLERS. | MDCCXC.
[variant, distinguishing two entirely different settings of the title-page: *PRINTED ... THOMAS*]

HT] [none]

Collation: (17.8 × 10.2) 12° A^6 b^2 B-D^6 E^6 (E2 + χ^2) F-R^6 [$3 (-b2) signed], 106 leaves, pp. [i-iii] iv-vi [vii] viii-x [xi] xii-xvi [1] 2-40 37*-40* 41-192 (= 196); frontispiece

Contents: frontispiece, Iconography No. IX. p. [i]: title-page. [ii]: blank. [iii]: introduction. [vii]: 'CONTENTS.'. [xi]: 'THE | PREFACE.'. On xvi: '*Birmingham*, 1783.'. [1]: heading 'INLAND NAVIGATION: | AN | *ODE*.' and text (138 pieces). On 192: 'FINIS.'.

RT] [none; page number (arabic numerals, no full point, within square brackets) in centre of headline; 37*-40*, with asterisks]

CW] A6v Burgoyne, b2v INLAND C3v So [And] D5v RECRUIT- [RECRUITING] F6v He I1r The [Afpiring] L6v Envy P6r On [The]

PF] E3v G6v: 1; B4r (in some copies: C1v) H6r (in some copies: I6r) K4r (in some copies: L3v) M3v N6r O6r (in some copies: P6r) Q1v: 4; A6r D4r F4v R3v: 5

Price: 3s 6d (Introduction, also wrapper No. 23, and *London Catalogue of Books*, 1791; 1s according to Preface, but note date, p. xvi).

JOHN FREETH

Note: Re printer *v.* No. 25n.
Copy: Horden (-B6 K2 N1.6)

21. Another issue, as in No. 20 except that here R6 (pp. 191-92) is followed by:
S², 2 leaves, pp. 193-96 (3 pieces, none duplicated in No. 22. First piece (p. 193): 'COMBINATION DEFEATED.')
[upper wrapper:] *Printed for the Author.*
Reviewed: (either this issue or No. 22) *Monthly Review*, IV (N.S.), 1791, p. 470.
Copies: BL (11632. de. 59.; frontispiece cropped), Bodleian (280 e. 3078 -frontispiece), BRL (413367, 233172 -frontispiece), Harding (uncut, wrappers)

22. Another issue, as in No. 20 except that here R6 (pp. 191-92) is followed by:
S², 2 leaves, pp. 193-96 (4 pieces, none duplicated in No. 21. First piece (p. 193): 'On LORD SHERARD's coming of AGE, the | 10th of October, 1788.'. On p. 196: 'FINIS.')
Reviewed: v. No. 21.
Copies: BL (11622. b. 44.), BRL (5880, frontispiece cropped)

23. Another issue, as in No. 20 except that here R6 (pp. 191-92) is followed by:
T-U*⁶ U⁶, 18 leaves, pp. 197-220 [221-32]
[upper wrapper:] *FREETH's* | POLITICAL SONGSTER. | [*spread rule*] | OF former Editions of this Work the | Monthly and Critical Reviewers have fpoken | as follows: | "J.FREETH is an honeft Publican of Birmingham, has | followed the feparate Bufineffes of Brewing and Ballad- | making with confiderable Succefs for more than twenty | Years; fome of his Songs abound with Humour, and in- | deed they are all above the common Style of Street Poetry. | *Monthly Review*, Dec. 1784. | "In Juftice to our Birmingham Pindar, we muft ob- | serve, that there is nothing Indecent in his TOUCH ON THE | TIMES; that though his Expreffions are fometimes Coarfe, | his Obfervations are often fhrewd, and that he poffeffes a | happy Knack at Verfification; we like his Humour, and | fincerely

wifh him Succefs. | *Critical Review, July* 1784. | *[short parallel rule]* | PRINTED FOR THE AUTHOR. | *[within square brackets:]* Price Three Shillings and Six-pence | MDCCXC.

Contents: p. 197: text (18 pieces; first piece: 'WAR and no WAR.'). [221]: 'A | *LIST* | OF | SUBSCRIBERS.'. [232]: blank.

CW] T6V This U*6r INVITA- [INVITATION] U*6v (no CW)

PF] U*4r: 4; T6r: 5

Notes: On sheet U* only U*1 has the asterisk, the other signatures consisting solely of letter and numeral.

The 'List of Subscribers' contains 396 names and calls for 516 copies.

On p. 220 is the text of invitation card No. 60.

Copy: BL (11622. b. 21.)

24. Another issue, as in No. 21 except that here S2 (pp. 195-96) is followed by:
T-U*⁶ U⁶, 18 leaves, pp. 197-220 [221-32](as in No. 23).

Copies: BBkC (-L4,5), BRL (233171; frontispiece cropped); PL (copy now missing)

25. THE | POLITICAL | SONGSTER, | WITH A | PREFACE ON THE TIMES. | *[short double rule]* | *By* J.FREETH. | *[short double rule]* | *[woodcut orn. (1.7 × 4.6 cms): trumpet, mouthpiece uppermost, and lyre upon an open volume backed by decorative foliage]* | *[short parallel rule]* | 𝔅irmingham, | PRINTED BY T.A.PEARSON, *FOR THE AUTHOR.* | *[short spread rule]* | MDCCXCVIII.

HT] THE | POLITICAL SONGSTER. | *[short ornamental spread rule]*

Collation: (17.1 × 10.1) 12°: A⁶ a² B-E⁶ [$3 (-a2) signed], 32 leaves, pp. [1-3] 4-16 [17] 18-64

Contents: p. [1]: title-page. [2]: blank. [3]: 'THE TIMES. | *[double rule]*'. On 16: '*October* 16, 1798.'. [17]: HT and text (27 pieces). On 64: 'FINIS.'.

RT] [none; page number (arabic numerals, no full point, within square brackets) in centre of headline]

CW] A6v Clofely   a2v (no CW)   B6v How   C6v Britain-D6v That

PF] C1v D6v: 1; B6v: 4; A6v E4v: 5

Price: (?) 3s 6d (*London Catalogue of Books,* 1799; this entry may refer to No. 20).

Notes: The woodcut ornament on the title-page is also found in Nos 36 and 37; re printer *v.* No. 36n.

During 1798 the printing-house responsible for this book changed its imprint (*v.* p. 15). The date of the change is reflected most precisely by *Aris's Birmingham Gazette,* a product of the same printing-house: the issue of 6 August 1798 being the last to have the old imprint (with Thomas Pearson's name), and the next issue, on the following 13 August, bearing the new imprint (with the name of Thomas Aris Pearson). If the change was observed at the same time with all the work of that printing-house then this edition of *The Political Songster* was presumably not published until after 6 August 1798.

Copies: BRL (57533; 5874)

Inland Navigation, an Ode

26. INLAND NAVIGATION, | AN | ODE. | HUMBLY INSCRIBED TO | The Inhabitants of *Birmingham,* | AND | Proprietors of the Canal. | [*rule*] | By J.FREETH. | [*parallel rule*] | BIRMINGHAM: | Printed for the AUTHOR. 1769. | [*within square brackets:*] Price SIX-PENCE.

HT] [*panel of type-orns*] | INLAND NAVIGATION: | AN | ODE. | [*row of type-orns*]

Collation: (18.0 × 13.7) 4°: *A*⁴ (*A*2 + B⁴) [$2 signed], 8 leaves, pp. [1-4] 5-16

Contents: p. [1]: title-page. [2]: blank. [3]: 'TO THE | PUBLIC.' (full point misaligned), signed 'J.F.', from '*BIRMINGHAM* | *November* 6, 1769.'. [4]: blank. 5: HT and text ('Inland Navigation' and 3 pieces).

RT] [none; page number (arabic numerals, no full point, within square brackets) in centre of headline]

CW] B4r BIR- [BIRMINGHAM] *A*3r (no CW) *A*3v *The*

Note: 'Inland Navigation' was revised and, under the title 'Birmingham Navigation, an Ode', reprinted in Nos 15 and 29.

Copy: BRL (386794)

27. Another issue, as in No. 26 except that here the title-page, for which the same type has been used, contains an additional line, thus:

... CANAL. | [*rule*] | The SECOND EDITION. | [*rule*] | By ...

Copy: BRL (63268)

Wilkes's Enlargement, an Ode

28. *Wilkes's Enlargement, an Ode,* 1770

Note: No copy known. An advertisement in *Aris's Birmingham Gazette,* 9 April 1770, announced the work as 'now being in the press, and on Wednesday the 18th. Inst. will be published *Wilkes's Enlargement, an Ode* with an occasional Song, in lieu of the old K.'s Ghost, which is deemed unsafe'. A week later, on 16 April, *Wilkes's Enlargement* was again advertised in the same paper. Its date of publication had been advanced by one day and was announced, on 16 April, as being at 'Twelve o'clock To-morrow', price 6d (*v.* also pp. 5-6).

The Warwickshire Medley

29. THE | Warwickſhire Medley: | OR, | CONVIVIAL SONGSTER. | BEING | A Collection of Original Songs, | Political, Humourous, and Satyrical. | TOGETHER WITH | MANY OTHER SELECT PIECES: | CALCULATED FOR THE TIMES. | By J.FREE. | BIRMINGHAM: | PRINTED FOR THE AUTHOR, BY PEARSON | AND ROLLASON; AND SOLD BY ALL THE | BOOKSELLERS IN TOWN AND COUNTRY. | [*within square brackets:*] Price Two Shillings.

HT] [*double row of type-orns*] | THE | Warwickſhire Medley. | [rule]

Collation: (15.5 × 9.2) 8°: A⁴ χ¹ B⁸ (± B1.8) C⁸ D⁸ (±D4) E-H⁸ I² K⁸ L² [$4 (-A4 C3,4 E4 L2 [+I2]) signed], 73 leaves, pp. [i-iii] iv-viii [*2*] [1] 2-136

Contents: p. [i]: title-page. [ii]: blank. [iii]: 'TO THE PUBLIC.'. On viii: 'J.FREE.'. [*1*]: 'INDEX.'. [1]: HT and text (41 pieces). 69: '[*row of type-orns*] | SONGS, | *Written during the* General Election *in the Year* 1774. | [*short spread rule*]' and text (6 pieces). 78: '[*row of type-orns*] | WORCESTERSHIRE CONTEST.' and text (6 pieces). 86: '[*row of type-orns*] | LEICESTERSHIRE CONTEST.' and text (6 pieces). On 94: '[*row of type-orns*] | SONGS, ODES, &c.' and text (13 pieces). On 116 (in some copies): 'FINIS.'. 117: '[*row of type-orns*] | GLOCESTERSHIRE ELECTION.' [GLOCESTERSHIRE] and text (7 pieces). 125: '[*row of type-orns*] | Herefordſhire Election.' and text (4 pieces). On 131: '[*row of type-orns*] | BIRMINGHAM NAVIGATION. | AN ODE.' and text (2 pieces). On 136: 'FINIS.'.

RT] [none; page number (arabic numerals, no full point, within parentheses) in centre of headline]

CW] B8v The D8v And F8v At K5r To [Who] K6r SONG [THE] K8v Of [The]

Notes: The most probable date of publication appears to be 1780, as Robert K. Dent has suggested (*Old and New Birmingham*, I, p. 210).

Re printers *v.* No. 31n.
Copy: BRL (57527 + cutting of No. 6 on free leaf at front)

30. Another issue, as in No. 29 except that here L2 (pp. 135-36) is followed by:
²χ⁴, 4 leaves, pp. [137] 138-9 [*1*] 140-2 [143] (3 pieces; first piece: 'DUDLEY ROUT.'; pp. [*1*] [143]: blank)
Copies: BL (11601. b. 44.; ²χ⁴ cropped), Bodleian (Gough Warw. 14 (7))

Modern Songs

31. MODERN SONGS, | ON | VARIOUS SUBJECTS: | ADAPTED TO COMMON TUNES. | WRITTEN ON THE | IMMEDIATE ARRIVAL OF THE ACCOUNTS | OF THE | DIFFERENT EVENTS. | By JOHN FREE. | BIRMINGHAM, | PRINTED FOR THE AUTHOR; | AND SOLD BY PEARSON AND ROLLASON. | MDCCLXXXII.

HT] A | COLLECTION | OF | NEW SONGS.

Collation: Printing demy 12°: A⁴ B-F⁶ [$3 (-A3) signed], 34 leaves, pp. [i-iii] iv-viii [1] 2-60

Contents: p. [i]: title-page. [ii]: 'CONTENTS.'. [iii]: 'THE | PREFACE.'. [1]: HT and text (32 pieces). On 60: '*FINIS.*'.

RT] [none; page number (arabic numerals, no full point, within square brackets) in centre of headline]

CW] B5r Then [Were]   D1r D3r (no CW)   E4v The [Then] F4v Bu [But]   F6r Though [Through]

Price: 1s (Preface).

Notes: In some copies p. 25 has (l.10) 'TOWE[R]' and (l.16) 'diſgra[ce]'.

For a manuscript of this work *v.* No. 96.

The typography here, and in No. 33 and Nos 17-18, suggests that Pearson and Rollason were the printers, and it may be that the imprint in each instance should be read as stating this.

Copies: BL (11623. aaa. 14.), Harding, ULC (7720 d. 457)

32. Another issue, as in No. 31 except that here F6 (pp. 59-60) is followed by
χ¹, 1 leaf, pp. [61-62]
Contents: p. [61]: 'AN | ADDITIONAL SONG.' and text (1 piece: 'TUTANIA.').

RT] (χ1v) ADDITIONAL SONG.

Copy: BRL (5876, uncut; χ1 misbound after C3)

A Touch on the Times

33. A | TOUCH ON THE TIMES: | OR, THE | MODERN SONGSTER, | ON | VARIOUS SUBJECTS: | ADAPTED TO COMMON TUNES. | By JOHN FREE. | BIRMINGHAM, | PRINTED FOR THE AUTHOR; | AND SOLD BY PEARSON AND ROLLASON. | MDCCLXXXIII.

HT] A | COLLECTION | OF | NEW SONGS.

Collation: (17.7 × 10.5) 12°: A^4 B-F^6 χ^1 ^{x}G^6 $^2\chi^2$ G^2 H^6 [$3 (-A3 G2) signed], 51 leaves, pp. [i-iii] iv-viii [1] 2-60 63-64 *61 ^{2}62-72 *57-*60 ^{3}61-76 (=94)

Contents: p. [i]: title-page. [ii]: 'CONTENTS.'. [iii]: 'THE | PREFACE.'. [1]: HT and text (50 pieces). On 76: 'THE END.'.

RT] [none; page numbers (arabic numerals, no full point, within square brackets) in centre of headline; 25 and 50, within parentheses; *61 and *57-*60, with asterisks]

CW] A4v A COL- [see HT] C6v After [The] D6v Tho' E6v Tho' F3v (no CW) G2v All

PF] ^{x}G3v: 2

Notes: This may be a later, enlarged, reissue of the original edition of 1783. There are allusions on χ^1 and ^{x}G^6 to events of 1785 and 1784 respectively (*v.* No. 17n.).

χ^1 and ^{x}G^6 are from the same setting of type as in No. 17.

Re printers *v.* No. 31n.

Copy: BRL (57534)

34. A | TOUCH ON THE TIMES; | BEING | A COLLECTION OF | *NEW SONGS* | TO OLD TUNES, | INCLUDING SOME FEW WHICH HAVE APPEARED | IN FORMER EDITIONS. | [*double rule*] | *BY A VETERAN* | In the Clafs of Political Ballad Street Scribblers, | Who, when good News is brought to town, | Immediately to Work fits down, | And Bufinefs fairly to go through, | Writes Songs, finds Tunes, and fings them too. | [*double rule*] | [*short ornamental spread rule*] | *Birmingham*, | PRINTED FOR THE AUTHOR, | AT THE OFFICE OF

THE EXECUTORS OF T.A.PEARSON, | *AND SOLD BY KNOTT & LLOYD.* | [*short spread rule*] | 1803.

[upper wrapper:] as title-page to 'VETERAN', then: < >Clafs of Political Ballad Street Scribblers. | [*double rule*] | EMBELLISHED WITH A HEAD OF THE AUTHOR. | [*short spread rule*] | *Birmingham,* | PRINTED FOR THE AUTHOR, | AT THE OFFICE OF THE EXECUTORS OF T.A.PEARSON, | *AND SOLD BY KNOTT & LLOYD.* | 1803 | [*short spread rule*] | PRICE ONE SHILLING.

HT] [*ornamental spread rule*] | A | TOUCH ON THE TIMES. | [*short ornamental spread rule*]

Collation: (18.0 × 10.9) 12°: A^2 B-E^6 F^4 [\$3 (-F_3) signed], 30 leaves, [*4*] [1] 2-56; frontispiece

Contents: frontispiece, Iconography No. IX. p. [1]: title-page. [2]: blank. [3]: 'TO THE PUBLIC.', signed 'J.FREETH.' on 'JUNE 28, 1803.'. [4]: blank. [1]: HT and text (38 pieces). On 56: 'THE END.'.

RT] [none; page number (arabic numerals, no full point, within parentheses) in centre of headline]

CW] B3r GOOD [*Written*] B3v True [Much] C6v CHORUS D6v (no CW) F1v NOTHING [FRENCH]

PF] E6r: 1; C6v D3v: 4

Note: Re printer *v.* No. 25n.

Copies: BL (11621. e. 15. + upper wrapper only, slightly mutilated), BRL (57531), Harding, PL (copy now missing)

A Collection of New Songs

35. A COLLECTION OF | NEW SONGS | ON THE | PRESENT TIMES, | *Adapted to common Tunes,* | [*short total rule*] | By J.FREETH. | [*short parallel rule*] | *BIRMINGHAM,* | Printed by T.CHAPMAN, 1793 | [*within italic parentheses:*] | *Price Threepence,* [*perhaps: Threepence. full point*]

HT] NEW SONGS | ON THE | PRESENT TIMES. | [*short spread rule*]

Collation: (16.9 × 9.8) 8°: A-B⁴ χ¹ [$2 signed], 9 leaves, pp. [1-3] 4-18

Contents: p. [1]: title-page. [2]: blank. [3]: HT and text (9 pieces). On 18: 'FINIS. | [*cruciform cluster of type-orns.*]'

RT] [none; page numbers (arabic numerals, no full point, within parentheses) in centre of headline]

CW] A4v But   B4v (no CW)

Copies: BRL (413428), Harding

The Annual Political Songster

36. THE | ANNUAL | POLITICAL SONGSTER, | WITH A | PREFACE ON THE TIMES. | [*short double rule*] | By *J.FREETH.* | [*short double rule*] | [*woodcut orn., as in No. 25*] | [*short parallel rule*] | *BIRMINGHAM,* | PRINTED BY THOMAS PEARSON, | *FOR THE AUTHOR,* | AND SOLD BY R.BALDWIN, PATER-NOSTER ROW, LONDON. | [*short spread rule*] | MDCCXCIV. [PATER-NOSTER]

HT] THE | *ANNUAL* | POLITICAL SONGSTER.

Collation: Printing demy 12°: A-E⁶ [$3 signed], 30 leaves, pp. [i-iii] iv-xii [1] 2-48

Contents: p. [i]: title-page. [ii]: blank. [iii]: [*underlined with a double rule:*] 'PREFACE.'. On [xii]: '*December*, 1793.'. [1]: HT and text (29 pieces). On 48: 'THE END.'.

RT] [none; page numbers (arabic numerals, no full point, within square brackets) in centre of headline]

CW] A6v (no CW)   B6r NAVIGATION. [NAVIGATION:] C6v Bob,   D6v O glorious   E2r RA- [RATIONALITY.]

PF] A6r B6r D6r E1v:1; C1v:5

Price: 1s (review).

Reviewed: Monthly Review, XIV (N.S.), 1794, pp. 348-49.

Notes: A copy belonging to Dr B. T. Davis of Birmingham is inscribed 'the gift of poet Freeth to J Clarke by the Hands of J.Pool Apl 6ᵗʰ 1794' (also described in *Old and New Birmingham*, II, p. 216, though Dent's version of the inscription is inaccurate in several details). This date, together with that of the Preface, gives a broad indication of the length of time the book was in the press, and narrows the probable date of publication to the first three months of the year.

The woodcut ornament on the title-page is also found in Nos 25 and 37. Its continued use is a reminder that the majority of Freeth's songsters were printed at the same press (*v.* pp. 15-16).

R. Baldwin, of Pater Noster Row (*v.* title-page), is the only London bookseller to be named as offering any of Freeth's works. According to Henry R. Plomer 'the literature sold by the house of Baldwin ... during the seventeenth and eighteenth centuries is a mirror of the political and social history of those times ... (*Dictionary of Printers and Booksellers, 1726-1775*, 1968, p. 14).

Copies: BRL (57584, uncut), Harding

New Ballads

37. NEW | BALLADS, | TO | OLD FAMILIAR TUNES. | [*short spread rule*] | BY | J.FREETH. | [*short spread rule*] | [*woodcut orn., as in No. 25, but here inverted*] | *BIRMINGHAM,* | PRINTED FOR THE AUTHOR, | AT KNOTT AND LLOYD'S OFFICE, HIGH-STREET | [*short rule*] | 1805.

HT] NEW BALLADS. | [*short ornamental spread rule*]

Collation: Printing demy 12°: A-B⁶ [$3 signed], 12 leaves, pp. [1-3] 4-24 [in some copies: 9 has failed to print, leaving an ink mark]

Contents: p. [1]: title-page. [2]: blank. [3]: HT and text (15 pieces). On 24: woodcut orn., as on title-page, but here not inverted; at foot: '[*rule*] | BIRMINGHAM, PRINTED BY KNOTT AND LLOYD.'.

RT] NEW BALLADS.

CW] [none]

Notes: The woodcut ornament on the title-page and on p. 24 is also found in Nos 25 and 36.

The BMAG copy is inscribed 'Given me by Miss Freeth 13th of Jany 1858' and 'E.H.Kempson 13 Bristol Road Edgbaston E.H.K.'. This Miss Freeth was probably the 'Poet's' daughter Jane (*v.* n.20); for E.H. Kempson (Edward Kempson?) *v.* Iconography No. VI.

Copies: BirmUL (MS BX5149.B2; bound with No. 96 and three other printed texts; uncut), BL (11622. bb. 34.(2.)), BMAG (uncut, wrappers), Bodleian (280 e. 4109), BRL (64732, uncut; 5875, uncut, wrappers), Harding, Johnson (uncut, wrappers)

Complete Collection of Songs

38. *A Complete Collection of Songs*, by the late John Freeth, with a memoir of the author and illustrative and explanatory notes by William Matthews, 1822.

Notes: No copy known. An advertisement in *Aris's Birmingham Gazette*, 23 December 1822, proposes the publication by subscription of the collection as a 12° volume, 'elegantly printed on fine wove paper'. The price to subscribers was to be seven shillings, one half to be paid at the time of subscribing, the remainder on delivery of the book. The work, it was promised, 'will be immediately put to press, and the price will be advanced to non-subscribers'.

Subscriptions were to be accepted by R. Hunter, 72 St Paul's Churchyard, London; Beilby and Knotts, Wrightson, and Belcher and Son, Birmingham.

The proposal is dated 21 December 1822.

INVITATION CARDS

Of the invitation cards described here (Nos 39-95) a collection of forty-five cards is in the BRL (press-mark: 523377), to which it was presented in 1937 by Mrs E. Hutton Clarke. One duplicate (No. 45) has since been added.

A further fourteen cards, three of them (Nos 59, 73, and 81) duplicating cards in the Clarke Collection, are in the archives of the BBkC.

BMAG has one card, a duplicate of No. 61 in the BRL.

The text of one invitation card (No. 60) is taken from a song-book of Freeth, and no card containing it is known to have survived.

Where no location is given it is to be assumed that one example of the card is found in the BRL, otherwise all locations are noted.

The verso of each card, with one exception (No. 40 q.v.) is blank (but for manuscript additions, *v.* p. 28).

To avoid over-elaboration in the quasi-facsimile transcriptions, the position to the left or right of centre on the card of certain recurring words and short sentences has not been indicated. These — the word 'Sir', the date, the address, and Freeth's signature — have been transcribed in order as though centered on the card. This should not prove misleading if it is remembered that at the top of a card the word 'Sir' is always on the left, and that when the address or date are also named at the top of the card they are invariably on the right. Similarly, at the foot of a card Freeth's signature (either name, pseudonym, or initials) is always on the right, while the address or date are always on the left. Where such words or sentences balance each other to left and right on the same line they have been transcribed as a single line with only the description '*to the right:*' inserted at the appropriate point. All passages of prose of more than one line are in paragraph form (except in No. 44 in which the first line is not indented). Otherwise all lines of type may be taken as centred on the card unless the contrary is indicated.

The descriptions include only the first and last lines of any passage of verse (with a turnover at the end of a line being indicated by a vertical line-ending stroke), and a note has been given of the total number of lines. With the exception of that omission each card has been fully transcribed.

Some cards are not quite symmetrical, and in such instances the measurements given (in cms, the vertical measurement first) are those of the longer of each pair of sides. Where the first word of the text is shown as being in two sizes of capitals, it is to be assumed that the first letter is a drop initial indenting the second line of text (with the exception of Nos 63 and 74, where the initial capital is on the base line). Where more than one example of a card is noted the dimensions given are those of the largest.

Since the cards convey invitations a note has been added, wherever possible, giving any details of the day and time of the invitation not contained in the transcript.

39. SIR, | [*14 ll. beginning:*] IN this wrangling fluctuating State-juggling Age. | [*last line:*] 'Tis exact Pudding-Time when St. Martin's ſtrikes One. | Nov.29, 1770. [*to the right:*] J.FREETH. 6.4 × 9.4 [*State-juggling*]

Note: Invitation is for 'to-morrow' (a Friday).

40. SIR, | [*10 ll. beginning:*] HE that would taſte of noble Fare, | [*last line:*] Twenty may dine as well as one. | Nov. 28, 1771. [*to the right:*] J.FREETH. [*perhaps:* Nov, 1771, FREETH,] 5.8 × 6.3

Notes: Invitation is for 'to-morrow' (a Friday).

Apparently printed on the back of half a playing-card. Its verso shows part of one of the suit of clubs.

41. BIRMINGHAM, Nov.24, 1774. | SIR, | [*10 ll. beginning:*] EXCUSE all Defects, 'tis a hurrying Time, | [*last line:*] May [t]he Toaſt of the Day be — Succeſs to a POCHIN. | J.FREE. | Dinner will be ready at Half an Hour paſt One o'Clock. [[t]he: *impression of* 't' *clear, but inking faint*] 6.3 × 9.5

Note: Invitation is for 'to-morrow' (a Friday).
Copy: BBkC

42. [*Within a frame largely of cruciform type-orns:*] SIR. | [*10 ll. beginning:*] As few when the Seaſon its kindneſs diſplays, | [*last line:*] Our good friends at BOSTON and thoſe at NEW YORK. | J.FREE. | Birmingham; June, 15th 1775. 6.3 × 9.4 (Plate 11.)

Note: Invitation is for 'to-morrow' (a Friday), 'pudding time is at One'.

43. [*Within a frame of type-orns, Straus-Dent 1:*] SIR. | [*12 ll. beginning:*] WHILST ſome to the Throne are ADDRESSES conveying, | [*last line:*] Be forc'd into Service, and mount

BUNKER's HILL. | J.FREE. | November 21ſt. 1775.
8.0 × 12.4 (Plate 11.)

Note: Invitation is for 'next Friday'.

44. SIR, | Friday next being FEAST DAY, | the Favour of
your Company is | humbly requeſted to DINE at J.FREE's, |
at ONE o'Clock. | June 12, 1776.
6.5 × 9.2 (Plate 11.)

45. SIR, | [*10 ll. beginning:*] In hopes this Card your Notice will
engage, | [*last line:*] Thoſe who regard good Cheer, may have
their Fill. | *Birmingham, June* 11, 1777. [*to the right:*] J.FREE.
6.3 × 9.3

Note: Invitation is for 'Friday next'.
Copies: BRL (two copies)

46. [*Within a frame of type-orns (v.* Notes*):*] SIR. [*to the right:*]
Birmingham, June 17th 1778. | [*12 ll. beginning:*] By Cuſtom
laid down, in the fair month of June, | [*last line:*] To Keppel a
Toaſt, and Succeſs to his Fleet. | J.FREE.
6.3 × 9.5

Notes: Invitation is for 'Friday'.
    The frame consists of Straus-Dent 10 with two units of Straus-
Dent 8. Also in the frame are other pieces of type including
'daggers' and 'double daggers'.

47. [*Within a frame of type-orns (v.* Notes*):*] *SIR.* [*to the right:*]
November, 25, 1778. | [*12 ll. beginning:*] Tho' as bad as Times
are, 'tis a folly to grieve, | [*last line:*] Thinks Danger is near if
he peeps out of Brest. | J.FREE. [are, (verse, l.1) *broken
comma;* FREE. *full point misaligned*]
6.4 × 9.6 (Plate 11.)

Notes: Invitation is for 'next Friday'.
    The frame is mainly of Straus-Dent 10, with pairs of units of
Straus-Dent 8 at the corners. Also included in the frame are two
semi-colons, a section sign, and a small 'double-dagger'.

48. SIR, | [*12 ll. beginning:*] On *the* Fifteenth *of* June, *as there's
much to be done,* | [*last line:*] For *Care, a Relief* --- *is to* drink *and be*

jolly. | Birmingham, *June* 13, 1781. [*to the right:*] J.FREE.
6.4 × 9.4

Note: Invitation is for the following Friday (15 June), with the proceedings, though possibly not the meal, due to commence at 1.30 p.m.

49. Sir, | [*12 ll. beginning:*] As a Glafs of good Port for the reigning Difeafe, | [*last line:*] Time of Action commences at Half after One. | Birmingham, | June 11, 1782. [*to the right:*] J.FREE.
6.4 × 9.5

Note: Invitation is for 'Friday'.

50. SIR, | [*14 ll. beginning:*] On Friday obferve, *Beef* and *Pudding*'s the Text, | [*last line:*] To ELIOTT the brave, and his Veteran Band. | Birmingham, Nov. 27, 1782. [*to the right:*] J.FREE.
6.4 × 9.3

51. [*Within a frame of fleuron type-orns:*] STAMP DUTIES. | SIR, | [*16 ll. beginning:*] For Friday prepare, the Enjoyment embrace, | [*last line:*] As the TOWER-HILL STAMP public Evils to cure. | Birmingham, June 18, 1783. [*to the right:*] J.FREE.
8.0 × 12.5

Note: Frame as in No. 62.

52. [*Within a frame of type-orns:*] SOCIETY FEAST. | SIR, | [*16 ll. beginning:*] FRIDAY next, if you've nothing material on Hand, | [*last line:*] Lefs Taxes, more Trade — and with all the World Peace! | *Birmingham, June 9th* 1784. [*to the right:*] J.FREE. | [*outside the frame, on the right, read from the outer edge of the card:*] Swinney, Letter Founder and Printer.
8.0 × 12.1 (Plate 11.)

Note: The frame consists of small 'diamonds' alternating with rows of tiny vertical lines (giving an effect comparable to that of the French rule), and has a single foliar ornament at each corner. No. 58, also printed by Swinney, has a similar frame.

53. [*Within a frame of floral type-orns:*] *SOCIETY FEAST.* |
SIR, | [*18 ll. beginning:*] AT a Time when ADVENTURERS,
braving the Sky, | [*last line:*] "That a Tax upon Dogs be the laft
we're to have." | Nov. 30, 1784 [*to the right:*] J.FREE.
7.9 × 12.2
Note: Invitation is for 'next Friday', exactly at 1.30 p.m.

54. SOCIETY FEAST. | SIR, | [*18 ll. beginning:*] On the
tenth day of June | [*last line:*] And letting the Females alone. |
BIRMINGHAM, | *June* 8, 1785. [*to the right:*] J.FREE.
9.4 × 6.4
Note: Invitation is for the following Friday (10 June).

55. [*Short double rule*] SOCIETY FEAST. | SIR, | [*18 ll.
beginning:*] *FRIDAY next is feftive Day,* | [*last line:*] *For* PITT *has
worn the* BUDGET *out.* | Birmingham, [*to the right:*] J.FREE, |
[*to the left:*] 23d Nov. 1785. [FREE,]
12.4 × 8.0 (Plate 11.)

56. SOCIETY FEAST. | SIR, | [*14 ll. beginning:*] MY regular
Summons I truft you'll obey, | [*last line:*] One Half keep at
home — let the Reft go to Sea. | J.FREETH | BIRMINGHAM,
June 13, 1786.
6.5 × 9.5
Note: Invitation is for 'sixteenth of June' (a Friday) at 1.30 p.m.

57. [*Within a frame of type-orns:*] SOCIETY FEAST. | [*to the
right:*] Dinner at Half after One. | SIR, | [*18 ll. beginning:*] THE
Gloom of November is apt, People fay, | [*last line:*] "Difturbers
of Peace fend to BOTANY BAY." | J.FREETH. | *Birmingham,*
Nov. 22, 1786. | M.Swinney, Printer.
12.3 × 8.0 (Plate 11.)
Note: Invitation is for 'Friday'.

58. [*Within a frame of type-orns:*] SOCIETY FEAST, | ON
FRIDAY NEXT. | [*short spread rule*] | [*within square brackets:*]
Dinner on Table at Half paft One. | [*18 ll. beginning:*] ONE Guinea
per ticket for MUSIC alone | [*last line:*] Long life to the KING —
to the PRINCE Reformation. | BIRMINGHAM, [*to the right:*]

J.FREETH. | [*to the left:*] June 6th, 1787. | [*outside the frame, at the foot of the card:*] Swinney, Printer.
12.1 × 7.8
Note: Frame as in No. 52.

59. SOCIETY FEAST. | [*fist, pointing to:*] Dinner exactly at Half paft One. | SIR, | [*16 ll. beginning:*] ON Friday next, St.ANDREW'S Day, | [*last line:*] And RELAXATION give the mind. | *Nov.* 28, 1787. [*to the right:*] J.FREETH.
9.2 × 6.3
Copies: BBkC, BRL

60. INVITATION CARD. | SIR, | [*18 ll. beginning:*] GEORGE GORDON may write, | [*last line:*] And SECONDS I always have ready. | *Birmingham Jan.* 22, 1788.
Notes: Invitation is for 'next Friday' at 1.30 p. m.
No card known. Text from *The Political Songster*, 1790, p. 220 (Nos 23-24).

61. SOCIETY FEAST. | [*short spread rule*] | *SIR,* | [*20 ll. beginning:*] I HAVE not a doubt but young GEESE and green PEAS, | [*last line:*] "That our Children may make the beft Ufe of their Days." | J.FREETH. | *Birmingham, June* 10, 1788.
12.2 × 7.8
Note: Invitation is for 'next Friday'.
Copies: BMAG, BRL

62. [*Within a frame of fleuron type-orns:*] SOCIETY FEAST, on FRIDAY next. | *DINNER at Half paft One o'Clock. .* | SIR, | [*12 ll. beginning:*] WHILST over the Land REVOLUTION's the Sound, | [*last line:*] I wifh to good Health, he may foon be reftor'd. | J.FREETH | *Birmingham, Nov.* 26, 1788.
6.3 × 9.2
Note: Frame as in No. 51.

63. SOCIETY FEAST, | [*type-orn.*] FRIDAY *next.* | *SIR,* | [*18 ll. beginning:*] IN this *Duelling* age, | [*last line:*] "And Freedom all o'er the world flourish!" | BIRMINGHAM, *June* 10, 1789. [*to the right:*] J.FREETH.

9.1 × 6.3

Note: Invitation is for 1.30 p.m.

64. SOCIETY FEAST — on FRIDAY next. | *Dinner at Half paſt One.* | [*short spread rule*] | SIR, | [*14 ll. beginning:*] My CONTEST, which full thirty minutes will hold, | [*last line:*] For the *ſtomach* much better than BANBURY | THUMPS. | J.FREETH. | *Nov. 25, 1789.*
9.3 × 6.2

65. SOCIETY FEAST, | ON FRIDAY NEXT. | [*fiſt, pointing to:*] *Dinner at Half paſt One.* | [*short spread rule*] | SIR, | [*18 ll. beginning:*] FOR once and away, | [*last line:*] All over the world be maintain'd. | J.FREETH. | [*two lines braced on right:*] *Birmingham,* | *June 9, 1790.*
9.3 × 6.3

66. SOCIETY FEAST. | *Dinner at Half paſt One.* | [*short rule*] | [*18 ll. beginning:*] NEXT Friday the charter of old to keep up, | [*last line:*] At PARLIAMENT WAKE -- which to-morrow comes | on. | J.FREETH. | *Birmingham, Nov. 24,* 1790.
12.5 × 7.8

67. SOCIETY-FEAST, | *ON FRIDAY NEXT.* | *Dinner at half paſt One.* | [*short spread rule*] | SIR, | [*18 ll. beginning:*] SOCIAL mirth to enjoy, | [*last line:*] And *fighting* without any blows. | [*two lines braced on right:*] *Birmingham,* | *June 8, 1791.* | [*to the right, on approximately the same line as 'Birmingham':*] J.FREETH.
9.3 × 6.4

68. SOCIETY FEAST, | ON FRIDAY NEXT. | [*fiſt, pointing to:*] *DINNER at Half paſt ONE o'Clock.* | SIR, | [*12ll. beginning:*] COME to the ſociable Board, and act your Part, | [*last line:*] "Plenty of Trade, and Peace with all the WORLD." | J.FREETH. | Birmingham, Nov. 23, 1791.
6.4 × 8.9

69. SOCIETY FEAST ON FRIDAY NEXT. | [*to the right:*] DINNER AT HALF PAST ONE | [*short spread rule*] |

SIR, | [*14 ll. beginning:*] IN troublefome times, when divifions are made, | [*last line:*] "The KING, CONSTITUTION, and Moderate Men." | Birmingham, Dec. 5, 1792. [*to the right:*] J.FREETH.
6.4 × 9.2

70. SOCIETY FEAST, | *ON FRIDAY NEXT.* | [*short spread rule*] | *Dinner at Half paft One.* | [*short spread rule*] | SIR, | [*12 ll. beginning:*] SOME fay 'tis the age of *Starvation*, | [*last line:*] "And fpeedy relief to the POLES." | J.FREETH. | *Birmingham, June* 12, 1793.
9.0 × 6.2

71. *SOCIETY FEAST,* | ON NEXT FRIDAY. | [*to the right:*] [*fift, pointing to:*] *Dinner at Half paft One o'Clock.* | SIR, | [*10 ll. beginning:*] THE World's in an uproar, and when it will ceafe, | [*last line:*] "FREE TRADE and GOOD FELLOWSHIP all the World o'er." | J.FREETH. | BIRMINGHAM, | November 27, 1793.
6.3 × 9.3

72. *SOCIETY FEAST,* | ON FRIDAY NEXT. — DINNER AT TWO O'CLOCK. | [*short spread rule*] | *SIR,* | [*12 ll. beginning:*] ON the Firft Day of June, gallant HOWE — right and tight, | [*last line:*] "Point the way to a fpeedy and permanent PEACE." | J.FREETH. | BIRMINGHAM, June 18, 1794.
6.3 × 9.2

73. *Society Feaft,* | [*short double rule*] | ON FRIDAY NEXT. | *Dinner on the Table at Half paft One.* | SIR, [*at centre:*] [*short spread rule*] | [*12 ll. beginning:*] AS ftrange as things feem, in this age of delufion, | [*last line:*] "And all the world over a PERMANENT PEACE." | *Birmingham, Nov.*26, 1794. [*to the right:*] J.FREETH.
6.3 × 9.1
Copies: BBkC, BRL

74. SIR, | THE Favour of your Company to | *Sup* at *J.Freeth's,* on FRIDAY next, will | much oblige, | Yours, |

December 2, 1794. *[to the right:]* Smith, Son, & Smith. | *[short rule]* | *[8 ll. beginning:]* A JOCULAR hour, with a good-natur'd Friend, | *[last line:]* "And all the world over, a PERMANENT PEACE." | J.F.
6.3 × 9.2

75. *SOCIETY FEAST*, | AND | *Sale of Books*, | on | FRIDAY NEXT. | *[fist, pointing to:]* Dinner at Half paft One o'Clock. | *[type-orn.]* | Sir, | *[8 ll. beginning:]* AS Food much in vogue, for the keen craving Mind, | *[last line:]* May the OLIVE BRANCH gladden the Land. | *J.Freeth.* | Birmingham, Jan. 21, 1795.
9.5 × 6.5 (Plate 10.)
Copy: BBkC

76. *Society Feast,* | ON FRIDAY NEXT, | *Dinner exactly at Two o'Clock.* | *[short spread rule]* | SIR, | *[16 ll. beginning:]* THE Stomach, if rightly in tune, | *[last line:]* "And HARMONY all the World o'er." | J.FREETH. | *Birmingham, June* 10, 1795.
9.4 × 6.3

77. SOCIETY FEAST, | On Friday next. | *Dinner exactly at Two o'Clock.* | SIR, | *[18 ll. beginning:]* IN thefe hard times, fome people fay, | *[last line:]* No padlock cramp the liberal mind. | J.FREETH, | Birmingham, Nov. 25, 1795.
9.5 × 6.2

78. *ANNUAL FEAST*, | ON | TUESDAY NEXT. | *[short spread rule]* | *[fist, pointing to:]* Dinner exactly at TWO o'Clock.* | SIR, | *[16 ll. beginning:]* HOWEVER hard the Times may be, | *[last line:]* If Peace comes feated on his Wing. | J.FREETH. | Birmingham, Feb.5, 1796.
9.1 × 6.1

79. Society Feaft, | ON FRIDAY NEXT. | Dinner on the Table exactly at Two o'Clock. | *[short spread rule]* | SIR, | *[22 ll. beginning:]* GEESE and Green Peas — luxurious Fare, | *[last*

line:] And Peace make happy BRITAIN'S ISLE. | *Birmingham, June* 8, 1796. *[to the right:]* J.F.
9.2 × 6.4

80. SOCIETY FEAST, | *On FRIDAY next. — Dinner exactly at Two o'Clock.* | *[short spread rule]* | PEACE & PLENTY. | SIR, | *[12 ll. beginning:]* OUR grand PLENIPO. is set out, | *[last line:]* But no more FAST-DAY PROCLAMATIONS. | *Birmingham, Nov.*23, 1796. *[to the right:]* J.F. [PLENIPO.]
6.5 × 9.3

81. SOCIETY FEAST, | ON FRIDAY NEXT. | *[double rule]* | *DINNER EXACTLY AT TWO O'CLOCK.* | *[double rule]* | SIR, | *[16 ll. beginning:]* WAITING for News to cheer the Land, | *[last line:]* Soon wafted to the BRITISH STRAND. | J.FREETH. | *Birmingham, June* 21, 1797.
9.3 × 6.4
Copies: BBkC, BRL

82. SOCIETY FEAST, | ON FRIDAY NEXT. | *[fist, pointing to:]* Dinner exactly at Two o'Clock.* | *[short spread rule]* | SIR, | *[18 ll. beginning:]* IN thefe uncommon fighting days, | *[last line:]* Than feel his TREBLE TAXES. | J.FREETH. | Birmingham, November 22, 1797.
9.2 × 6.4

83. SOCIETY FEAST. | *[short spread rule]* | SIR, | *[18 ll. beginning:]* IN this duelling age, | *[last line:]* And SECONDS I always have ready. | *J.FREETH.* | Birmingham, June 6, 1798.
9.3 × 6.5
Note: Invitation is for 'next Friday ...when St.Martin's strikes two'.
Copy: BBkC

84. SOCIETY FEAST, | ON FRIDAY NEXT. | *[short parallel rule]* | *Dinner at Two o'Clock.* | *[short spread rule]* | SIR, | *[12 ll. beginning:]* 'TIS a plentiful time all allow, | *[last*

line:] "Brave NELSON, the LORD of the NILE." | J.FREETH. |
BIRMINGHAM, *Nov.* 28, 1798.
9.3 × 6.5

85. *Annual Feaſt, and Sale of Books,* | ON FRIDAY NEXT. |
[*short rule*] | DINNER AT TWO o'CLOCK. | SIR, | [*18 ll.*
beginning:] IN theſe plentiful days, | [*last line:*] "GOOD
FELLOWSHIP all the World o'er." | Birmingham, Jan. 23, 1799.
[*to the right:*] J.F.
9.2 × 6.3 (Plate 10.)
Copy: BBkC

86. SOCIETY FEAST, | *On FRIDAY next.* — *Dinner at Two
o'Clock.* | SIR, | [*14 ll. beginning:*] WHEN SIXPENNY LOAVES
but two pounders appear, | [*last line:*] Will Pleaſure uncommon!
ſpread over the LAND. | Birmingham, Nov. 27, 1799.[*to the
right:*] J.FREETH. | [*short spread rule*] | Birmingham, printed
at T.A.Pearſon's Printing Office, High-ſtreet.
6.5 × 9.4
Note: Re printer *v.* No. 25n.
Copy: BBkC

87. *SOCIETY FEAST, AND SALE OF BOOKS.* | [*fist,
pointing to:*] DINNER AT TWO o'CLOCK. | SIR, | [*12 ll.
beginning:*] THO' dear as things are, o'er the ſociable cup, | [*last
line:*] For no Man can live without moiſt'ning his Clay. |
Birmingham, January 29, 1800. [*to the right:*] J.FREETH.
6.3 × 9.1
Note: Invitation requests 'on Friday attend'.
Copy: BBkC

88. SOCIETY FEAST — On FRIDAY next. | [*fist, pointing to:*]
Dinner at TWO o'Clock. | [*short ornamental spread rule*] | SIR, |
[*16 ll. beginning:*] I MUCH the Word *Scarcity* hate, | [*last line:*]
"And good Beef at Four-pence per Pound." | BIRMINGHAM,
Nov. 24, 1800. [*to the right:*] J.FREETH.
6.5 × 9.3

89. *Annnal Feaſt and Sale of Books* — *on Friday next.* | DINNER
AT TWO o'CLOCK. | [*16 ll. beginning:*] Reſpecting mankind's

old habitual fare, | [*last line:*] BETTER TIMES be the Toaſt of the Day. | Birmingham, Jan. 27, 1801. [*to the right:*] J.FREETH. [*Annnal*]
6.4 × 9.0 (Plate 10.)
Copy: BBkC

90. SOCIETY FEAST, | ON FRIDAY NEXT. | [*short spread rule*] | [*fist, pointing to:*] Dinner at TWO o'Clock. | [*spread rule*] | SIR, | [*12 ll. beginning:*] IN Egypt the French whilſt the Engliſh are banging | [*last line:*] And Peace be at Hand, a rich Harveſt to crown | *Birmingham, July* 27, 1801. [*to the right:*] J.FREETH. [*perhaps:* crown. (*full point*)]
6.5 × 9.3

91. COMING OF AGE. | [*short ornamental spread rule*] | SIR, | YOUR Company is deſired at | J.FREETH's on FRIDAY next. — Dinner at | Two o'Clock. | [*short spread rule*] | "LIFE is a Jeſt, and all Things ſhow it; | "I thought ſo once, but now I know it." | [*16 ll. beginning:*] On cool Reflection ſo ſaid GAY, | [*last line:*] Of *precious* Minutes make the beſt. | *Birmingham, Sept.* 16 1801. [*to the right:*] J.F.
9.3 × 6.5
Note: The motto, 'Life is a Jest...', is John Gay's epitaph, written by himself, and found on his tomb in Westminster Abbey.
Copy: BBkC

92. SOCIETY FEAST. | [*short double rule*] | SIR, | YOUR Company is deſired at J.FREETH's on FRIDAY | next. | [*short spread rule*] | [*fist, pointing to:*] DINNER at TWO o'Clock. | [*short spread rule*] | [*8 ll. beginning:*] MY Houſe has been thoroughly warm'd, never fear, | [*last line:*] The DEFINITIVE TREATY be ſign'd. | J.FREETH | *BIRMINGHAM, NOVEMBER* 24, 1801.
6.4 × 9.3 (Plate 11.)

93. SOCIETY FEAST, | AND | *SALE OF BOOKS,* | ON FRIDAY NEXT. | [*short rule*] | [*fist, pointing to:*] Dinner at Two o'Clock. | [*short ornamental rule*] | [*16 ll. beginning:*] THO' moſt Things are grievouſly dear, | [*last line:*] The BOOKS much the better may fell. | J.FREETH. | Birmingham, Jan. 26, 1802.

9.4 × 6.4

Copy: BBkC

94. SHROVE TUESDAY FEAST. | [*short spread rule*] | DINNER AT TWO O'CLOCK. | [*ornamental spread rule*] | SIR, | [*16 ll. beginning:*] COME and take at my table a feat, | [*last line:*] "GOOD FELLOWSHIP all the world o'er." | J.FREETH. | *Birmingham, February 25, 1802.*

9.0 × 6.2

Note: Shrove Tuesday 1802 fell on 2 March.

Copy: BBkC

95. SOCIETY FEAST, | *And Sale of Books, on Friday next.* | DINNER AT TWO O'CLOCK. | SIR, | [*10 ll. beginning:*] THO' much *blood* and treasure the war must have cost, | [*last line:*] Be "FRIENDSHIP & ADDINGTON , PLENTY & PEACE." | *J.FREETH.* | *Birm. Jan. 25,* 1803.

6.2 × 9.1 (Plate 10.)

Copy: BBkC

MANUSCRIPT

96. (194.0 × 158.0) 4°, 65 leaves, MS pp. [2] 1-98 [99-128]

Contents: p. [1]: Accessions Cat. No. : 4°, 1022. [2]: portrait of Freeth mounted in (Iconography No. IX), and some later annotations. 1: text. 84: blank. 95: text. 98: blank. [128]: text (not Freeth's).

WM] 'Britannia' with the motto: 'PRO PATRIA EJUSQUE LIBERATE', similar to Heawood No. 201 (*Watermarks*, 1950), with a countermark, 'GR and crown', similar to that of Heawood No. 205. There is some variation in the watermark.

Notes: For provenance, a description of the contents, and of compositorial markings *v.* pp. 11-13.

JOHN FREETH

The identification of the hand as Freeth's is based upon the assumptions that the manuscript is the printer's copy for *Modern Songs*, 1782 (No. 31), and that the various emendations show the writer to have been the author of the songs. The manuscript bears no contemporary indications of authorship (the portrait of Freeth not being published until 1788, *v.* Iconography No. IX). BirmUL (MS BX5149.B2)

LINES ATTRIBUTED TO FREETH

97.　Oliver's Tap is Strong and Good,
　　　None in the Kingdom can out-do it;
　　　And if to taste your Heart's inclined,
　　　Step down this Lane, you'll soon come to it.

Note: It is believed that this was the inscription on a signboard at the corner of Fish Lane, Harborne, Birmingham, where a tavern was kept by Oliver Shaw. Freeth is said to have gone there with friends 'at least once a week' (*v.* Jennings, p. 73). Traditionally attributed to Freeth.

98.　Free and easy through Life 'twas his wish to proceed,
　　　Good men he revered be whatever their Creed:
　　　His pride was a sociable evening to spend,
　　　For no man lov'd better his Pipe and his Friend.

Note: Found on Freeth's tombstone, originally in the burial ground of the Old Meeting House, Birmingham, but since 1882 in the City of Birmingham Cemetery at Witton. Traditionally attributed to Freeth.

INDEXES

Because Freeth's work was occasional and essentially ephemeral, and since so much of it was, nevertheless, republished several times with numerous difference, emendations, and substitutions, the text has many variants. A large proportion of these appear to be incidental and without significance; for example, the alternative use of 'or' and 'on' to introduce the same sub-title in different issues is seemingly random. Similarly, there are many instances of personal and proper names being given in substanially different forms in identical contexts. Only the ready accessibility of a critically edited text would justify the inclusion of all variants in the indexes of song titles, first lines, and tunes; without it, even the most sophisticated index would either be unacceptably cumbersome or would produce ambiguities. Therefore, certain kinds of variant have not been individually represented here, and the following general points should first be noted:

(a) Demonstrable error has been silently corrected.

(b) No attempt has been made to reflect the typography of the originals.

(c) With the exception of certain words that invariably appear in a form now unorthodox, spelling has been standardized.

(d) Punctuation has been standardized.

(e) The manuscript (Bibliography No. 96) has not been indexed.

Exceptions to these rules, and an explanation of the treatment of particular aspects of an index, are to be found in the appropriate rubric.

JOHN FREETH

Table of Contents of Songsters

The various editions and issues of Freeth's songsters (and similar works) are listed here in chronological order, as in the Bibliography, each preceded by its entry number there.

Entries list the titles of songs in the order of their appearance in the songster. Numbers are those of song titles, as given in the *Index of Song Titles* (pp. 93-108), followed, where appropriate, within parentheses by the number of the tune or tunes, as given in the *Index of Tunes* (pp. 122-27), specified on that occasion.

Wherever more than one tune is indicated as accompanying a song it must be borne in mind that the first tune cited is not necessarily that to which the beginning of the song is set (v. rubric p. 108).

14. *The political songster*, 1766: 160 (84), 162 (21), 349, 290 (107), 324, 95 (115), 280 (136), 264 (43), 153, 269 (138), 185 (121), 195, 121 (36), 343, 304 (80), 12 (177), 344 (28), 52 (115), 201 (20, 115, 142, 84), 200, 302, 150, 72

15. Another edition, 1771: 305 (117), 51 (122), 99 (121), 135 (112), 371 (9), 160 (84), 162 (21), 349, 18 (177), 269 (138), 52 (115), 343, 195, 332 (128), 134, 335 (138), 11 (118), 64 (152), 290 (107), 324, 40, 233, 192 (97), 182, 88 (64), 374 (46), 176 (136), 177, 107 (164, 42, 4, 159, 93), 119 (128), 24, 219, 227 (143), 71 (141), 91 (40), 171 (71), 19 (159), 7 (93), 92, 78, 83 (175), 61, 299 (108), 288, 37, 151, 297, 379, 138, 21

16. Another issue, 1771: as in No. 15, but with the addition of 13.

17. Another edition, 1784: 141 (116), 333 (120), 163 (22), 80 (45), 215 (53), 356 (79), 48 (90), 294 (32), 166 (106), 179 (157), 272 (136), 94 (173), 168 (75), 329, 213 (88), 187 (17), 139 (128), 316 (161), 39 (151), 2 (164), 36 (3), 372 (51, 15), 82 (102), 41 (128), 382 (8), 377 (56), 357 (79), 337 (23), 147 (30), 63 (114), 204 (111, 4, 62), 383 (144), 375 (81), 266 (100), 118 (70), 136 (115), 70 (168), 218 (85), 66 (73), 225 (156, 179, 35, 34), 25 (145), 236 (80), 158 (158)

18. Another edition, 1786: 349 (119), 221 (76), 42 (38), 242 (79), 160 (93), 75, 159 (170), 46 (60), 267, 354 (110), 259 (59), 273

Numbers refer to: (left margin) *Bibliography*; (without parentheses) *Index of Song Titles*; (within parentheses) *Index of Tunes*

CONTENTS OF SONGTERS

Numbers refer to: (left margin) *Bibliography*; (without parentheses) *Index of Song Titles*; (within parentheses) *Index of Tunes*

(83, 113, 67, 61), 377 (56), 65 (73), 329, 213 (116), 272 (136), 187 (17), 168 (75), 2 (164), 356 (79), 316 (161), 39 (151), 36 (3), 382 (8), 357 (79), 204 (111, 4, 62), 238 (145), 235 (80), 274 (119), 16 (148), 170 (170, 164, 53), 158 (158)

19. Another issue, 1786: as in No. 18, but with the addition of 284, 208, 27, 96, 271, 128 (tunes not known for any of these songs; copy now missing)

20. Another edition, 1790: 161, 338 (77), 31 (9), 135 (112), 40, 64 (57), 172 (103), 4, 88 (64), 51 (122), 233, 240 (93), 224, 26 (87), 48 (90), 49 (26, 62), 282 (25), 94, 179, 294 (32), 89 (110), 166 (144), 329, 168 (75), 102 (154), 23, 42 (38), 259 (59), 316 (161), 39 (168), 2 (164), 36 (3), 356 (79), 163 (22), 54, 227 (143), 141 (116), 256 (99), 80 (45), 216 (53), 82 (102), 103 (155), 67 (135), 211 (34), 213 (88), 187 (17), 337 (23), 327, 372 (51, 15), 143 (144), 365 (73), 74 (115), 348 (38, 23), 41 (128), 59 (138), 1, 334 (92), 44 (94), 98 (64, 52), 137 (162), 196 (98), 333 (137), 382 (8), 377 (56), 375 (81), 75 (168), 159 (170), 47 (60), 354 (110), 357 (130), 65 (73), 221 (76), 349 (119), 242 (79), 184 (148), 109 (165), 383 (144), 235 (80), 96 (16), 165, 17 (66), 351 (116), 70 (168), 118 (70), 136 (115), 389 (156, 179, 35, 34), 260 (19), 331 (53), 33 (28), 79 (40), 43 (124), 158 (158), 170 (54, 164, 53), 147 (30), 139 (128), 266 (100), 271 (88), 28 (25), 160 (93), 34 (44), 273 (83, 113, 129, 61), 274 (119), 129 (80), 167 (125), 310 (106), 317 (114), 117, 358, 319 (8), 253 (110), 306, 360 (12), 291, 320 (50), 321 (32), 328, 202 (62), 287 (160), 156 (25), 22 (65, 125, 163, 153), 116 (145), 276 (48), 190 (147), 362 (115), 301 (105), 77, 380 (149), 29 (21), 57 (150), 5, 231 (18), 255 (120), 347 (176), 307 (33), 292 (96), 62 (39), 258 (166), 204 (82), 124 (47)

21. Another issue, 1790: as in No. 20, but with the addition of 68 (30), 126 (123), 144 (4)

22. Another issue, 1790: as in No. 20, but with the addition of 239, 229 (72), 249 (39), 123 (178)

23. Another issue, 1790: as in No. 20, but with the addition of 373 (144), 145, 323, 346 (64, 37), 100 (115), 152, 361, 305 (149), 53, 370 (158), 173, 203, 326 (14), 286 (132), 315, 289 (5), 164, 246

24. Another issue, 1790: as in No. 21, but with the addition of 373 (144) to 246 as in No. 23

25. Another edition, 1798: 87 (8), 130 (29), 205 (95), 207 (89), 3 (2), 248 (13), 342 (58), 369 (33), 247 (79), 261 (86), 355 (22),

Numbers refer to: (left margin) *Bibliography*; (without parentheses) *Index of Song Titles*; (within parentheses) *Index of Tunes*

363 (120), 106 (25), 140 (149), 366 (1), 50 (110), 120 (27), 58 (133), 15 (53), 341 (116), 300 (106), 132 (101), 20 (33), 234 (3), 154 (4), 155, 178 (73)

26-27. *Inland navigation, an ode*, 1769: 161, 19 (160), 7 (93), 250 (55)

28. *Wilkes's enlargement, an ode*, 1770: no copy known, but see 379

29. *The Warwickshire medley* [1780]: 4, 162 (21), 361, 143 (120), 257, 298, 281 (8), 146, 305 (117), 51 (122), 285, 48 (90), 160 (84), 135 (112), 349, 18 (177), 269 (138), 40, 53.5, 52 (115), 332 (128), 233, 88, 374 (46), 176 (136), 177, 119 (128), 219, 227 (143), 171 (71), 19 (159), 7 (93), 78, 61, 95 (115), 153, 335 (138), 38, 308 (63), 186 (121), 60 (159), 14, 311 (159), 169 (73), 181 (51), 69 (93), 127 (123), 283 (140), 157 (124), 381 (93), 90, 81, 241, 93, 279 (128), 376, 228, 263, 55, 26 (87), 370 (158), 244, 6, 254, 388, 113, 114, 224, 150, 217, 151, 138, 9 (172), 73, 278 (70), 352, 95, 251, 237 (127), 183 (171), 76, 175 (9), 314 (107), 21, 112

30. Another issue, [1780]: as in No. 29, but with the addition of 104, 309 (131), 268

31. *Modern songs*, 1782: 35 (32), 89 (110), 179 (157), 166 (120), 111 (8), 272 (136), 94, 282 (25), 74 (115), 168 (75), 329, 213 (116), 187 (17), 345 (5), 139 (128), 378 (24), 337, 351 (116), 17 (66), 82 (102), 327, 165, 102 (179, 73), 226 (64), 296 (93), 23 (72), 84, 2 (164), 77, 210 (120), 141 (174), 356 (79)

32. Another issue, 1782: as in No. 31, but with the addition of 364 (74)

33. *A touch on the times*, 1783: 333 (120), 163 (22), 80 (45), 215 (53), 356 (79), 48 (90), 282 (25), 294 (32), 89 (110), 166 (144), 179 (157), 272 (136), 94, 168 (75), 329, 213 (116), 187 (17), 139 (128), 337 (23), 327, 316 (161), 82 (102), 54 (93), 39 (151), 2 (164), 141 (116), 103 (155), 36 (3), 172 (103), 211 (34), 25 (145), 236 (80), 118 (70), 136 (115), 70 (168), 218 (85), 66 (73), 225 (156, 179, 35, 34), 227 (143), 41 (128), 367 (126), 357 (79), 256 (99), 67 (135), 365 (73), 372 (51, 15), 74 (115), 143 (144), 348 (38, 23), 198 (111, 4, 62), 382 (8)

34. Another edition, 1803: 307 (58), 359, 252 (167), 354 (110), 275 (7), 387 (79), 386 (88), 206 (89), 265 (149), 191, 336, 124 (47), 110 (71), 390 (4), 149, 196 (98), 148 (30), 45 (73), 193 (49), 325, 385 (39), 292 (96), 167 (125), 289 (5), 36 (3), 313 (139), 62 (39), 57 (150), 205 (95), 213 (116), 340 (5), 214 (120), 212 (78), 2 (164), 133 (104, 110, 166, 6), 56 (146), 293, 295, 312 (68)

35. *A collection of new songs*, 1793: 212 (78), 180 (89), 222 (116), 30 (109), 209 (88), 193 (49), 189, 270 (106), 115 (79)

36. *The annual political songster*, 1794: 188 (133), 209 (88), 97 (128), 180 (89), 193 (49), 108 (116), 212 (78), 105 (169), 30 (109), 10 (72), 384 (65), 85, 144 (4), 313 (139), 353 (134), 289 (5), 2 (164), 36 (3), 29 (21), 124 (47), 125 (54, 164, 53), 174 (41), 62 (39), 292 (96), 245 (33), 197 (29), 350 (105), 339 (10), 8 (31)

37. *New ballads*, 1805: 277 (7), 142 (149), 32 (120), 330 (2), 101 (76), 131 (11), 86 (157), 368 (116), 199 (69), 303 (52), 158 (158), 45 (73), 149, 220 (95), 377 (91)

Index of Song Titles

The titles listed are those of printed pieces attributed to Freeth in the *Bibliography*, whether cited there as separate works or recorded in the *Table of Contents of Songsters* (pp. 90-93) as constituents of songsters or similar publications. Invitation cards (Nos 39-95) have not been noticed here since they are without individually relevant titles or headings (though they may easily be identified from the *Index of First Lines*, pp. 108-22).

Each entry refers to those entry numbers of the *Bibliography* (here in bold type) which indicate where the given piece is to be found.

The number in parentheses after a title is that of the first line as given in the *Index of First Lines*. Variant first lines have been recorded individually in this manner, but when more than one such first line number has been cited within the same parentheses it indicates either that the song is a medley (or akin to one) or that a change of tune has been specified in the course of a single text (see rubric p. 108).

Wherever a song has been printed untitled, and lacks a heading that can serve as a title (of the sort which may be found with newspaper publications, e.g. *Bibliography* No. 4), then the first line has been taken as a substitute. This is given in upper and lower case letters within inverted commas.

All titles are given in their most extended form. Wherever minor variants are equally valid, that which has been most commonly used is adopted here. In some instances (e.g. the use of 'or' and 'on', *v.* rubric p. 89) an arbitrary choice has been necessary. Occasionally, narrowly differing versions of the same title are significant in their separate contexts, and each version has then been recorded. All alternative titles have been included, but because they may indicate substantially different texts they have not been cross-referenced. A few titles are duplicated, as may be seen where a title is followed by more than one first line number, each of them having different references to the *Bibliography* (e.g. *Index of Song Titles* No. 95).

1. Address of condolence to His Majesty on the death of the Princess Amelia (428): **20, 21, 22, 23, 24**
2. Admiral Parker's engagement with the Dutch Fleet (238): **17, 18, 19, 20, 21, 22, 23, 24, 31, 32, 33, 34, 36**
3. Alarms of war in the spring of 1794 (299): **25**
4. American contest (199): **20, 21, 22, 23, 24, 29, 30**
5. Amor et Concordia, an occasional song, set to music, and sung by J. Probin, at the annual meeting of the Military Association, at the Hotel, in Manchester (283): **20, 21, 22, 23, 24**
6. Amorous Antinomian (The), (162): **29, 30**
7. Artists' Jubilee (The), (445): **15, 16, 26, 27, 29, 30**
8. Arts reviv'd (The); or, the Queen's birthday (217): **36**
9. Atkinson's ghost (24): **29, 30**
10. Bagshot Camp (5): **36**
11. Ballad-singer's ramble to London (A), (84): **15, 16**
12. Beer drinkers' objection to the repeal of the Cyder Act (The), (49): **14**
13. Belzebub's tour to Leicester (15): **16**
14. Belzebub's trip to Warwick (342): **29, 30**
15. Billy Pitt's timepiece (335): **25**
16. Billy's quite too young (373): **18, 19**
17. Birmingham ale tasters (219): **20, 21, 22, 23, 24, 31, 32**
18. Birmingham beer, a new song (452): **2, 15, 16, 29, 30**
19. Birmingham lads (316): **15, 16, 26, 27, 29, 30**
20. Birmingham Loyal Association: a martial glee, adapted for the fourth of June 1798 (195): **25**
21. Birmingham navigation, an ode (86): **15, 16, 29, 30**

Numbers refer to: (within parentheses) *Index of First Lines*; (in bold type) *Bibliography*

Numbers refer to: (within parentheses) *Index of First Lines*; (in bold type) *Bibliography*

22. Birmingham overseers (The), (418, 289, 102, 355): **20, 21, 22, 23, 24**

23. Birmingham recruits (83): **20, 21, 22, 23, 24;** (183): **31, 32**

24. Birmingham riot (The), (111): **15, 16**

25. Birmingham Tradesmen's Society song (60): **17, 33**

26. Birmingham tranquility, 1776 (148): **20, 21, 22, 23, 24, 29, 30**

27. Bishops turn'd navigators (*): **19**

28. Bishops turn'd navigators (The). A song, on the Worcester intended Canal Bill being thrown out of the House of Peers (207): **20, 21, 22, 23, 24**

29. Blood-Royal (354): **20, 21, 22, 23, 24, 36**

30. Blue and Orange united (405): **35;** (175): **36**

31. Boiling of the vintner's wig (The), (25): **20, 21, 22, 23, 24**

32. Bonaparte's coronation (123): **37**

33. Botany Bay (29): **20, 21, 22, 23, 24**

34. Bowling Green Festival (The), (154): **20, 21, 22, 23, 24**

35. Britain's glory (67): **31, 32**

36. Britannia triumphant: on the glorious victory of April 12, 1782 (33): **17, 18, 19, 20, 21, 22, 23, 24, 33, 34, 36**

37. Britannia's complaint (384): **15, 16**

38. Britannia's complaint, an elegy on the death of the Marquis of Granby (384): **29, 30**

39. British Salamanders (The), (235): **17, 18, 19, 20, 21, 22, 23, 24, 33**

40. Bromwich Masquerade (The), (307): **15, 16, 20, 21, 22, 23, 24, 29, 30**

41. Budget (The), (39): **17, 20, 21, 22, 23, 24, 33**

42. Budget Day (236): **18, 19, 20, 21, 22, 23, 24**

43. Budget without any tax (The), (305): **20, 21, 22, 23, 24**

44. Budget worn out (The), (37): **20, 21, 22, 23, 24**

45. Bull-baiting (47): **34, 37**

46. Bumper toast (A), (126): **18, 19**

47. Bumpers toast (A), (126): **20, 21, 22, 23, 24**

48. Bunker Hill; or, the soldier's lamentation (134): **17, 20, 21, 22, 23, 24, 29, 30, 33**

*First line not known; copy now missing

Numbers refer to: (within parentheses) *Index of First Lines*; (in bold type) *Bibliography*

49. Burgoyne's defeat on the Plains of Saratoga (368, 380): **20, 21, 22, 23, 24**

50. Call to the brave (A), (399): **25**

51. Call to the Bucks (A), (74): **15, 16, 20, 21, 22, 23, 24, 29, 30**

52. Camp (The), (424): **14, 15, 16, 29, 30**

53. Cannibals (The): on the partition of Poland (329): **23, 24**

53.5 Cannibals (The); or, the division of Poland (329): **29, 30**

54. Captain Carver's Militia (341): **20, 21, 22, 23, 24, 33**

55. 'Cease your idle humdrum prating': **29, 30**

56. Change of times (417): **34**

57. Changes of fashion (The), (430): **20, 21, 22, 23, 24, 34**

58. Changes of fashion in politics (336): **25**

59. Charles Town Bar; or, the Cabinet Council's lamentation. A song (414): **20, 21, 22, 23, 24**

60. Christmas Eve (274): **29, 30**

61. Clear the house; or, the ranting Lords (437): **15, 16, 29, 30**

62. Coach Drivers (The); or, Billy's not too young (113): **20, 21, 22, 23, 24, 34, 36**

63. Coalition flight (375): **17**

64. Cock lane ghost (The), (301): **15, 16, 20, 21, 22, 23, 24**

65. Colliers' Fete-Champêtre (The), (365): **18, 19, 20, 21, 22, 23, 24**

66. Colliers' Fete-Champêtre (The). A stroke at the Budget (365): **17, 33**

67. Colliers' march (The), (36): **20, 21, 22, 23, 24, 33**

68. Combination defeated (61): **21, 24**

69. 'Come all ye sons of liberty': **29, 30**

70. Commutation (129): **17, 20, 21, 22, 23, 24, 33**

71. Complaint (The), (271): **15, 16**

72. Conjuror (The), (411): **14**

73. Consultation (The), (69): **29, 30**

74. Contest (The), (401): **20, 21, 22, 23, 24, 31, 32, 33**

75. Contractors (The), (255): **18, 19, 20, 21, 22, 23, 24**

76. Contractor's canvass (The), (367): **29, 30**

77. Contrast (The), (184): **20, 21, 22, 23, 24**; (455) **31, 32**

78. Convention (The), (412): **15, 16**; (413) **29, 30**

Numbers refer to: (within parentheses) *Index of First Lines*; (in bold type) *Bibliography*

79. Convicts' departure (The), (385): **20, 21, 22, 23, 24**

80. Corruption defeated; or, the Premier routed (108): **17, 20, 21, 22, 23, 24, 33**

81. Corruption's cavalcade (454): **29, 30**

82. Cottager's complaint (The): on the intended bill for enclosing Sutton Coldfield (130): **17, 20, 21, 22, 23, 24, 31, 32, 33**

83. Covent Garden murmurs (144): **15, 16**

84. Coventry Raree Show (54): **31, 32**

85. Cruize (The), (158): **36**

86. Curious events of the day (40): **37**

87. Dance of the day (The), (171): **25**

88. Defaulter's retreat (The), (444): **15, 16, 20, 21, 22, 23, 24, 29, 30**

89. Defeat of D'Estaing at Savannah (The), (115): **20, 21, 22, 23, 24, 31, 32, 33**

90. Demireps (The), (449): **29, 30**

91. Departure (The), (371): **15, 16**

92. Devil among the tailors (The), (402): **15, 16**

93. Devil and the Pope (The), a conference (410): **29, 30**

94. Diaboliad (The), (406): **17, 20, 21, 22, 23, 24, 31, 32, 33**

95. Dialogue (A), (347): **14, 29, 30**; (309): **29, 30**

96. Diamond cut diamond (*): **19**; (206): **20, 21, 22, 23, 24**

97. Disappointment (The); or, the dashing daily prints (190): **36**

98. Diversion of quoits playing (The), (194, 59): **20, 21, 22, 23, 24**

99. Dog-act (The), (220): **15, 16**

100. Dog-tax (The), (339): **23, 24**

101. Drilling; or, warring without blows (110): **37**

102. Droitwich Annual Festival (68): **20, 21, 22, 23, 24**; (87) **31, 32**

103. Dudley riot (The), (363): **20, 21, 22, 23, 24, 33**

104. Dudley rout. A song. On the celebration of the victory on Long Island (73): **30**

105. Duke and no Duke (432): **36**

106. Duke of Brunswick's retreat (The), (263): **25**

107. Dumb administration (The). A burlesque cantata (372, 170, 42, 254, 43, 425): **15, 16**

*First line not known; copy now missing

JOHN FREETH

Numbers refer to: (within parentheses) *Index of First Lines*; (in bold type) *Bibliography*

108. Dumourier's retreat (119): **36**
109. Dutch patriotism; or, castles in air (388): **20, 2i, 22, 23, 24**
110. English cock (The), and the jovial cockers (227): **34**
111. English lion (The) (188): **31, 32**
112. Epilogue written by Mr. Free, for his benefit, and spoken on Wednesday evening last, by Mr. Penn, with great judgement and propriety to a very crowded and respectable audience at the New Theatre in this town (174): **5, 6, 29, 30**
113. Epistle from Windsor (461): **29, 30**
114. Epistle to a friend in London (An), (20): **29, 30**
115. 'Ev'ry mind a continual anxiety wears': **35**
116. Extension of trade (The), (435): **20, 21, 22, 23, 24**
117. False alarm (The), (1): **20, 21, 22, 23, 24**
118. Female canvasser (The). On the Westminster election (395): **17, 20, 21, 22, 23, 24, 33**
119. Fishermen (The), (361): **15, 16, 29, 30**
120. Flanders wake (216): **25**
121. Foibles of dress (The), (451): **14**
122. Following (The), amongst other songs upon the occasion was sung before a numerous company on the Thanksgiving Day, by that well-known songster of the times J. Free (292, 215): **7**
123. For the Earl of Harborough's birthday (456): **22**
124. Free and easy English traveller (The), (355): **20, 21, 22, 23, 24;** (356): **34;** (358): **36**
125. [Free and easy English traveller (The)]: on the same subject (30, 326, 293): **36**
126. Freedom triumphant (241): **21, 24**
127. Freedom triumphant; or, the downfall of the Lords! On chairing Sir Charles Holte and Mr Skipwith (394): **29, 30**
128. Freedom's fair-ground (*): **19**
129. Freedom's fair-ground. A song on the Treaty of Commerce (441): **9, 20, 21, 22, 23, 24**
130. French folly (95): **25**
131. French invaders (The), (91): **37**

*First line not known; copy now missing

Numbers refer to: (within parentheses) *Index of First Lines*; (in bold type) *Bibliography*

132. French invaders; or, the Gallican bugbear (426): **25**

133. French invasion. A comic medley (38, 76, 252, 280): **34**

134. French tonsor (The), (203): **15, 16**

135. Gamblers (The), (442): **15, 16, 20, 21, 23, 24, 29, 30**

136. Game laws (The), (352): **17, 20, 21, 22, 23, 24, 33**

137. Game of fives (The), (298): **20, 21, 22, 23, 24**

138. Gamester's soliloquy (The), (364): **15, 16**; (272): **29, 30**

139. General election (The), (72): **17, 20, 21, 22, 23, 24, 31, 32, 33**

140. General Mack (225): **25**

141. Georges (The); or, Lord Sackville's promotion (223): **17, 20, 21, 22, 23, 24, 31, 32, 33**

142. Going for too much (77): **37**

143. Gold Coin Act (The), (145): **20, 21, 22, 23, 24, 33**; (396): **29, 30**

144. Golden days of George the Third (The), (417): **21, 24, 36**

145. Grand expedition (The), (158): **23, 24**

146. Hard times (234): **29, 30**

147. Harvest home (62): **17, 20, 21, 22, 23, 24**

148. Harvest home (for the year 1802) (62): **34**

149. High-born cattle (261): **34, 37**

150. Hospitality (393): **14, 29, 30**

151. Hudibrastic epistle (An). Addressed to Anonymous, Objector, &c. (345): **15, 16, 29, 30**

152. Hudibrastic epistle to a friend (An), (345): **23, 24**

153. Hum (The), (264): **14**; (265): **29, 30**

154. Humbug (The); or, the hero of the Alps (172): **25**

155. [Humbug (The); or, the hero of the Alps.] The supplement (317): **25**

156. 'In Bedworth and Handsworth, one cause to uphold': **20, 21, 22, 23, 24**

157. Independent Freeman's invitation to the poll (The): on Sir Watkin's second arrival (447): **29, 30**

158. India Bill (The). A constitutional song (114): **17, 18, 19, 20, 21, 22, 23, 24, 37**

159. India game (118): **18, 19, 20, 21, 22, 23, 24**

160. Inland navigation (369): **14, 15, 16, 29, 30**; (100): **18, 19, 20, 21, 22, 23, 24**

JOHN FREETH

Numbers refer to: (within parentheses) *Index of First Lines*; (in bold type) *Bibliography*

161. Inland navigation, an ode (86): **20, 21, 22, 23, 24, 26, 27**
162. Ins and outs (The), (382): **14, 15, 16, 29, 30**
163. Ins and outs (The); or, the State Jockies (381): **17, 20, 21, 22, 23, 24, 33**
164. Invitation card ('George Gordon may write') (106): **23, 24**
165. Invitation to Vauxhall Gardens (287): **20, 21, 22, 23, 24, 31, 32**
166. Jersey Expedition (The): (52, 350): **17, 20, 21, 22, 23, 24, 31, 32, 33**
167. John Wesley's prophecy (312): **20, 21, 22, 23, 24**; (311): **34**
168. Jolly Dick and Jemmy Twitcher. A dialogue (376): **17, 18, 19, 20, 21, 22, 23, 24, 31, 32, 33**
169. 'Jolly sons of mirth and freedom': **29, 30**
170. Jolly travellers (The), (30, 326, 294): **18, 19**; (30, 326, 293): **20, 21, 22, 23, 24**
171. Jovial cocker (The), (228): **15, 16, 29, 30**
172. Jovial cockers (The). Written by desire (228): **20, 21, 22, 23, 24, 33**
173. Junction (The); or, triple alliance (438): **23, 24**
174. Katterfelto (186): **36**
175. Kidnappers (The), (370): **29, 30**
176. King of Denmark's arrival (The), (450): **15, 16, 29, 30**
177. King of Denmark's masquerade (The), (167): **15, 16, 29, 30**
178. Lammas Day (78): **25**
179. Langara's defeat; or, the British flag triumphant (427): **17, 20, 21, 22, 23, 24, 31, 32, 33**
180. Less paper credit, and more Tower guineas (332): **35**; (333): **36**
181. Liberty's call (121): **29, 30**
182. London addressors (The), (107): **15, 16**
183. London cast off (The), (2): **29, 30**
184. Londoners' petition against the Shop Tax (The), (373): **20, 21, 22, 23, 24**
185. Lord G–E S–E's promotion (398): **14**
186. Lord G–E S–E's promotion; or, Minden bravery rewarded (398): **29, 30**
187. Lord G. Gordon's procession (233): **17, 20, 21, 22, 23, 24, 31, 32, 33**; (232): **18, 19**

INDEX OF SONG TITLES

Numbers refer to: (within parentheses) *Index of First Lines*; (in bold type) *Bibliography*

188. Lord Macartney's embassy to China (416): **36**
189. Lord Macartney's embassy to China. A Warwickshire ballad (416): **35**
190. Lord SH–D's retreat from Coventry (330): **20, 21, 22, 23, 24**
191. Lord Warwick and a large loaf (457): **34**
192. Lottery Club (The), (291): **15, 16**
193. Love and unanimity (404): **34, 35, 36**
194. Loyal song which poet Freeth wrote for old Job Nott (The) (403): **13**
195. Magisterial promotions in the town of Birmingham (128): **14, 15, 16**
196. Marble playing (290): **20, 21, 22, 23, 24**; (150): **34**
197. March (The), (327): **36**
198. Marvellous alliance (The). A mock cantata (155, 318, 159, 315): **33**
199. Marvellous leap (The), (191): **37**
200. Masquerade (The), (307): **14**
201. Medley (A), (295, 390, 319, 41): **14**
202. Mendoza (18): **20, 21, 22, 23, 24**
203. Mendoza's trip to Birmingham (279): **23, 24**
204. Mock cantata (A), (155, 318, 48, 315): **17, 18, 19**; (155,315): **20, 21, 22, 23, 24**
205. Money and men at home (4): **25, 34**
206. More guineas & less paper (281): **34**
207. More guineas, and less paper credit (334): **25**
208. Much ado about nothing; or, Peg Nicholson's knights (*): **19**
209. National convention (343): **35, 36**
210. Navigation (28): **31, 32**
211. Navigation contest (209): **20, 21, 22, 23, 24, 33**
212. Navigation; or, the canal fever (208): **34, 35, 36**
213. Ned Dennis, commonly called Jack Ketch (391): **17, 18, 19, 20, 21, 22, 23, 24, 31, 32, 33**; (392): **34**
214. Negotiation; or, the French invaders (210): **34**
215. New administration (The), (189): **17, 33**

*First line not known; copy now missing

JOHN FREETH

Numbers refer to: (within parentheses) *Index of First Lines*; (in bold type) *Bibliography*

216. New administration, in 1783 (The), (189): **20, 21, 22, 23, 24**
217. New epilogue (A), (400): **29, 30**
218. New window tax (The), (137): **17, 33**
219. News from Elysium (147): **15, 16, 29, 30**
220. No continental war: money and men at home (4): **37**
221. Nothing at all. An Hibernian dialogue on the propositions (379): **18, 19, 20, 21, 22, 23, 24**
222. 'Now hark what tidings from the Hague' : **35**
223. 'Now no more to distant lands' (233): **7**
224. Ode on the birthday of the Marquis of Granby (85): **20, 21, 22, 23, 24, 29, 30**
225. Ode: written and sung on the evening of the Thanksgiving Day for a general peace (308, 259, 292, 215): **17, 33**
226. Old English hospitality. In honour of the Duke of Rutland's birthday (415, 340): **31, 32**
227. Old King's ghost (The), (53): **15, 16, 20, 21, 22, 23, 24, 29, 30, 33**
228. Old ranting blues (The), (27): **29, 30**
229. Old St Michael's Day, 1788 (275): **22**
230. On a benefaction of five hundred pounds being presented to The General Hospital by a lady unknown (226): **8**
231. On a famous Lincolnshire horse called Rodney (written by desire) (6): **20, 21, 22, 23, 24**
232. On a late verdict (306): **1**
233. On a play-house being turned into a Methodist Meeting-House (139): **15, 16, 17, 20, 21, 22, 23, 24, 29, 30**
234. On Admiral Nelson's victory: Britannia triumphant (101): **25**
235. On Blanchard's aerial voyage to the Continent (431): **18, 19, 20, 21, 22, 23, 24**
236. On Blanchard's aerial voyage to the Continent. A balloon song (431): **17, 33**
237. On chairing Mr Berkeley (275): **29, 30**
238. On commerce (435): **18, 19**
239. On Lord Sherard's Coming of Age, the 10th October, 1788 (440): **22**
240. On Sir Charles Holt's election (55): **20, 21, 22, 23, 24**

INDEX OF SONG TITLES

Numbers refer to: (within parentheses) *Index of First Lines*; (in bold type) *Bibliography*

241. On Sir Watkin's being chaired (275): **29, 30**
242. On the Bachelor's Tax (344): **18, 19, 20, 21, 22, 23, 24**
243. On the Bill depending for removing public nuisances. Epigram (465): **3**
244. On the B–ll for preventing the killing of dogs. P–T Wake (221): **29, 30**
245. On the bravery of the British Guards on the Plains of Lincelles (386): **36**
246. On the death of the truly facetious Mr Job Hart (70): **10, 23, 24**
247. On the defeat of the Dutch (34): **25**
248. On the discovery of the Wicklow Golden Mountain (99): **25**
249. On the Earl of Harborough's birthday, November 1, 1786 (140): **22**
250. On the first arrival of the barges with coals (443): **26, 27**
251. On the Frenchified procession of the Blues (409): **29, 30**
252. On the happy prospect of peace (104): **34**
253. On the illumination for His Majesty's recovery. A loyal glee (266): **20, 21, 22, 23, 24**
254. On the installation at Windsor (120): **29, 30**
255. On the petitions for the abolition of the slave trade (178): **20, 21, 22, 23, 24**
256. On the prospect of peace (212): **20, 21, 22, 23, 24, 33**
257. On the Royal Marriage Act (462): **29, 30**
258. On the rumour of a French war in 1787 (23): **20, 21, 22, 23, 24**
259. On the Speaker's casting voice against fortifications (351): **18, 19, 20, 21, 22, 23, 24**
260. On the Treaty of Commerce (104): **20, 21, 22, 23, 24**
261. On the uncommon dearness of corn (460): **25**
262. On the uncommon rise and fall in the price of bread (272): **12**
263. Origin of an Old Blue (397): **29, 30**
264. Paper shop (The), (198): **14**
265. Paper war (258): **34**
266. Parliament wake (117): **17, 20, 21, 22, 23, 24**
267. Parliamentary reform (257): **18, 19**
268. Parody on the jolly young waterman (8): **30**

JOHN FREETH

Numbers refer to: (within parentheses) *Index of First Lines*; (in bold type) *Bibliography*

269. Patagonians (The), (374): **14, 15, 16, 29, 30**
270. Patentee pads (82): **35**
271. Patrolling (*): **19**; (89): **20, 21, 22, 23, 24**
272. Paul Jones (224): **17, 18, 19, 31, 32, 33**
273. Paviers (The). A Birm . . . am cantata (302, 11, 112, 231): **18, 19, 20, 21, 22, 23, 24**
274. Paviers music (The), (218): **18, 19, 20, 21, 22, 23, 24**
275. Peace and plenty (306): **34**
276. Peg Nicholson's knights (436): **20, 21, 22, 23, 24**
277. Piebald coalition (The), (244): **37**
278. Pistol Blues defeated (51): **29, 30**
279. Pochin and plenty (459): **29, 30**
280. Political chase (The), (444): **14**
281. Pope's address to his good friends in England (The), (160): **29, 30**
282. Prescott's breeches; or, the old soldier's voyage to America (378): **20, 21, 22, 23, 24, 31, 32, 33**
283. Pride of Worcester (The): on Sir Watkin Lewes's arrival (230): **29, 30**
284. Prince in Fitz (The),(*): **19**
285. Prorogation (116): **29, 30**
286. Publicans of Birmingham to the churchwardens (The), (285): **23, 24**
287. Pugilists (The); or, Banbury thumps (181): **20, 21, 22, 23, 24**
288. Punch's opera (423): **15, 16**
289. Quarter day (187): **23, 24, 34, 36**
290. Queen's little mare (The), (250): **14, 15, 16**
291. Raree Show (The); or, march to St. Paul's (213): **20, 21, 22, 23, 24**
292. Rationality (192): **20, 21, 22, 23, 24, 34, 36**
293. Recruiting song (67): **34**
294. Recruiting song: on the commencement of hostilities with the French (67): **17**; (66): **20, 21, 22, 23, 24, 33**
295. [Recruiting song.] Supplement (278): **34**

*First line not known; copy now missing

296. Recruiting songs. Captain Carver's militia (341): **31, 32**

297. Red Lion Society (The), (98): **15, 16**

298. Regatta (419): **29, 30**

299. Return (The), (240): **15, 16**

300. Richard Brothers the Prophet (46): **25**

301. Rights of mankind all the world over (The), (348): **20, 21, 22, 23, 24**

302. Riot (The), (111): **14**

303. Road to church preferment (The), (58): **37**

304. Rose and Thistle (The), (270): **14**

305. Royal commodore (The), (434): **15, 16, 23, 24, 29, 30**

306. Royal festivity (453): **20, 21, 22, 23, 24**

307. Sailors' rouse (The), (125): **20, 21, 22, 23, 24**; (12): **34**

308. St Andrew's Day, a Scotch air (304): **29, 30**

309. Second rout (A); or, the proceedings of the Dudley Council, on an insult offer'd to their conspicuous loyalty (177): **30**

310. Seven devils in the tailor (277): **20, 21, 22, 23, 24**

311. Skipwith, Holte, and independency (458): **29, 30**

312. Sociability (30): **34**

313. Social friend (The), (389): **34, 36**

314. Soldiers' complaint (The), (157): **29, 30**

315. Song. – For the British tars: on sailing for the Baltic (57): **23, 24**

316. Song for the British tars: on the sailing of Lord Howe's fleet (93): **17, 18, 19, 20, 21, 22, 23, 24, 33**

317. Song ('George Gordon by profession'): **20, 21, 22, 23, 24**

318. Song: on obtaining the Birmingham and Worcester Canal Bill (58): **11**

319. Song on the Regency Bill (132): **20, 21, 22, 23, 24**

320. Songs written for the 4th of November, 1788: unanimity's call (269): **20, 21, 22, 23, 24**

321. Songs written for the 4th of November, 1788: unanimity's call. Song II ('British hearts the call obey'): **20, 21, 22, 23, 24**

322. 'Sons of trade for mirth prepare' (292): **7**

323. Spanish convention (The), (90): **23, 24**

JOHN FREETH

Numbers refer to: (within parentheses) *Index of First Lines*; (in bold type) *Bibliography*

324. Spanish riot (The), (9): **14, 15, 16**
325. Speculation on the present day (168): **34**
326. Spiritual inquisition (The): on Mr Bastard's Bill (273): **23, 24**
327. Staffordshire fox-chase (The), (161): **20, 21, 22, 23, 24, 31, 32, 33**
328. Stage boxing (360): **20, 21, 22, 23, 24**
329. State beggars (The), (222): **17, 18, 19, 20, 21, 22, 23, 24, 31, 32, 33**
330. State game (362): **37**
331. State game; or, the road to church preferment (58): **20, 21, 22, 23, 24**
332. State jockeys (The), (448): **15, 16, 29, 30**
333. State pensioners (The), (310): **17, 20, 21, 22, 23, 24, 33**
334. State trial (359): **20, 21, 22, 23, 24**
335. Statesmen (The), (7): **15, 16, 29, 30**
336. Strange times (151): **34**
337. Stream of corruption (The), (205): **17, 20, 21, 22, 23, 24, 31, 32, 33**
338. Strolling ballad-singer's ramble to London (A), (84): **20, 21, 22, 23, 24**
339. Subsidy money (179): **36**
340. Sudden alarm (The). An extempore glee (31): **34**
341. Sunday duel (The), (260): **25**
342. Tars of Old England (The). (Written on the day the news came of Lord Howe's victory) (349): **25**
343. Taste (446): **14, 15, 16**
344. Taxation (323): **14**
345. Taxation; or, the courtier's creed (135): **31, 32**
346. Tax-trade minister (The), (256, 75): **23, 24**
347. Test (The), (322): **20, 21, 22, 23, 24**
348. Threescore jolly anglers (The), (64, 197, 44): **20, 21, 22, 23, 24, 33**
349. Times (The), (383): **14**; (338): **15, 16**; (166): **18, 19, 20, 21, 22, 23, 24**; (338): **29, 30**
350. Times as they go (The), (80): **36**

Numbers refer to: (within parentheses) *Index of First Lines*; (in bold type) *Bibliography*

351. Times (The): on stopping the circulation of dollars (133): **20, 21, 22, 23, 24, 31, 32**

352. Tom and Nell. An election dialogue (19): **29, 30**

353. Trade at low ebb (297): **36**

354. Trade in England ne'er shall die (313): **18, 19, 20, 21, 22, 23, 24, 34**

355. Trade, tranquillity, and a large loaf for sixpence (17): **25**

356. Trading War (The); or, a dip in the Loan (346): **17, 18, 19, 20, 21, 22, 23, 24, 31, 32, 33**

357. Trinity Tax (The), (141): **17, 18, 19, 33;** (142): **20, 21, 22, 23, 24**

358. Trip from Dublin in search of a Regent (A). An English song to an Irish tune (284): **20, 21, 22, 23, 24**

359. Trip to Calais (127): **34**

360. Trip to Cheltenham (262): **20, 21, 22, 23, 24**

361. Trip to Portsmouth (408): **23, 24, 29, 30**

362. Troubles of France (The), (32): **20, 21, 22, 23, 24**

363. True British loyalty (196): **25**

364. Tutania (an additional song) (71): **32**

365. Tutania buckles (71): **20, 21, 22, 23, 24, 33**

366. Unfortunate monarch (The), (193): **25**

367. Union (The), (328): **33**

368. Upstart emperors (149): **37**

369. Valentine's Day; or, the drubbing of the Dons (246): **25**

370. Vicar of Brentford (The), (152): **23, 24, 29, 30**

371. Vintner's wig (The), (26): **15, 16,**

372. Volunteer's rouse (The): on the call for arming, (122, 314): **17, 20, 21, 22, 23, 24, 33**

373. War and no war (387): **23, 24**

374. Warwickshire Militia (The), written in the year 1761 (303): **15, 16, 29, 30**

375. Watermen (The). An Hibernian harangue about places (200): **17, 20, 21, 22, 23, 24**

376. 'Whilst some are endeav'ring the land to enslave': **29, 30**

377. Whipcord; or, the walking stationers (268): **17, 18, 19, 20, 21, 22, 23, 24, 37**

378. White-wash (The); or, King's-Bench wake (185): **31, 32**

379. Wilkes's enlargement, an ode (366): **15, 16 [28]**

380. Wimbledon Curl (The), (353): **20, 21, 22, 23, 24**

381. Windmill Tavern (The), (439): **29, 30**

382. Wonderful coalition (The), (21): **17, 18, 19, 20, 21, 22, 23, 24, 33**

383. Wonders; or, the man of the moon (229): **17, 20, 21, 22, 23, 24**

384. Worcester and Birmingham Canal Bill (63): **36**

385. World as it wags (The), (331): **34**

386. World turn'd upside down (The), (written in the year 1800) (3): **34**

387. Written at the request of a Leicestershire hosier (245): **34**

388. Written extempore, on hearing that Mr Skipwith, Member for Warwickshire, was remarkably active in preventing the exportation of wheat, by opposing the motion in the House of Commons (156): **4, 29, 30**

389. Written on the Day of Thanksgiving for a general peace (308, 259, 292, 215): **20, 21, 22, 23, 24**

390. Year ninety-five (The), (460): **34**

Index of First Lines

The first lines listed are those of pieces attributed to Freeth in the *Bibliography*, whether cited there among *Ephemera* (Nos 1-13), noticed in the *Table of Contents of Songsters* (pp. 90-93) as constituents of a songster or similar publication, or included among *Invitation Cards* (Nos 39-95) and *Lines Attributed to Freeth* (Nos 97-98). Only the manuscript (No. 96) has not been indexed. An entry indicates the location of the piece.

The reference numbers are of two kinds. The first is the song-title number as recorded in the *Index of Song Titles* (pp. 93-108). The second kind, in bold face, is the entry number in the *Bibliography* for any song or verse found elsewhere than in a songster – appearing, for instance, in newspapers and on invitation cards – and which is most conveniently identified thus.

Wherever a fresh tune has been introduced by name into the continuous text of a piece (which is not, that is, a medley or akin to one), the line immediately following its introduction has similarly been noticed here. Frequently this occurs where no

INDEX OF FIRST LINES

tune has been named at the commencement of the song, and consequently the first tune cited (in the *Table of Contents of Songsters*) with a piece is not necessarily that to which the opening lines are set.

Every first line and its substantive variant forms have been recorded, except for the differing use of elision, and where an initial definite or indefinite article is involved as an alternative.

1. About Britain's monarch how great the surprize: 117
2. Alderman strongly connected (An): 183
3. All Europe still convuls'd appears: 386
4. All to no purpose, such is the case: 205, 220
5. Always some fond recreation: 10
6. Amongst the brute beings the world doth produce: 231
7. Amongst the rulers of the State: 335
8. And did you not hear of a dexterous Minister: 268
9. As a fav'rite abroad: 324
10. As a glass of good port for the reigning disease: **49**
11. As along the broad way, I happen'd to stray: 273
12. As Englishmen finding our rights are at stake: 307
13. As few when the season its kindness displays: **42**
14. As food much in vogue, for the keen craving mind: **75**
15. As Satan who always his agents employs: 13
16. As strange as things seem, in this age of delusion: **73**
17. As thousands but lately their hard fate were mourning: 355
18. As tight a lad Mendoza was: 202
19. As tippling Tom the other night: 352
20. As you seem'd in your last very pressing to know: 114
21. At a period when all public virtue is lost: 382
22. At a time when adventurers, braving the sky: **53**
23. At once to realise estates: 258
24. At solemn midnight hour, when owls: 9
25. Attend my jolly hearts of gold: 31
26. Attend, ye jolly Fellows all: 371
27. Attend ye jolly hearts of gold: 228
28. Away with all party contention: 210
29. Away with all whimsical bubbles of air: 33

JOHN FREETH

Numbers refer to: (plain type) *Index of Song Titles*; (bold type) *Bibliography*

30. Away with contention, the toast send about: 125, 170, 312
31. Awhile the horizon may lower: 340
32. Behold Britain's monarch – grown fond of the deep: 362
33. Behold from afar, what glad tidings are brought: 36
34. Block'd up in the Texel best part of a year: 247
35. British hearts the call obey: 321
36. Britons for news upon tip-toe were got: 67
37. Britons now your murmuring cease: 44
38. Britons to make a glorious stand: 133
39. Budget's disclos'd – fresh taxes impos'd (The): 41
40. But a few months ago: 86
41. But cease all this wrangling, disputing and jangling: 201
42. But if truth may be spoke: 107
43. But of all the grand Robin Hood ranters: 107
44. But though the river has its charms: 348
45. By custom laid down, in the fair month of June: **46**
46. By many it oft has been said: 300
47. By the poor, hard times forgetting: 45
48. By two of the greatest extremes coalescing: 204
49. Can a cause be assign'd why the lads in the West: 12
50. Cease your idle humdrum prating: 55
51. Cheer up my jolly hearts of gold: 278
52. Christmas gambols to make, being valiant and stout: 166
53. Clock had struck twelve, old Morpheus's hour (The): 227
54. Colours flying, music playing: 84
55. Come all ye sons of liberty: 69, 240
56. Come and take at my table a seat: **94**
57. Come cheer up my lads - still be valiant and stout: 315
58. Come, come, my boys, the sport pursue: 303, 331
59. Come, come my boys to sport away: 98
60. Come, come my jolly hearts, let mirth abound: 25
61. Come haste to the chairing, our hearts are delighted: 68
62. Come lay by the sickle till next summer season: 147, 148
63. Come, now begin delving, the Bill is obtain'd: 384; **11**
64. Come rouse, brother sportsmen, the clock has struck four: 348

INDEX OF FIRST LINES

Numbers refer to: (plain type) *Index of Song Titles*; (bold type) *Bibliography*

65. Come to the sociable board, and act your part: **68**
66. Come ye lads, that wish to shine: 294
67. Come ye lads who wish to shine: 35, 293, 294
68. Contests holding in derision: 102
69. Council met (The) – the chiefs were call'd: 73
70. Death who to all must give the fatal stroke: 246; **10**
71. Disregarding wind or weather: 364, 365
72. Dissolution's the word, and the writs are all out: 139
73. Dudley's a loyal spot: 104
74. Dusk of the evening began to appear (The): 51
75. Enormous bills to get defray'd: 346
76. Erskine appearing in the van: 133
77. Ever since about Malta a bustle arose: 142
78. Ever since the House of Brunswick: 178
79. Ev'ry mind a continual anxiety wears: 115
80. Ev'ry mind an uncommon anxiety wears: 350
81. Excuse all defects, 'tis a hurrying time: **41**
82. False emblems which actresses wear: 270
83. Fife and drum afford enjoyment: 23
84. First of April 'sixty-three (The): 11, 338
85. Fond of the honours that were nobly won: 224
86. For ancient deeds let history unfold: 21, 161
87. For concord to shew our affection: 102
88. For Friday prepare, the enjoyment embrace: **51**
89. For lenity let who will plead: 271
90. For more than six months with anxiety keen: 323
91. For more than threescore years ago: 131
92. For once and away: **65**
93. Fort to save, the Fleet is gone (The): 316
94. Free and easy through life 'twas his wish to proceed: **98**
95. French boasters by way of false cover: 130
96. Friday next, if you've nothing material on hand: **52**
97. Friday next is festive day: **55**
98. From care and toil to sooth the mind: 297
99. From England, as times go, who would not away: 248
100. From pinching cold when friends retire: 160

101. From the mouth of the Nile, flush'd with glory, behold: 234
102. From the sumptuous living met with: 22
103. Geese and green peas – luxurious fare: **79**
104. Genius of England had long droop'd her head (The): 252, 260
105. George Gordon by profession: 317
106. George Gordon may write: 164; **60**
107. Give attention to my ditty: 182
108. Give round the word, resign, resign: 80
109. Gloom of November is apt, people say (The): **57**
110. Go where you will there is nothing but drilling: 101
111. God prosper long our noble King: 24, 302
112. Good cattle and good roads, good Sirs: 273
113. Good old coach, Britannia, still (The): 62
114. Grecian bards may sing about (The): 158
115. Hark! from o'er the Western main: 89
116. Hark, hark, the voice of royalty: 285
117. Hark, hark to the call! – Dissolution's the word: 266
118. Hark, hark to the summons – behold what a rout: 159
119. Hark! Hark! what tidings from the Hague: 108
120. Hark! the call of the day: 254
121. Hark to liberty's call, how it darts through the air: 181
122. Hark to liberty's call – how it echoes around: 372
123. Haste, haste to the grand Raree-show: 32
124. He that would taste of noble fare: **40**
125. Hearts of Oak, with vigour rouse: 307
126. Here's to the tradesman, who social and gay: 46, 47
127. His Consulship having resolv'd in his mind: 359
128. How happy are we in these troublesome days: 195
129. How happy for that company: 70
130. How sweetly did the moments glide: 82
131. However hard the times may be: **78**
132. Huntsman who goes to the fields with his hounds (The): 319
133. I am a jolly Bacchanal: 351
134. I am a jolly soldier: 48
135. I am the Premier's scholar bred: 345
136. I have not a doubt but young geese and green peas: **61**

INDEX OF FIRST LINES

Numbers refer to: (plain type) *Index of Song Titles*; (bold type) *Bibliography*

137. I'll block up lights ere Christmas Day: 218
138. I much the word Scarcity hate: **88**
139. I sing not of battles, nor sing of the state: 233
140. I will maintain it to be true: 249
141. In a beggarly state that is held up to scorn: 357
142. In a State for its follies oft held up to scorn: 357
143. In Bedworth and Handsworth, one cause to uphold: 156
144. In British dominions, did ever mankind: 83
145. In country, as well as in town: 143
146. In Egypt the French whilst the English are banging: **90**
147. In Elysium by latest of tidings that came: 219
148. In England's fair capital every year: 26
149. In fickle France, where monarchy: 368
150. In former times the rustic game: 196
151. In France when American broils were made known: 336
152. In George the Third's illustrious reign: 370
153. In hopes this card your notice will engage: **45**
154. In life's merry round – with hearts that are sound: 34
155. In merry Old England, there once was a time: 198, 204
156. In nervous, animated, lays: 388; **4**
157. In pitiful plight: 314
158. In pleasure's round – 'twas always found: 85, 145
159. In principle two grand extremes coalescing: 198
160. In Rome's rigid clime when it came to be known: 281
161. In seventeen hundred and seventy-nine: 327
162. In these days of pleasure, when amorous sport: 6
163. In these hard times, some people say: **77**
164. In these plentiful days: **85**
165. In these uncommon fighting days: **82**
166. In this age of dissipation: 349
167. In this blessed land of plenty: 177
168. In this busy wrangling age: 325
169. In this duelling age: **63, 83**
170. In this pitiful condition: 107
171. In this up and down world, where mankind daily skip: 87
172. In this whimsical age, which some call in derision: 154

Numbers refer to: (plain type) *Index of Song Titles*; (bold type) *Bibliography*

173. In this wrangling fluctuating State-juggling age: **39**
174. In times of old it often has been said: 112; **5, 6**
175. In times of peace their zeal to shew: 30
176. In troublesome times, when divisions are made: **69**
177. It happened upon a certain day: 309
178. It must be allow'd there are slaves: 255
179. It strange may appear that the Minister coolly: 339
180. Jocular hour, with a good-natur'd friend (A): **74**
181. Johnsonian method of fighting (The): 287
182. Jolly sons of mirth and freedom: 169
183. Jolly sons of mirth and spirit: 23
184. King in the hearts of his subjects that reigns (The): 77
185. Let those through life who'd fondly stray: 378
186. Let those who wit and genius prize: 174
187. Life's turnpike fairly to get through: 289
188. Lion of England, a score years ago (The): 111
189. Long had the vessel of the state: 215, 216
190. Long in suspense many thousands had been: 97
191. Long pull, a strong pull, and pull altogether (A): 199
192. Man that wears an honest heart (The): 292
193. Mankind still by thousands the war sweeps away: 366
194. Mankind will their favourite pleasures pursue: 98
195. Martial strains proclaim the day: 20
196. Mayor of Bath – God bless him (The): 363
197. Morn is fair – serene the air (The): 348
198. Mother England of late a strange dust has kick'd up: 264
199. Mother England's own child, a fine lusty grown lass: 4
200. Murdock, says Patrick, I cannot make out: 375
201. My contest, which full thirty minutes will hold: **64**
202. My house has been thoroughly warm'd, never fear: **92**
203. My name it is Taste, from Paris in haste: 134
204. My regular summons I trust you'll obey: **56**
205. My song is of corruption's stream: 337
206. National debt is Britannia's mill-stone (The): 96
207. Navigation's a lottery frequently had: 28
208. Navigation's become such a trade: 212

INDEX OF FIRST LINES

Numbers refer to: (plain type) *Index of Song Titles*; (bold type) *Bibliography*

209. Navigators, haste, away: 211
210. Negotiating's all done away: 214
211. Next Friday the charter of old to keep up: **66**
212. Now away with pining care: 256
213. Now begins the raree show, Sir: 291
214. Now hark what tidings from the Hague: 222
215. Now no more to distant lands: 225, 389; **7**
216. Now, now my boys, the sport pursue: 120
217. Now to glad the infant year: 8
218. Now to labour haste my crony: 274
219. Of all civil officers annually chose: 17
220. Of all Penal Laws that enacted have been: 99
221. Of all the grand plans that have lately been laid: 244
222. Of all the jolly beggars: 329
223. Of great and glorious names to speak: 141
224. Of heroes and statesmen I'll just mention four: 272
225. Of heroes when speaking, to single one out: 140
226. Of Russell, though much has been said: **8**
227. Of the different kinds of game: 110
228. Of the jovial sons of game: 171, 172
229. Of wonders the English will prate: 383
230. Of Worcester the worthy Sir Watkin's the pride: 283
231. Off with a bumper, jollity shew: 273
232. Old England, alas! what has come to thy sons: 187
233. Old England, alas! what is come to thy sons: 187
234. Old England, I cannot but pity thy fate: 146
235. Old Gib. is safe, with care away: 39
236. Old scores to pay, we've been so much: 42
237. Oliver's tap is strong and good: **97**
238. On a summer's Sunday morning: 2
239. On cool reflection so said Gay: **91**
240. On Dover's high cliffs, in a deep plaintive tone: 299
241. On E'sham's fair and fertile ground: 126
242. On Friday next, St Andrew's Day: **59**
243. On Friday observe, beef and pudding's the text: **50**
244. On political grounds, let who will rule the roost: 277

245. On the axis of time as the world whirls about: 387
246. On the eve of Valentine: 369
247. On the Fifteenth of June, as there's much to be done: **48**
248. On the first day of June, gallant Howe – right and tight: **72**
249. On the tenth day of June: **54**
250. Once a creature brought o'er: 290
251. One guinea per ticket for music alone: **58**
252. Our Empire still upon the main: 133
253. Our grand Plenipo. is set out: **80**
254. Our statesmen so much are the subject of ridicule: 107
255. Our troops abroad when many said: 75
256. Parliament meets, and a bustle is made (The): 346
257. Parliamentary reform is the plan to pursue: 267
258. Peace is accomplish'd (A) – but what of all that: 265
259. People were seiz'd with a frenzy (The): 225, 389
260. Point of honour to decide (A): 341
261. Politics getting out of fashion: 149
262. Pomona's sweet climate a visit to pay: 360
263. Prussia inveigled by Austria set out: 106
264. Push about the brisk bowl, and let freedom abound: 153
265. Push about the brisk bowl, and let pleasure abound: 153
266. Quickly ye bards your songs prepare: 253
267. Respecting mankind's old habitual fare: **89**
268. Reuben and Moses, two poor walking stationers: 377
269. Revolution's the sound which to pleasure gives birth: 320
270. Rose of Old England, so dearly caress'd (The): 304
271. Say my noble Laird of Bute: 71
272. Scarce break of day, retiring from the game: 138
273. Scene is laid open, and nothing but spirit (The): 326
274. Season for fond recreation (The): 60
275. See the legal Member comes: 237, 241
276. See what plenty stands before us: 229
277. Seven Devils in Bristol 'tis said: 310
278. Short-liv'd Peace begone awhile: 295
279. Since bear-garden sport of the times is the rage: 203
280. Since England was England, a still happy nation: 133

INDEX OF FIRST LINES
Numbers refer to: (plain type) *Index of Song Titles*; (bold type) *Bibliography*

281. Since forgery so much has spread: 206
282. Since freedom each pow'rful opponent repels: **1**
283. Since now no more to distant lands: **5**
284. Six chosen ambassadors valiant and stout: 358
285. Social companion's a foe to contention (The): 286
286. Social mirth to enjoy: **67**
287. Soft Spring, the proclaimer of rural delights: 165
288. Some say 'tis the age of starvation: **70**
289. Some years ago, the case was such: 22
290. Some years ago the rustic game: 196
291. Sons of mirth and jollity: 192
292. Sons of trade for mirth prepare: 225, 389; **7**
293. Soon as we reach the happy spot: 125, 170
294. Soon as we've reached the happy spot: 170
295. Sorely griev'd through vile oppression: 201
296. Speculation much varied 'twixt June and September: **12**
297. Sprightly Bob was a lad open-hearted and steady: 353
298. Sprightly sons of manly sport: 137
299. Spring is commencing with dire alarms! (The): **3**
300. Stomach, if rightly in tune (The): **76**
301. Stories of phantoms in history long have stood: 64
302. Stout rustic blade that can handle a spade (The): 273
303. Strike up the song, my jovial lads: 374
304. Strike up the tabor, ye lads and be frisky: 308
305. Tables are turning, rejoice at the measure (The): 43
306. Tables are turning - there's cause to rejoice (The): 275
307. Talk no more of vain romances: 40, 200
308. Thanksgiving days so rarely come: 225, 389
309. That Freeholders good we've rejected: 95
310. That miracles never will cease: 333
311. That sage divine, John Wesley, said: 167
312. That sage divine, John Wesley, says: 167
313. That trade is dead, we're apt to say: 354
314. Then quickly away: 372
315. Things have strangely veer'd about: 198, 204
316. This day, for our new navigation: 19

JOHN FREETH

Numbers refer to: (plain type) *Index of Song Titles*; (bold type) *Bibliography*

317. This Gallic commander, as bold as any Grecian: 155
318. This marvellous union, 'mongst other debates: 198, 204
319. This world is a bubble and full of deceit: 201
320. Tho' as bad as times are, 'tis a folly to grieve: **47**
321. Tho' dear as things are, o'er the sociable cup: **87**
322. Tho' fond variety to taste: 347
323. Tho' in peaceable times, 'tis a cruel vexation: 344
324. Tho' most things are grievously dear: **93**
325. Tho' much blood and treasure the war must have cost: **95**
326. Tho' we cheerfully together: 125, 170
327. Though commerce has much been declining: 197
328. Though many at the match may frown: 367
329. Three ravenous creatures: 53, 53.5
330. Three years ago, or thereabout: 190
331. Thro' life promiscuously we stray: 385
332. Through false suspicion and distrust: 180
333. Through false suspicion and mistrust: 180
334. Through serious doubts, and sad distrust: 207
335. Time-taxing Will, Britannia's guide: 15
336. Times are now so ticklish grown (The): 58
337. 'Tis a plentiful time all allow: **84**
338. 'Tis a shame to the land! and a cursed vexation: 349
339. 'Tis an unpleasant thing – about taxes to sing: 100
340. 'Tis freedom's fair call: 226
341. To arms, to arms, hark! hark the drum: 54, 296
342. To Beelzebub soon as the tidings were brought: 14
343. To Britain's much lov'd happy shore: 209
344. To find out a tax that is certain to please: 242
345. To find the way to Heaven's gate: 151, 152
346. To get a snug penny, since fighting began: 356
347. To judge at this crisis which England's the best: 95
348. To mortals who genuine liberty prize: 301
349. To Old England's glory, behold from the West: 342
350. To St Malo was sent an express: 166
351. To the man let a bumper go cheerfully round: 259
352. To the sports of the field: 136

118

353. To Wimbledon, bloods of high style may away: 380

354. Toast if I offer, pray do not be cruel (A): 29

355. Trace all the towns the Kingdom round: 22

356. Traveller full forty years have I been (A): 124

357. Traveller full forty years I have been (A): 124

358. Traveller many long years I have been (A): 124

359. Trial's begun, and I'll venture to say (The): 334

360. True art of boxing – the old English game (The): 328

361. True jolly anglers of ev'ry degree (The): 119

362. 'Twas always the case when scrambling for power: 330

363. 'Twas at a place call'd Dudley: 103

364. 'Twas break of day, retiring from the Game: 138

365. 'Twas in sultry summer weather: 65, 66

366. 'Twas in the blessed reign of G--rge the Third: 379

367. 'Twas in the land of cyder: 76

368. 'Twas in the year of 'seventy-seven: 49

369. 'Twas just at the time when in sorrowful strain: 160

370. 'Twas when that contest had begun: 175

371. 'Twas when the business of the state: 91

372. 'Twas when the Lords were met, a noble sight: 107

373. 'Twas when the odious shop-tax had: 16, 184

374. 'Twas when the times were peaceable: 269

375. 'Twas when the war was ended: 63

376. Two Statesmen, who were seldom known: 168

377. Waiting for news to cheer the land: **81**

378. We set sail from Portsmouth on Candlemas-day: 282

379. Well met, brother Peter! Now do not deceive me: 221

380. Were ever British forces in: 49

381. What a noise has there been, what a confounded pother: 163

382. What a noise has there been, what a strange consternation: 162

383. What a shame to the land! What a cursed vexation: 349

384. What grief must the kingdom sustain: 37, 38

385. What if the parting day is at hand: 79

386. What in France by valour done: 245

387. What means all this rub-a-dub rattle: 373

388. What means all this tumult, and noise about fighting: 109

Numbers refer to: (plain type) *Index of Song Titles*; (bold type) *Bibliography*

389. What mortal can more happy be: 313
390. What nation like Britain was ever tormented: 201
391. Whate'er in justice may be said: 213
392. Whatever truly may be said: 213
393. When Birmingham's illustrious town: 150
394. When Britons to distress were stung: 127
395. When Charles in contest hard was run: 118
396. When commerce is on the decay: 143
397. When contentions are spread: 263
398. When dastards are plac'd in the list of promotions: 185, 186
399. When deeds atrocious have transpir'd: 50
400. When Garrick and Colman, our two great commanders: 217
401. When luxury reign'd, and court panders obtain'd: 74
402. When Parliment business was near at an end: 92
403. When party feuds and crafty wiles: **13**
404. When party feuds and hateful broils: 193
405. When plenty smiles throughout the land: 30
406. When Pluto, as told: 94
407. When sixpenny loaves but two pounders appear: **86**
408. When summer days were long and fair: 361
409. When the Blues each morn parade: 251
410. When the fam'd Stuart race had deserted the Crown: 93
411. When the grandees of Birmingham's grand undertaking: 72
412. When the tidings were brought that Port Egmont was gone: 78
413. When tidings arriv'd that Port Egmont was gone: 78
414. When vile mishaps had judg'd it fit: 59
415. Where Old English true hospitality reigns: 226
416. Whilst busy minds are o'er and o'er: 188, 189
417. Whilst changes the world is continually ringing: 56, 144
418. Whilst friendship I boast of, and truth is my guide: 22
419. Whilst in spite of pension'd pleading: 298
420. Whilst over the land revolution's the sound: **62**
421. Whilst some are endeav'ring the land to enslave: 376
422. Whilst some to the Throne are Addresses conveying: **43**
423. Whilst your hearts with ardour glow: 288

Numbers refer to: (plain type) *Index of Song Titles*; (bold type) *Bibliography*

424. Who has e'er been at camp, must admit without doubt: 52
425. Who'd e'er have thought that Warwickshire: 107
426. With credulous mortals – invasions's the sound: 132
427. With party away: 179
428. With the King for the loss of his aunt to condole: 1
429. Wonder not that this contention: **3**
430. World – and what creature knows when it will stop (The): 57
431. World to amaze, and keep fancy alive (The): 235, 236
432. World's a stage – the cheerful glass (The): 105
433. World's in an uproar, and when it will cease (The): **71**
434. Ye brave jolly tars, who delight o'er your cheer: 305
435. Ye British artists still exert your skill: 116, 238
436. Ye citizens so fond and free: 276
437. Ye coffee-house cits: 61
438. Ye E'sham boys, from whose rich soil: 173
439. Ye free-born souls who nobly dare: 381
440. Ye friends and ye neighbours, come share of the bounty: 239
441. Ye friends to fair freedom, and sons of true worth: 129; **9**
442. Ye gambling vile banditti: 135
443. Ye good fellows all: 250
444. Ye hunters so bold, who delight in a chase: 88, 280
445. Ye jovial lads come join with me: 7
446. Ye Ladies so prim, and ye Jemmies so gay: 343
447. Ye lads for the contest again be preparing: 157
448. Ye lads who delight in a whip and a spur: 332
449. Ye lasses that so fondly see: 90
450. Ye mortals so fond of the baubles of state: 176
451. Ye mortals who aim to be wonderful wise: 121
452. Ye mortals who never in all your wild trips: 18; **2**
453. Ye musical lads and ye lasses: 306
454. Ye slaves who would wish to enforce the example: 81
455. Ye steady supporters of honour and worth: 77
456. Ye strangers to care and vexation: 123
457. Ye Warwickshire lads free and hearty: 191

458. Ye Warwickshire lads, true and steady: 311
459. Ye worthy electors who dare to be free: 279
460. Year 'ninety-five of all others to mention (The): 261, 390
461. You can't but have heard of the grand installation: 113
462. Young Harry, a prince of less wisdom than wealth: 257

Index of Tunes

The tunes listed are all those named in any published piece attributed to Freeth in the *Bibliography*. An entry indicates those songs for which the given tune is specified.

The reference numbers are of two kinds. The first is the song-title number as recorded in the *Index of Song Titles* (pp. 93-108); the second kind, in bold type, is the entry number in the *Bibliography* for any song found elsewhere than in a songster – in fact, solely in newspapers – and which is most conveniently identified thus.

For the greater part the name of each tune has been recorded in the form in which it appears (except that the omission of the frequently used '&c.' has not been noticed). Where both short and extended forms have been variously employed the latter alone has been given, provided that the evidence for equating them is convincing; otherwise each form has been shown (e.g. Nos 50, 52-53, 56-57).

1. Alknomook: 366
2. All of them Kings in their turn: 3, 178, 330
3. All shall yield to the mulberry tree: 36, 234
4. Ally Croaker: 107, 144, 154, 198, 204, 390
5. And a-hunting we will go: 289, 340, 345
6. As I was a riding up Highgate: 133
7. As I was driving my waggon: 275, 277
8. As I was driving my waggon one day: 87, 111, 281, 319, 382
9. As Jack the brisk young drummer: 31, 175, 371

Numbers refer to: (plain type) *Index of Song Titles*; (bold type) *Bibliography*

INDEX OF TUNES

Numbers refer to: (plain type) *Index of Song Titles*; (bold type) *Bibliography*

10. As riding through Highgate: 359
11. Away to the downs: 131
12. Away with contention: 360
13. Ballinamoni oro: 248
14. Banks of the Dee (The): 326
15. Belle Isle March (The): 372
16. Billy Pitt the Tory: 96
17. Black joke (The): 187
18. Black Sloven: 231
19. Bright Phoebus has mounted the chariot of day: 260
20. Brother debtor: 201
21. Caesar and Pompey: 29, 162
22. Caesar and Pompey were both of them horned: 163, 355
23. Cassini: 337, **348**
24. Cassino: 378
25. Chase of Killruddy (The): 28, 106, 156, 282
26. Chevy Chase: 49
27. Clock had struck, I can't tell what (The): 120
28. Cobbler there was (A): 33, 344
29. Come all hands ahoy to the anchor: 130, 197
30. Come haste to the wedding: 68, 147, 148
31. Come let us dance and sing – in Inkle and Yarico: **8**
32. Come then all ye social powers: 35, 294, 321
33. Come ye lads who wish to shine: 20, 245, 307, 369
34. Come ye party jangling swains: 211, 225, 389; **7**
35. Drink and set your hearts at rest: 225, 389
36. Drink deep of the stream: 121
37. Duralin: or female volunteers: 346
38. Dusky morn (The): 42, **348**
39. Dusky night (The): 62, 249, 385
40. Early one morn a jolly brisk tar: 79, 91
41. Female volunteers: 174
42. Free and Accepted Mason (A): 107
43. Gee woo Dobbin: 264
44. General election (The): 34
45. Give round the word, dismount, dismount: 27, 80

46. Glorious first of August (The): 374
47. Go patter to lubbers: 124
48. Grecian Bard (The): 276
49. Hardy tar (The): 193
50. Hark away: 320
51. Hark the echoing horn: 181, 372
52. Hark, hark away: 98, 303
53. Hark, hark away, away to the Downs!: 15, 125, 170, 215, 216, 331
54. Hark, hark to the summons: 125, 170
55. Harvest Home: 250
56. Have you not read a book call'd Tristram Shandy: 377
57. Have you not read a book call'd Tristram Shandy, Ma'am.: 64
58. Heart of oak: 307, 342
59. Heart of oak are our ships: 259
60. Here's to the maiden of bashful fifteen: 46, 47
61. Highgate and horns: 273
62. Highland laddie (The): 49, 198, 202, 204
63. Hooly and fairly: 308
64. Hounds are all out (The): 88, 98, 226, 346
65. How happy a state: 22, 384
66. How happy a state does a miller possess: 17
67. I'll maintain of Englishmen: 273
68. In Liberty Hall – out of liberty's bowl: 312
69. Irish hay-makers (The): 199
70. Jack the brisk young drummer: 118, 278
71. Jolly angler (The): 110, 171
72. Jolly mortals: 10, 23, 229
73. Jolly mortals fill your glasses: 45, 65, 66, 102, 169, 178, 273, 365
74. Jolly sons of mirth and spirit: 364
75. Jovial beggar (The): 168
76. Larry Grogan: 101, 221
77. Last week in Lent I came to town: 338
78. Let us all be unhappy together: 212

Numbers refer to: (plain type) *Index of Song Titles*; (bold type) *Bibliography*

79. Liberty Hall: 115, 242, 247, 356, 357, 387
80. Lilies of France (The): 129, 235, 236, 304; **1, 9**
81. Lilliburlero: 375
82. Lowland lads (The): 204
83. Maid of the mill for me (The): 273
84. Marquis of Granby: 160, 201
85. Master Pol, &c. in Midas: 218
86. Merry sons of freedom push about the pitcher: 261
87. Miller of Mansfield (The): 26
88. Moggy Lauder: 209, 213, 271, 386
89. Mrs Casey: 180, 206, 207
90. Muffled bells of Bow and Bride (The): 48
91. Murdock O'Blaney: 377
92. Myself betwixt Bacchus: 334
93. Nancy Dawson: 7, 54, 69, 107, 160, 240, 296, 381
94. Navigators haste away: 44
95. Near to a place call'd Dover in Kent: 205, 220
96. Newton talk'd of lights and shades: 292
97. Now to pant on Thetis's breast: 192
98. Now we are free from College rules: 196
99. Now's the time for mirth and glee: 256
100. Of heroes and statesmen I'll just mention four: 266
101. Of heroes when speaking: 132
102. Oh the broom, the bonny bonny broom: 82
103. Oh the jolly angler's life: 172
104. Old Highland laddie (The): 133
105. Old Homer, but what: 301, 350
106. Old woman clothed in grey (An): 166, 270, 300, 310
107. Old woman of Grimstone (The): 290, 314
108. On the white cliffs of Albion: 299
109. One evening at ambrosial feast: 30
110. Over the hills and far away: 50, 89, 133, 253, 354
111. Over the water to Charley: 198, 204
112. Pilgrim blithe and jolly (A): 135
113. Prate like a parrot, a parrot: 273
114. Princess lost her shoe (The): 63, 317

JOHN FREETH

115. Push about the brisk bowl: 52, 74, 95, 100, 136, 201, 362
116. Push about the jorum: 108, 141, 213, 222, 341, 351, 368
117. Queen's ass (The): 305
118. Rag-fair: 11
119. Rakes of Malta (The): 274, 349
120. Religion's a politic law: 32, 143, 166, 210, 214, 255, 333, 363
121. Roast beef of Old England: 99, 185, 186
122. Rouse, rouse, brother sportsman: 51
123. Rule, Britannia: 126, 127
124. Rural felicity: 43, 157
125. St David's Day: 22, 167
126. Same as the Georges [i.e. Push about the jorum, No. 116]: 367
127. See the conquering hero comes: 237
128. Shawnbree: 41, 97, 119, 139, 278, 332
129. Sing, I'll maintain of Englishmen: 273
130. Sing tantarara rogues all: 357
131. Sir John why will you go fight-a: 309
132. Sit down neighbours all: 286
133. So merrily danc'd the Quaker: 58, 188
134. Spanking Jack was so comely: 353
135. Staffordshire fox-chase (The): 67
136. Stick a pin there: 176, 272, 280
137. Strange rumours of war: 333
138. Sun was in the firmament (The): 59, 269, 335
139. Sweet lass of Richmond Hill: 313
140. Sweet Willy O: 283
141. Take me Jenny: 71
142. Tantarara: 201
143. Teague's ramble to London: 227
144. That miracles never will cease: 143, 166, 373, 383
145. Then sling the flowing bowl: 25, 116, 238
146. There liv'd a man in Ballymycrazy: 56
147. There's na good luck for me: 190
148. There's na luck about the house: 16, 184
149. Time enough yet: 140, 142, 265, 305, 380

Numbers refer to: (plain type) *Index of Song Titles*; (bold type) *Bibliography*

150. To get a snug penny: 57
151. Trip to Portsmouth (A): 39
152. Tristram Shandy: 64
153. 'Twas at a place call'd Dover in Kent: 22
154. 'Twas in sultry summer weather: 102
155. 'Twas in the land of cyder: 103
156. Two Welshmen partners in a cow: 225, **389**
157. Vicar and Moses (The): 86, **179**
158. Vicar of Bray (The): 158, **370**
159. Warwickshire lad (The): 19, 60, 107, **311**
160. Warwickshire lads: 19, 287
161. We are the boys, who fear no noise, where thundering cannons roar: **316**
162. Welcome every friendly guest: 137
163. Welcome, welcome: 22
164. Welcome, welcome, brother debtor: 2, 107, 125, 170
165. Well met Brother Peter: 109
166. When first to Cambridge we do come: 133, 258
167. When Phoebus had mounted the chariot of day: 252
168. When summer days were long and fair: 39, 70, 75
169. Whilst busy minds: 105
170. Whilst o'er the mountains: 159, 170
171. Widow bewitch'd with her passion (A): **183**
172. William and Margaret: 9
173. With party away: 94
174. Yankee Doodle: 141
175. Ye belles and ye flirts: 83
176. Ye citizens so fond and free: **347**
177. Ye prigs who are troubled with conscience's qualms: 12, 18; **2**
178. Ye Warwickshire lads: 123
179. Ye Warwickshire lads and ye lasses: 102, 225, **389**

A SELECTION OF
FREETH'S SONGS AND OTHER PIECES

The compositions are in the order of the first published appearance
of the version selected. The date of publication is given in square
brackets after the title. The seven songs that were removed from the
manuscript of *Modern Songs*, 1782 (*v.* pp.11–12) have been indicated
by '[MS. 1782]'; six of those songs are here published for the first
time.

Significant substantive variants found in other versions of a few
songs have been appended. Letters purposely omitted from some
proper names (and a few other words) have been supplied within
square brackets.

Titles of compositions and tunes, and the heading 'Chorus', have
been given in a uniform manner, manifest errors have been silently
corrected, and spelling and punctuation have been normalized,
although Freeth's spelling of some French words has been preserved. The first word or words of a few songs have been put into
capital letters to conform with the majority of the songs. Otherwise
the use of upper case and italic type in the text reflects that of the
originals, though no other attempt has been made to represent their
typography.

The events and persons referred to have been documented elsewhere, and it has seemed best, therefore, not to burden the text with
annotations. The glosses on 'The diversion of quoits playing' are
Freeth's (pp. 189–90).

JOHN FREETH

A DIALOGUE
Tune: *Push about the brisk bowl*
[1766]

TO judge at this crisis which *England's* the best,
　　This tott'ring *Old State*, or the *New*;
The story I tell, not devis'd as a jest,
　　Very clearly the matter will shew.

To a *Briton* in point of dispute t'other day,
　　An *American* made this reply:
'Those measures which bring your dear land to decay,
　　Are the Deeds which we boldly defy.

'The fruits of our country we freely enjoy,
　　And when any disturbances rise;
In a body we join, and disdain to comply,
　　To be stung by that monster Excise'.

'I grant ev'ry mortal in freedom delights,
　　Yet the State which your greatness did raise,
That protected your lives and defended your rights,
　　Sure in taxing may do as they please.

'As our Blood and our Treasure were lavish'd away,
　　To secure you from insults of France;
Pray, why should you grumble those Levies to pay?
　　Which we in proportion advance'.

Then the *Colonist* frown'd in the wrangling debate,
　　And reply'd as in anger he wax'd:
'Ye *Britons* have always been fool'd by your State,
　　But *Americans* scorn to be tax'd.

'You're tax'd in your Lights, and how shocking to think!
　　That you two-pence must pay to the K[ing],
For ev'ry twelve penn'worth of Stingo you drink,
　　Which, by Bacchus, I swear's not the thing.

'Now, if you are minded to live at your ease,
　　Ride o'er the wide ocean with me;
Leave cavilling courtiers to do as they please,
　　And with us you shall ever be free'.

Old England's decline, thus embarrass'd with cares,
　　Caus'd the Briton no longer to stand;
For he not to this Tale only laid down his ears,
　　But bid fair adieu to the land.

[In a later version of this song, first published in *The Wawickshire Medley*,
[1780], the last two stanzas are replaced by:

'Now if you in peace, ease, and safety would live,
　　Sail o'er the wide ocean with me;
There America yields what Old England can't give,
　　The blessings of true Liberty'.]

HOSPITALITY
[1766]

WHEN Birmingham's illustrious town
Remark'd for opulence was grown,
The sons of eminence began,
To think upon some noble plan,
That to their honour might redound,
As well as serve the country round;
Some talk'd of *Inland Navigation*,
And told how much 'twould serve the nation
If *Trent* and *Severn* were united,
The cost would amply be requited;
And that its great utility,
All that had eyes might clearly see.
　　The sages of the sober sort,
Who seldom with their money sport,
Unless convinc'd the plan would tend,
To serve some good and useful end,
Propos'd a scheme for building up,
A firm and lasting Gospel-shop;
As such a laudable intent,
Would be a graceful ornament,
Where those, who room for worship wanted,
Might have their pious wishes granted.
　　But matters of a public kind,
Will always some opposers find;

Tho' the design be e'er so good,
Or e'er so clearly understood;
This made the former schemes protracted,
'Tis hop'd, not totally rejected;
But as the sequel tends to shew,
A motive of a different view;
Excuse me whilst I deign to speak,
What with our leaders seem'd to take.

A mighty Ruler of the town,
Whose fame has many years been known,
(An *Esculapian*, and some say,
As great as *Galen* in his way,)
Express'd the goodness of his mind,
And tender feeling for mankind;
Long time the people plainly saw,
What e'er he said was counted law,
So numbers join'd his noble call,
And voted for an HOSPITAL.

Now that his name rever'd shall be,
And honour'd by posterity,
A stately edifice shall rise,
T'extol his goodness to the skies;
The poor, the sick, the lame and blind,
By this grand work relief shall find;
Paupers, and ballad-singers too,
With all the tag-rag tatter'd crew,
That often at the glass-house swarm,
To keep their wretched bodies warm,
Shall leave their dens and hither come,
To find a lasting asylum;
Discarded tars who lurk about,
To trace the charitable out,
With tuck'd-up limbs, or artful wounds,
Shall enter here and quit their rounds;
The brick-kiln girls, and cinder dames,
Who harbour where a furnance flames,
Their habitations shall forsake,
In hopes their quarters here to take;
Incurables of *Doctor Lock*,
From distant parts shall hither flock,
The gipsy tribe of fortune-tellers,
Match-mongers and old rag retailers,

With brats upon their backs shall crawl,
To find this GENERAL HOSPITAL;
Of every county round, the scum,
Shall leave their huts and hither come,
Upon the generous bounty feed,
And like the *Scots* who cross the *Tweed*,
Finding a better clime shall ne'er
Return into their native air;
Here lose the Itch, shake off their Lice,
And call the land a paradise,
Each bound to bless his happy lot,
In gaining such a bounteous spot.
    And every beggar's daily pray'r
Shall be for its peculiar care.

INLAND NAVIGATION
Tune: *Marquis of Granby*
[1766]

'TWAS just at the time when in sorrowful strain,
  Old *England* was grievously groaning;
Her natives in sadness to add to the scene,
  The loss of their trade were bemoaning;
To give some redress, in this age of distress,
  Some Worthies (tho' few in the nation)
As a scheme that might tend, to a fav'rable end,
  Were resolv'd to promote NAVIGATION.
               Tol, lol, &c.

The lovers of commerce will freely combine,
  Without any kind of evasion,
To strengthen so noble and brave a design,
  And gladly embrace the occasion;
Not a *Briton* that knows, what opulence flows
  From this art, but with free approbation,
And spirit alert will his int'rest exert,
  To support and extend NAVIGATION.
               Tol, lol, &c.

'Tis this makes our isle in the eyes of the world,
    A bulwark of terror and wonder;
No state when our shipping their sails have unfurl'd,
    But what is oblig'd to knock under;
In war or in peace, all commerce would cease,
    Was it not for a free NAVIGATION;
'Tis of riches the source, when such plans we enforce,
    And of freedom our dear preservation.
                Tol, lol, &c.

In *Lancashire*, view what a laudable plan,
    Is brought into fine execution,
By *Bridgwater's Duke*; let us copy the man,
    And stand to a good resolution;
If the waters of *Trent*, with the *Severn* have vent,
    What mortal can have an objection?
So they do not proceed, to cut into the *Tweed*.
    With the SCOTS to have greater connection.
                Tol, lol, &c.

A free intercourse with our principal ports,
    For trade must be certainly better;
When traffic's extended, and goods easy vended,
    In consequence things must be cheaper;
Our commerce will thrive, and the arts will revive,
    Which are now in a sad situation;
If we follow this notion, from ocean to ocean,
    To have a complete NAVIGATION.
                Tol, lol, &c.

To the land what advantages then will proceed,
    As soon as we've open'd our sluices?
Our cattle, and even the ground where they feed,
    Will be turn'd into far better uses;
'Tis this will enable our merchants abroad
    To vie with each neighbouring nation;
Who now as they tell us, in fact under sell us,
    For want of this free NAVIGATION.
                Tol, lol, &c.

[In a later version of this song, first published in *The Warwickshire Medley*, [1780], the last two stanzas are conflated to read:

To the land what advantages then will proceed,
    As soon as we've open'd our sluices;
Our cattle, and even the ground where they feed,
    Will be turn'd into far better uses;
Our commerce will thrive, and the arts will revive,
    Which are now in a sad situation;
If we follow this notion, from ocean to ocean,
    To have a complete Navigation.]

TAXATION
Tune: *A cobbler there was*
[1766]

THO' in peaceable times, 'tis a cruel vexation!
To talk of devising new modes of taxation;
Yet if the design be well-founded, why may not
This honest proposal take place in the Senate?
                Derry down, &c.

I hope no offence in declaring my mind,
And wish that our rulers were this way inclin'd,
'Twould certainly be for the good of the nation,
I mean for a tax to promote Propagation.
                Derry down, &c.

By taxing our Lights, and by taxing our Beer,
We feel them as burdens too heavy to bear;
But where'd be the harm, if a duty was laid
In proportion on ev'ry old Bachelor's head?
                Derry down, &c.

No doubt, but each Miser, Coquet, and old Prude,
May think my design is maliciously rude;
But good *English Dames*, who to wedlock have took,
Will approve of the Scheme, and will laugh at the joke.
                Derry down, &c.

JOHN FREETH

For Marriage we know, is a precept divine,
The Scripture informs us therewith to enjoin,
And bids us to conjugal pleasure give birth,
In order thereby to replenish the earth.
                                    Derry down, &c.

Don't think that I mean to deprive 'em of choice,
For Liberty's cause be for ever my voice;
Yet still as the annual supplies we must raise,
What people so proper to pay 'em as these.
                                    Derry down, &c.

But among all degrees, let it not be forgot,
This old standing order to bring in the plot;
Nor think me too hard, if I mean to imbibe
Double Duty on those of the Fumbling Tribe.
                                    Derry down, &c.

Then judge, if this maxim should pass approbation,
How they'd vie with each other in strong emulation!
To avoid being tax'd, many husband and wife,
Would find out fresh springs to the vitals of life.
                                    Derry down, &c.

Then now, my good fellows, take hold of the can,
Give a fatherly toast to encourage the plan;
For if no young sprouts from the old ones should spring,
Pray, what would become of our Country and King.
                                    Derry down, &c.

WILKES'S ENLARGEMENT
An Ode
[1771]

RECITATIVE

'TWAS in the blessed Reign of G[EO]RGE the Third,
When Sycophants were at the Helm preferr'd,
And good NEWC[ASTL]E, at Ambition's Stride,
Wept for the Land, and broken-hearted dy'd;
When from the courtly Catalogue were rais'd,
The Names of those who for their Deeds were prais'd,

Whose valiant FATHERS nobly bled, to place
ENGLAND'S bright Crown upon the BRUNSWICK Race,
'Twas then that FREEDOM'S CHAMPION boldly dar'd
To speak — what others wish'd to have declar'd.

AIR

England *cannot but revere him*
For his PATRIOTIC *Stand,*
    Lordly Tyrants still shall fear him,
    And his faithful numerous Band.
Since Integrity has mark'd him,
Steadfast to the People's Rights,
    In the Cause he has embark'd in,
    Every honest Heart unites.

In deep Distress, BRITANNIA long has moan'd,
Her ancient Courage dwindled into nought,
    Under Oppression have her Natives groan'd,
    And for Redress in vain, alas! have sought:
Unhappy Diff'rences abroad arise,
Whilst home-bred Discords every Day increase,
    And they — on whom our chiefest TRADE relies —
Forbid our Merchandise to cross the Seas.
    HIBERNIA'S Sons, to bitter Wrath provok'd,
Spurn at the Load of PENSIONS which they bear,
    And boldly cry — no longer they'll be yok'd,
To prop the Pride of each disgusted Peer.

Designing FRANCE, with watchful Eyes,
    Observes the Weakness of OUR STATE;
The jarring Discords that arise
    Their hidden HOSTILE Views create;
Nor better pleas'd than when intestine Broils
Inflame this ONCE styl'd happiest of Isles —
    In close compact
    With SPAIN — to act,
Behold their growing Armaments!
    In solemn Leagues,
    And dark Intrigues,
Planning for — desperate Events.

JOHN FREETH

AIR

The COCK *may well crow,*
And be forming a Blow,
When he sees England's LION *asleep;*
The MULE *may advance,*
And have Reason to prance,
When BRITANNIA *does nothing but weep.*

The EAGLE *may watch,*
And be on the Catch,
When his Neighbours are plung'd into War;
Too subtle to find
Which Way he's inclin'd,
And who his Proceedings can bar.

Howe'er Things appear,
What have Statesmen *to fear*
Whose Pride's o'er the Beacon *to jerk it?*
What care W[es]t *or* G[owe]r,
About foreign Power,
So they win but the Odds at Newmarket.

Spite of every bold Epistle,
  Big with each atrocious Wrong,
Till old Time shall crop the *Thistle,*
  England must with Grief be stung.

Had the *Caledonian* Bridle
  Ne'er been introduc'd above,
He who was the People's Idol,
  Might have still retain'd their Love.

King and Subject small Connexion
  Cannot but expect to find,
Till the *Freedom of Election*
  Is to Truth and Right consign'd.

BRITONS never want Allegiance,
  When protected by their Prince;
Nor are prone to Disobedience,
  But when shameful Wrongs commence.

By the glorious REVOLUTION
Was our FREEDOM *fairly gain'd;*
On that Plan *the* CONSTITUTION
Shall for ever be maintain'd.

THE FRENCH TONSOR
[1771]

MY Name it is *Taste*, from *Paris* in haste,
    Intent on procuring a Fortune,
To *London* I came, and publish'd my Fame,
    My great Skill and Practice for certain;
By oft advertising, the People surmising,
    Read over my fam'd Reputation,
With *Locks*, *Braids*, and *Tails*, on Ladies I wait,
    Who call me the Man of the Fashion.
                  Tol, lol, &c.

On *Sundays* to tell, I trip o'er the *Mall*,
    'Mongst Numbers of Gentry parading,
My Beaver and Wand, I hold in my Hand,
    My Topping to keep from all Shading;
The Folks as they pass, look full in my Face,
    As an Object of much Speculation,
The *Beaus* and the *Jemmies*, cry 'this a new Whim is,
    And certainly must be the Fashion'.
                  Tol, lol, &c.

To gain a by-Job, I put on my Bob,
    And round *Covent Garden* I ramble,
If farther I stretch, I slip on a Scratch,
    And 'mongst *Bacchanalians* assemble;
Sometimes by good Luck, I meet with a *Buck*,
    Divested of faint Hesitation,
When toasting his Dame, sets his Wig on a Flame,
    And wish it was more in the Fashion.
                  Tol, lol, &c.

For *Bishops*, and *Proctors*, *Attornies*, and *Doctors*,
    Full Bottoms, I have in great Plenty,
Each Head they go on, looks grave as a *Don*,
    Tho' in Years they may not have seen Twenty;

Besides, I assure it, for *Sexton* or *Curate*,
  I've Cuts, that admit no Evasion,
With Bows I salute 'em, and tell 'em I'll suit 'em,
  With neatest and best in the Fashion.
                              Tol, lol, &c.

I make them in Troth, exact to your Cloth,
  That when the Dust drops on your Shoulder,
The same you appear, as tho' none was there,
  By Means of my excellent Powder;
Newcastle, or *Bute*, may here themselves suit,
  Or any of different Persuasion,
My Colours are *Plaid*, *Green*, *Orange*, or *Red*,
  To match every Whim in the Fashion.
                              Tol, lol, &c.

My *Queues*, and my *Demi-queues*, had such a Run,
  That could I have made them much faster,
They all would have sold, for glittering Gold,
  So fond are the *English* of Taste, Sir;
The Son of great *Mars*, return'd from the Wars,
  Bald-headed, may make an Oration,
But surely a Copy, that's *Martial*, will not be,
  'Mongst peaceable People of Fashion.
                              Tol, lol, &c.

At Cutting and Dressing, my Knack is so pleasing
  The Actors of *Drury* adore me,
The Dancers and Singers, admire my fine Fingers,
  And place themselves daily before me;
For Nipping and Snipping, for Furling and Curling
  A Puff, and a little Flirtation,
They tip me a Fee, I return a *Congee*,
  That's decent, and just in the Fashion.
                              Tol, lol, &c.

I've got a Compound, nowhere else to be found,
  And those who are mindful of trying,
May have just a Lick, of my *Six-penny* Stick,
  And my Wash-Ball is well worth your buying,
If your Skin be as brown as an *African* Loon,
  That's a Slave in a Sugar Plantation,
From a deep Sooty-dun, you'll be fair as a Nun,
  And as spruce as the best in the Fashion.
                              Tol, lol, &c.

As through *Middle Row*, I chanced to go,
   The Cry was, 'Who buys my fine Caxon?
Here's long Bobs, and short Bobs, best Bobs and major Bobs,
   Ramillies whiter than Flaxen';
A Sweep standing near, cry'd, 'Club Wigs, I swear
   Give Credit to our Occupation';
So his Bag he let slip, and a Two-penny Dip
   Wrapt up his black Pate in the Fashion.

THE JOVIAL COCKER
Tune: *The jolly angler*
[1771]

OF the jovial Sons of Game,
Scatter'd o'er the Nation,
From the highest Rank of Fame,
To the lowest Station,
   None there are,
   That can compare,
To Cockers for a Spirit;
   Old and Young, of the Throng,
   When they hear, far or near,
   Of a Fight, take a Flight,
   Free and bold, sport their Gold,
'Mongst their Brethren of the Band;
   Winning, losing, ne'er refusing,
To discount a just Demand,
Whilst of Cash their Pockets stand,
   Stout enough to bear it.

Not a Country save our own,
Can such Sort be found in,
But in *Britain's* Isle alone,
Doth such Bloods abound in,
   True-bred Stags,
   Like *English* Lads,
Win the Fight or die, Sir;
   If by Chance the Breed of *France*,
   Mix among our feather'd Throng,
   Those we lot, for Spit or Pot,

For to feel, the Prick of Steel,
Makes 'em cow'r and turn Tail,
   Hasting, shifting, running, mourning,
British Fowl, Boys, never fail,
Over *French* Cocks to prevail,
   Or to make them fly, Sir.

'Tis a comely pleasing Sight
On a Summer's Morning,
To behold in Splendour bright,
All in Bloom adorning,
      Chanticleer,
      Devoid of Fear,
In Pride the World out-vying;
   Claps his Wings, then he sings,
   Now he walks, then he stalks,
   Turns his Head, of Coral Red,
   For to hear, if any near,
Answer to his thrilling Sound,
   Cawing, crowing, rutting, strutting,
Braving all his Neighbours round,
Combats those that's ever found
   On his Bound'ry prying.

When the Time approaches nigh
That there's Sport ensuing
For the Pit away we fly,
Fancy's Will pursuing,
   I hold a Crown,
   Before they're down,
Take of each your Liking;
   Standers by, loudly cry,
   'Odds the Grey, wins the Day',
   But in a While, the Ginger Pile,
   Foremost gets, now the Bets,
Turn about from Side to Side;
   Panting, breathing, bleeding, dying,
There's a Contest bravely try'd,
Grey was Bottom tho' he dy'd,
   And a true-bred Chicken.

Soon as e'er a Battle ends,
From the Fight retiring,
All sit down as jovial Friends,
What is more desiring,
    Than to see,
    Quick, frank, and free,
Social Mirth combining?
    Now we brag, of Duck-wing Stag,
    Make a Match, sing a Catch,
    Drink and smoke, pass a Joke,
    Then again, to the same;
Thus the Hours glide away,
    Gentle, simple, wicked, ragged,
All delight in sport and play,
And their Losings freely pay,
    Ne'er at Fate repining.

Let the rest of different Scenes,
Boast their greatest Pleasure,
Of the Turf, or pictur'd Queens,
Sporting free their Treasure,
    Let them prefer
    Inferior
Delights of Recreation;
    English Blood, staunch and good,
    Love to cock, drink, and smoke,
    And resort, for the Sport,
    To and fro, high or low,
Winds about each different Shire;
    Cutting, trimming, heeling, betting,
Care not for what Point we bear,
Cockers always meet and fare
    With the best in fashion.

THE ROYAL COMMODORE
Tune: *The Queen's ass*
[1771]

YE brave jolly Tars, who delight o'er your Cheer,
To fighting Transactions of lending an Ear,
Attend whilst I sing of the Wounds and the Scars,
That a *Commodore* met with in *Venus's* Wars.

JOHN FREETH

Of *Pocock* and *Keppel*, old Sailors may talk,
Or tell what Exploits have been done by a *Hawke*;
Yet none like our Commodore ever before,
In War or in Peace caus'd so great an Uproar.

The Name of a *Cumberland* once was rever'd,
Because he *Bellona's* loud Thunder ne'er fear'd;
But this is a quite different Genius I trow,
For the Weapon he fights with is young Cupid's Bow.

He often, when cruising in Search of a Prize,
False Colours will hoist by the Way of *Disguise*;
Tho' young in Commission, he ranks of the Line,
And to board a small *Frigate*, had laid a Design.

This *Frigate*, no Matter by whom she was mann'd,
By the G[ros]v[eno]r was rigg'd, and lay under Command;
Tho' the *Commodore* lately lays Claim to a Share,
And calls it in Raptures his '*dear little Hair*'.

If chance to be catch'd in a contraband Trade,
Ne'er tells where the choice smuggled Goods have been laid;
And for *Letters* so famous, as some People tell,
That he'd swear *by his Bible* before he could *spell*.

One Night near the Shore as at Anchor they lay,
Not dreading the Fury or Foams of the Sea,
A *Tender* unlook'd for, rush'd into the Creek,
Expecting the Frigate was springing a Leak.

A Tempest arose, drove the Vessels aground,
And the *Commodore's Damage* was *Ten thousand Pound*',
Yet sure for the Sake of his *Mother*, the Land
Will not scruple to pay such a trifling Demand.

But, Sirs, if the Public must pay for the Fun,
'Tis fit Something more in the Cause should be done;
On both Sides to get the Thing decently cook'd,
Let the Gr[os]v[eno]r be duk'd and the Commodore duck'd.

Ye learned Scotch Tutors, pray let there be shewn
Some Pains when instructing the Sons of the Crown,
And a whole Nation's Thanks you shall have for the Deed,
When you've hit on the Method of mending the Breed.

[In a later version of this song, first published in *The Warwickshire Medley* [1780], the last stanza has been omitted and in the eighth stanza 'Highness' has been substituted for '*Mother*'. In a yet later version, first published in *The Political Songster*, 1790 (No. 23), the last two stanzas are omitted and the last two lines of the eighth stanza (now the concluding lines) emended to read:

The Voyage is ended — enough has been said,
And the D[uk]e for his frolic has handsomely paid.]

BUNKER HILL
Or, The Soldier's Lamentation
Tune: *The muffled bells of Bow and Bride*

[1780]

I AM a jolly soldier,
    Enlisted years ago,
To serve my king and country,
    Against the common foe;
But when across th'Atlantic
    My orders were to go,
I griev'd to think that English hearts,
    Should draw their swords on those
Who fought and conquer'd by their side,
    When Frenchmen were their foes.

In drubbing French and Spaniards,
    A soldier takes delight;
But troops coop'd up in Boston,
    Are in so sad a plight,
That many think their stomachs more
    Inclin'd to eat than fight,
And like us would be loth to stir;
    For ev'ry vet'ran knows,
We fought and conquer'd side by side,
    When Frenchmen were our foes.

'Twas on the seventeenth of June,
  I can't forget the day,
The flower of our army,
  For Charlestown sail'd away.
The town was soon in ashes laid,
  When bombs began to play;
But, oh! the cruel scene to paint,
  It makes my blood run chill;
Pray heaven grant, I never more,
  May climb up Bunker Hill.

America to frighten,
  The tools of power strove,
But ministers are cheated,
  Their schemes abortive prove.
The men they told us would not fight,
  Are to the combat drove,
And to our gallant officers,
  It prov'd a bitter pill,
For numbers dropp'd before they reach'd
  The top of Bunker Hill.

I should not be amaz'd to hear
  Wolfe's ghost had left the shades,
To check that shameful bloody work,
  Which England's crown degrades.
The lads who scorn to turn their backs,
  On Gallia's best brigades,
Undaunted stood, but frankly own,
  They better had lain still,
Than such a dear-bought victory gain,
  As that of Bunker Hill.

Did they who bloody measures crave,
  Our toil and danger share,
Not one to face the Riflemen,
  A second time would dare.
Ye Britons, who your country love,
  Be this your ardent pray'r:
'To Britain and her colonies,
  May peace be soon restor'd,
And knaves of high and low degree,
  Be *destin'd to the cord*'.

[In a later version of this song, found only in *A Touch on the Times*, 1784, the third line of the last stanza reads:

    Not one to cross th'Atlantic,]

LIBERTY'S CALL
Tune: *Hark the echoing horn*
[1780]

HARK to liberty's call, how it darts through the air,
    Take horse, my brave boys, and away;
With courage advance, for the contest prepare,
    The time will admit no delay.
All hungry dependants of government shun,
    And act like your ancestors bold;
When the placeman appears, bid the traitor be gone,
    'An Englishman scorns to be sold'.

With heart, hand, and voice, for Sir Charles we'll unite,
    Britannia applauds the design;
We've long been oppress'd, and to do ourselves right,
    With freedom must nobly combine;
'Tis liberty's call, can a Briton refrain,
    His gen'rous assistance to lend?
Our country commands, and we'll bleed ev'ry vein,
    So glorious a cause to defend.

When freedom's at stake, and the land is oppress'd,
    Their duty they're acting who go
With resolute hearts to contribute their best,
    To crush the attempts of our foe!
Like Britons of old, may they courage display,
    Success their endeavours ensure;
And the dastard who barters his birthright away,
    In slav'ry for ever endure.

JOHN FREETH

SKIPWITH, HOLTE, AND INDEPENDENCY
Tune: *The Warwickshire lad*
[1780]

YE Warwickshire lads, true and steady,
For voting come get yourselves ready;
The signal is given, the time is at hand,
And Englishmen-like for your liberties stand.
   Liberties stand,
   Join the band,
And Englishmen-like for your liberties stand.

The sound to our ears is discordant,
Which echo's the name of a M[ordaun]t;
'Twould madness be counted to look for support
From him that's a tool to an infamous court.
   Tool of the court,
   Mark the sort,
And nobly disdain ev'ry tool of the court.

To do an old character justice,
This, this a true portrait I trust is;
At the Minister's beckon obsequious he bow'd,
And said aye or no with the sycophant crowd;
   Sycophant crowd,
   Who do proud?
And said aye or no with the sycophant crowd.

Can Englishmen choose the descendant
Of any such courtly dependant,
'Pray where is the freedom of voice in this case?
If he speaks from his conscience he loses his place'.
   Loses his place,
   Sore disgrace.
If he speaks from his conscience he loses his place.

Who wishes such myrmidons seated,
Deserves like a slave to be treated;
To Old England's welfare the basest of foes,
Are they who such dupes for our members propose.
   Members propose,
   Worst of foes,
Are they who such dupes for our members propose.

Some rotten grown borough may choose him,
True Warwickshire lads will refuse him;
The sprig of corruption a few friends may find,
But Skipwith and Holte are with freedom combin'd;
Freedom combin'd,
Well inclin'd,
But Skipwith and Holte are with freedom combin'd.

THE PRIDE OF WORCESTER
On Sir Watkin Lewes's arrival
Tune: *Sweet Willy O*
[1780]

OF Worcester the worthy Sir Watkin's the pride;
The best that came down,
He gladden'd the town,
For all in his promise could safely confide.

He came to our aid in a time of distress;
And each honest heart
Did freely impart
The kindest of wishes towards his success.

Hark! hark! to the sound of the fife and the drum;
No music so sweet
Could a Handel repeat,
As that which first told us a third man was come.

Newcastle may boast of her favourite Glynn;
And Worcester reviv'd,
When Lewes arriv'd,
And show'd the same spirit to welcome him in.

A scene more enliv'ning there could not be crav'd;
Where'er he came near
Much joy did appear,
For deeply his name on our hearts is engrav'd.

JOHN FREETH

A contest so noble must soon fire the land;
    And long as the tide
    Of Severn shall glide,
The name of Sir Watkin on record shall stand.

BRITISH VOLUNTEERS
Tune: *The Belle Isle March*
[MS: 1782]

COME on my brave Boys, 'tis no time to delay,
Our COUNTRY commands, let us quickly away;
In defence of our rights we'll undauntedly go,
Our best Blood to part with or vanquish the foe.

    Chorus
    Then quickly away
    Manly zeal to display,
Haste, haste, where the STANDARD of glory appears;
    In defence of your Land,
    When call'd on to stand,
'Tis an honour to rank with the brave Volunteers.

On MINDEN'S fair plains when to glory led on,
Remember my WORTHIES what wonders were done;
The BRITISH BRIGADES in such order arrang'd,
So firm were their Lines — a few Shot were exchang'd,
And full Sixty thousand BRAVADING MONSIEURS,
Gave way to Six REGIMENTS of brave VOLUNTEERS,
    and full Sixty thousand &c.

Of old in the Field as our ANCESTORS fought
'Their SONS, and their SONS' SONS by Nature are taught';
Their Valour to show, and their Deeds to record,
When Insults are offer'd — REVENGE is the word.
    Chorus — Then quickly away, &c.

Then rouse at the call all that's dear to defend,
With numerous foes tho' we have to contend,
In our Breasts shall this old ENGLISH MOTTO be wore
'The greater the DANGER — the HONOUR the more'.

Chorus
Then quickly away
Manly zeal to display,
Haste, haste, where the STANDARD of glory appears;
In defence of your Land,
When call'd on to stand,
'Tis an honour to rank with the brave VOLUNTEERS.

ON THE GLORIOUS SUCCESS OF THE ENGLISH PRIVATEERS

Tune: *Heart of Oak*

[MS: 1782]

YE bold British Tars who are strangers to fear,
And ne'er flinch your Colours if Danger is near;
Your Country commands, to her Standard advance,
And humble once more the Ambition of France.

Chorus
Then away my brave Boys, see what ardour appears,
Whilst Fame truth conveying,
Is daily displaying,
The glorious success of our brave PRIVATEERS.

Already observe the kind fortune that glads,
The Hearts of the BRISTOL and LIVERPOOL Lads;
The produce of INDIA rewards well their toil,
What mortal would wish to bring home better spoil?

Chorus — Then away, &c.

Bold Britons still able their Coast to defend,
To Gallic Intrusion were ne'er known to bend;
To fight and to conquer by Nature are taught,
And will till MONSIEURS to repentance are brought.

Chorus — Then away, &c.

Our PORTS swarm with prizes, the SAILOR'S delight,
And Commerce revives at so pleasing a Sight;
On Neptune's Sons Fortune propitiously smiles
And Britain shall still be the wealthiest of Isles.

JOHN FREETH

Chorus
Then away my brave Boys, see what ardour appears,
Whilst Fame truth conveying,
Is daily displaying,
The glorious success of our brave PRIVATEERS.

ON THE THREATEN'D INVASION AT THE BREAKING
OUT OF THE SPANISH WAR
Tune: *The jolly young waterman*
[MS: 1782]

IN spite of treacherous base combination,
    The loud Gasconading and threats of our foes,
No clamour about an intended Invasion,
    Can ever disturb a bold BRITON'S repose;
Come when they will, to receive 'em we're ready,
Our SOLDIERS are brave and our SAILORS are steady;
To rue they are certain, who dare to intrude,
For ENGLAND, old ENGLAND, will ne'er be subdu'd.

Of all the strange rumours who takes a perusal
    Must laugh at the talk of their Flat Bottom'd boats,
When touch'd to the Quick it is nothing unusual,
    To swear by St DENNIS, they'll cut all our Throats;
Much better at home 'tis their Int'rest to tarry,
Than projects attempt, which are sure to miscarry;
To SOUP-MAIGRE WARRIORS 'twould be sudden death,
Such Battalions to face as encamp on *Cox Heath*.

Now party, Contention, and Discord are dying,
    A true British Spirit success ever crowns;
The TARS on strong hope of fresh glory relying,
    On SPAIN'S waging War, cry, 'Have at their GALLEONS!
Then give but their FLOTA a thundering volley,
The insolent DONS will repent of their folly;
For insults of old, from the LORDS of the MAIN,
Chastisement they've felt, and shall feel it again.

152

SCALE OF TALENT
A political cantata
Tune: *Chevy Chase*
[MS: 1782]

'TWAS in the *year of 'Seventy-seven*
   All British hearts must own,
To England's crown fell such mishaps,
   The like was never known.

A mighty boasting Man of War
   To Canada was sent;
What pity that so bold a Knight
   On such a project went.

Eight thousand chosen Troops he led,
   'In armour bright and gay',
Which being told, one Arnold swore
   He would dispute the way.

'Where is the rebel that has dar'd,
   To mock the words I've said;
I'll give that Man a thousand Crowns,
   Who brings to me his head'.

'Twas nobly spoke, but whilst the Chief
   Of Vict'ry was in quest,
The rebels to his Quarters came,
   And took away his Chest.

The cruel Fates sent forth a GATES,
   And hard must be the task,
That of Foe he held so *cheap*,
   B[ur]g[oyne]e should mercy ask.

JOHN FREETH

Tune: *The Highland laddie*

Since never British Troops were in,
    A more unhappy situation;
Nor was by Mortal ever seen,
    A more Bombastic proclamation.

— Chorus —
Was ever Army so surrounded;
Was ever General so confounded;
The Boaster strikes, tho' none more gallant,
Ever fought by *Scale of Talent*.

He cross'd the Lakes and scour'd the Grounds,
    Stoutly fighting for provision;
Till almost brought within the bounds
    Of unconditional Submission.
        Chorus — Was ever Army &c.

Full of vigour this vaunting Commander set out,
    And vow'd he would soon put his Foe to the rout;
How the Tables were turn'd, when this Hero alas!
    Was himself taken up, and sent home with a Pass.
        Derry down.

To make his way over a wild Wilderness,
    He ardently strove, but in vain did he press;
On *retrograde motions* was given to frown,
    Nor Danger beheld till a Tumbrel broke down.
        Derry down.

'Twas said in the place where wise Senators meet,
    That the rebels should bend at the Minister's feet;
On such like affairs, only think how absurd,
    It must be for a Man to be worse than his word.
        Derry down.

Ye humble Addressors, who crave Blood and Slaughter,
    In readiness get to go over the water;
Your Lives and your Fortunes you've promised the King,
    I wish in the end you don't give him the fling.
        Derry down.

The Manchester Heroes, and other stout Fellows,
　For the good House of Stuart who've ever been zealous;
To deceive and betray, may call George their Defender,
　But they'd much rather fight for their King — the Pretender.
　　　　　　　Derry down.

The Man years ago, who his Country betray'd,
　Of this ruinous war is still kept at the head;
And whilst he is scheming, and dreaming of wonders,
　Each Season brings on a succession of Blunders.
　　　　　　　Derry down.

THE PLAYERS' MARCH
On information being laid for performing
[MS: 1782]

FOR the March every Son of the Buskin prepare,
The longer we tarry, the worse we shall fare;
Since labour we cannot, nor suffer'd to play,
What have we to do but scamper away?
　　Sing Tantararara hard case.

From Covent and Drury, the North and the West,
With hearty intentions of doing our best;
By Engagement we came, each with Cash in his Fob
But how to get back again — there lies the rub.
　　Sing Tantararara hard case.

So truly propitious was fortune last year,
In plenty we revell'd, and rich was our cheer;
On Ven'son we feasted, with Claret got mellow,
And each play'd the part of a good hearty Fellow.
　　Sing Tantararara brave Times.

But now only think how the Tables are turn'd
We snap at that *prog* which not long since we spurn'd;
For Justice runs rusty, and talks of a flogging,
Which makes many think 'tis high time to be jogging.

But why at our going should any complain
In a Town so divided who'd wish to remain;
For Comedy must be an unwelcome Guest
Till a patent's obtain'd and Commotion has ceas'd.

> Care our Bosoms ne'er can sting,
> If our Chiefs good Wages pay;
> And when marching — thus we'll sing,
> 'Over the Hills and far away'.

> Sturdy Beggars come along,
> Brothers of the Buskin throng;
> Here we can no longer stay,
> 'Over the Hills and far away'.

> Father Brookes and all the Train
> Fiddlers, Dancers, Grave and Gay;
> All shall aid the marching strain,
> 'Over the Hills and far away'.

> Farewell, Town to wrangling prone,
> We've no License here to stay;
> Barnshaw wet your pipes and tune
> 'Over the Hills and far away'.

THE TRIPE EATERS
[MS: 1782]

OF all the Towns in England
    For TRIPE that's fat and fair;
There is not one — I trow that can
    With BIRMINGHAM compare.
            And a-Triping we will go, &c.

When bak'd well, young, and tender
    Nor think I speak in Jest;
So rich the Food — by all that's good
    It beats a *Bailiff's feast*.
            And a-Triping, &c.

Observe what stands before us
  From Oven piping hot;
We'll on it fall — Hoofs, Heels and all,
  And fairly drain the pot.
              And a-Triping, &c.

My Worthy, in a moment,
  Hand up the Mustard cup;
For patience ne'er, is suffer'd here,
  Till all is eaten up.
              And a-Triping, &c.

The CAP is tore to pieces,
  The SELVAGE almost gone;
My Boys take care — your Elbows square,
  The work will soon be done.
              And a-Triping, &c.

The King's Beef-eating Heroes
  No doubt good Souls may be;
But neither they — nor *Majesty*
  Make better Meals than we.
              And a-Triping, &c.

The Prince of jolly Tripers
  Before he quits the cloth;
Tucks down the Belly of an Ox,
  And sups up all the *Broth*.
              And a-Triping, &c.

A Bumper to Tom Reynolds,
  His Tripe is sweet as Nuts;
And what I call — the best of all
  He gives us *Lumping Cuts*.

JOHN FREETH

THE VOLUNTEERS
Tune: *Here's to the maiden of bashful fifteen*
[MS: 1782]

BRITONS advance with a resolute mind,
  See where the COLOURS are flying;
Throw labour *aside* and give care to the wind,
  And let us our Fortunes be trying.

> Chorus
> Come my Boys come,
> Follow the Drum,
> We ne'er shall get Riches by staying at home.

Give me the Lad in his Bosom that wears
  A Heart that to grief is a stranger;
Free-hearted, fresh-looking true VOLUNTEERS,
  Knowing nothing of Sorrow or Danger.

> Chorus — Come my Boys come, &c.

Our Country commands, and we'll stand to the Test,
  Manfully, cheerful and clever;
Fear has no place in an Englishman's Breast
  'King George and old England for ever'.

> Chorus
> Come my Boys come,
> Follow the DRUM,
> We ne'er shall get riches by staying at home.

A SELECTION OF SONGS

ADMIRAL PARKER'S ENGAGEMENT WITH THE DUTCH FLEET

Tune: *Welcome, welcome, brother debtor*

[1782]

ON a summer's SUNDAY morning,
  'Ere the Sun has shown his face,
Gallant PARKER, danger scorning,
  'Spy'd a sail, and call'd to chase;
For the ACTION all get ready,
  Seeming fear no breast beset;
CHIEFS more brave, and MEN more steady,
  Never on the OCEAN met.

Now begins the deadly thunder,
  Noise and rage disturb the flood;
Bullets rending limbs asunder,
  Every deck runs down with blood;
Stout the vessels, great the slaughter;
  Many from the bloody fray,
Lay like WRECKS upon the water,
  Masts and rigging torn away.

Close and fierce began the firing,
  Briskly answering gun for gun,
Every moment lives expiring,
  Not a ship attempts to run;
Forty minutes 'bove three hours,
  Did this dreadful combat hold;
And of two contending powers,
  Which prevail'd, could scarce be told.

FAME, to honour each bold SAILOR,
  Through the world shall make it known,
On the waves, that British valour,
  Never more conspicuous shone;
From his colours no one shrinking;
  But upon the STORMY MAIN,
DUTCHMEN saw the HOLLAND sinking,
  Ne'er, alas! to rise again.

Tho' no CONQUEST great is sounded,
    Let the heart of pity crave,
Speedy comfort for the wounded,
    For the dead, a wat'ry grave!
COMMERCE, at the conflict weeping,
    Cries, 'My SONS, your rage give o'er;
Faith in TREATIES henceforth keeping,
    Close the BREACH, and war no more'.

BIRMINGHAM ALE TASTERS
Tune: *How happy a state does a miller possess*
[1782]

OF all civil officers annually chose,
There's none in the kingdom are equal to those,
Whose duty requires, little more than to rove,
And taste at the pleasure, what ENGLISHMEN love.

From Bord'sley to Hockley our PROVINCE extends,
I wish we had time to address all our friends;
Of houses all free-cost, to visit, 'tis clear,
The Number is more than are days in the year.

We carry no truncheons, our power to shew,
With government matters have nothing to do;
We drink with the common, yet rank with the best,
And like ALDERMEN live at a LOW BAILIFF'S FEAST.

Our good BROTHER OFFICERS strangers must be,
When beating our rounds, to the pleasures we see;
From office of CONSTABLE troubles ensue,
But that of a TASTER is joy the year through.

For when upon duty, as custom has taught,
We call for a TANKARD, 'tis instantly brought;
And how pleasing it is for a Landlord to say,
'You're welcome, kind sir, — there is nothing to pay'.

We visit the MARKETS, and traverse the STREETS,
Our CHIEF to assist, in adjusting the weights;
And wish 'twere the practice, in all kind of sales,
To down with the steelyards, and up with the scales.

The BUTCHERS may throw out their *marrow-bone* spite,
But reason informs us 'tis nothing but right;
For JUSTICE relying on TRUTH as her guide,
When pictur'd, has always the SCALES by her side.

Fill a bumper to TRADE, 'tis the TASTER'S request,
With plenty may BRITAIN for ever be blest;
Where discord abounds, may true friendship commence,
And BIRMINGHAM 'flourish a thousand years hence'.

BRITAIN'S GLORY

Tune: *Come then all ye social powers*

[1782]

COME ye lads who wish to shine
    Bright in future story,
Haste to arms and form the line
    That leads to martial glory.

    Chorus
Charge the MUSQUET, point the LANCE,
    Brave the worst of dangers;
Tell the blustering sons of France
    That we to fear are strangers.

Britain, when the LION'S rous'd,
    And her FLAG is rearing,
Always finds her sons dispos'd
    To drub the foe that's daring.
        Chorus — Charge the musquet, &c.

Heart of oak with speed advance,
    Pour your naval thunder
On the trembling shores of France,
    And strike the WORLD with wonder.
        Chorus — Charge the musquet, &c.

JOHN FREETH

HONOUR for the BRAVE to share
    Is the noblest booty;
Guard your coast, protect the fair,
    For that's a BRITON's duty.
        Chorus — Charge the musquet, &c.

What if SPAIN (for which she smarts)
    Forms a base alliance;
All unite, and British hearts
    May bid the world defiance.

    Chorus
Beat the DRUM, the TRUMPET sound,
    Manly and united;
Danger face, maintain your ground,
    And see your COUNTRY righted.

LORD G. GORDON'S PROCESSION
Tune: *The black joke*
[1782]

OLD ENGLAND, alas! what is come to thy sons,
Such rioting over the CAPITAL runs,
    As never was seen in the kingdoms before;
A strange set of beings as ever were found,
Or known to assemble on fair English ground,
All zealously bent, in a body rush on,
To make at *St Stephen's* their grievances known,
    Concerning the progress of Babylon's whore.

From the Fields of *St George*, when speaking, at least,
To see fifty thousand march just six-a-breast,
    The city might well in confusion be thrown;
Cockades of *True Blue* never more were display'd,
And to grace the procession, the *Bagpipes* were play'd;
A mixture more curious did never appear,
LORD GEORGE in the van, and JACK KETCH in the rear,
    'Crying, down, down, with popery down!'.

As the PEERS were assembling this RIOT begins,
Without blushing they broke the LORD PRESIDENT'S shins,
    And the BISHOPS' silk robes were shamefully tore;
From PARLIAMENT WIGS clouds of powder flew out,
For bags, and full bottoms, were bandied about,
And GERMAIN very fain would have mended his pace
When a full pot of *porter* came dash in his face,
    Who never but ONCE was so frightened before.

But heaven be prais'd, the disturbance is o'er,
LORD GEORGE safe and snug, is lodg'd in the TOWER
    Long waiting for Justice to settle the case;
From hence over BRITAIN may harmony reign,
And *London* the like ne'er experience again;
When warring abroad, divisions at home,
By beating RELIGION'S fanatical drum,
    On the kingdom has brought the greatest disgrace.

PRESCOTT'S BREECHES
Or, the old soldier's voyage to America

Tune: *The Chase of Killruddy*

[1782]

WE set sail from PORTSMOUTH on Candlemas-day,
The wind at North-east, and a moderate sea;
In forty-four hours of the Channel got clear,
And when under convoy, what had we to fear?
We stopp'd for provisions a few days at CORK,
Then making the best of our way to New York,
In less than six weeks the ATLANTIC got o'er,
And wrought in good health the AMERICAN SHORE.

For more than two months in the JERSEYS we lay,
When we'd nothing to eat, then we hasted away;
And whilst ENGLAND through, expectations beat high,
That HOWE would by thousands the REBELS destroy;

When just at those troops he had taken a peep,
Who before were compar'd to an army of SHEEP,
He took 'em for WOLVES, turn's his back, chang'd his tone,
And thought the best way was to let 'em alone.

Now up the CHESAPEAKE gently we steer,
Then back to NEW YORK, in a woundy career;
Wonders CORNWALLIS'S veterans reap,
Whilst CLINTON and WASHINGTON play at bo-peep:
I pity poor PRESCOTT, his case must be hard,
To be nabb'd in his quarters, but where was his guard?
One would think his whole CORPS must be dead or asleep,
Or he'd not been so easily hauled o'er the deep.

The chief from his bed, when commanded to rise,
With horror was struck — you may guess the surprise,
And doubtless might think, 'ere he wak'd from his fright,
When ent'ring the boat, in the dead of the night,
That the Fates had determin'd his doom so to fix,
And old CHARON was wafting him over the STYX;
More unpolite usage sure never was known,
Not to stop, just to let him his BREECHES slip on.

I wish from my heart the contention was o'er,
I long to approach my own country once more;
For plaguy hard biscuit, SALT PORK, and SOUR CROUT,
Ne'er pleasingly go down an ENGLISHMAN'S throat.
Ye beer-drinking souls, who, in moist'ning your clay,
Fight *battles*, storm *forts*, and cross *lakes* every day,
Pity the SOLDIER that's sent to these parts,
And drink to the welfare of all honest hearts.

A SELECTION OF SONGS

THE COTTAGER'S COMPLAINT
On the intended bill for enclosing Sutton Coldfield

Tune: *Oh the broom, the bonny bonny broom*

[1782]

HOW sweetly did the moments glide!
    How happy were the days!
When no sad fear my breast annoy'd,
    Or e'er disturb'd my ease;
Hard fate! that I should be compell'd,
    My fond abode to lose,
Where threescore years in peace I've dwell'd,
    And wish my life to close.
        Chorus
  Oh the TIME! the happy, happy TIME,
    Which in my COT I've spent;
  I wish the CHURCHYARD was his doom,
    Who murders my content.

My EWES are few, my STOCK is small,
    Yet from my little store,
I find enough for Nature's call,
    Nor would I ask for more;
That word, ENCLOSURE! to my heart,
    Such evil doth bespeak,
I fear I with my All must part,
    And fresh employment seek.
        Chorus — Oh the time, &c.

What little of the spacious plain,
    Should power to me consign,
For want of means, I can't obtain,
    Would not long time be mine:
The STOUT may combat fortune's frowns,
    Nor dread the rich and great;
The YOUNG may fly to market-towns,
    But where can I retreat?
        Chorus — Oh the time, &c.

What kind of feelings must that man
   Within his mind possess,
Who, from an avaricious plan,
   His neighbours would distress?
Then soon, in pity to my case,
   To Reason's ear incline;
For on his HEART it stamps disgrace,
   Who form'd the base design.

Chorus
   Oh the TIME! the happy, happy TIME,
     Which in my COT I've spent;
   I wish the CHURCHYARD was his doom,
     Who murders my content.

BRITANNIA TRIUMPHANT
On the glorious victory of April 12, 1782
Tune: *All shall yield to the mulberry tree*
[1783]

BEHOLD from afar, what glad tidings are brought,
What glorious exploits in the *Indies* are wrought;
The darling of *Neptune*, of *Britain* the pride,
Strikes terror to *France*, and her schemes has annoy'd.

Chorus
   All shall yield to thy maritime sway,
   Blest *Britannia* homage pay;
   Gallia's proud Sons shall trembling own,
   The glorious deeds by *Britons* done.

Of *Russell's* achievements, tradition may boast,
And tell at *La Hogue* how his fleet swept the coast;
But the conquest which RODNEY so nobly has won,
All the deeds of the fam'd '*Ninety-two* has outdone.
      Chorus — *All shall yield, &c.*

The late glorious war, noble conquests were made,
And *Saunders*, and *Hawke*, British valour display'd;
They fought, and they conquer'd, true glory to share,
But the Glory of RODNEY is past all compare!
          Chorus — *All shall yield, &c.*

The Sun never witness'd, 'till this rising year,
A contest so lasting, so close, and severe;
The stoutest built vessels the world e'er beheld,
To strike to the brave *British Flag* were compell'd.
          Chorus — *All shall yield, &c.*

Unpitied her folly shall *Gallia* mourn,
Her *Fav'rite* is captur'd, her *Lilies* are torn;
Her hopes are defeated, her schemes have been cross'd,
And her GRAND NAVAL CITY for ever is lost.

        Chorus
    All shall yield to thy sov'reignty,
    Blest *Britannia*, bend to thee;
    Matchless and free, thou still shalt be,
    And mistress reign of every sea.

THE FEMALE CANVASSER
On the Westminster election
Tune: *Jack the brisk young drummer*
[1783]

WHEN Charles in contest hard was run,
    And something more than drinking,
Was judg'd expedient to be done,
    To keep the cause from sinking;
The fairest Fair of Westminster,
    Her brilliant standard rearing,
The dubious kind, of votes to bind,
    Set out electioneering.

JOHN FREETH

Not more amaz'd were some than pleas'd,
    To see her Grace of Devon;
How must she strike, who looks so like,
    A Goddess dropp'd from heaven!
On common ground, when agents found
    No prospect of succeeding,
Deep game to plan, of course began,
    The art of female pleading.

'Twas in a dram-shop near the Strand,
    No matter who the keeper,
It seems the Duchess by the hand
    Had ta'en a chimney-sweeper;
Whilst glass for glass, *hob-nobbing* pass'd,
    In transports o'er his bumper,
'I must be free; a kiss', says he,
    'Will gain Charles Fox a plumper'.

The smearing of her cheek, 'tis clear,
    She not a rush regarded;
His vote was all, the joke was fair,
    And that her pains rewarded;
For when he on the hustings sprung,
    He gave the board a thumper,
Then wav'd his brush, and boldly sung,
    'I give Charles Fox a plumper'.

The Covent Garden nymphs of trade,
    Observing this manoeuvre,
For joy huzza'd, and, smiling, said,
    'Sir Cecil is done over;
Alike her study is to please,
    The port and porter-drinker;
Nor more respect a goldsmith pays,
    Than what she does a tinker'.

A group of dames, with borrow'd names,
    And dress'd in men's apparel,
Poll'd twice told o'er, and roundly swore,
    That Fox should wear the laurel;
By faces stain'd, and voices feign'd,
    Such members 'scap'd detection,
That many said, among the dead,
    There'd been a resurrection.

168

Ye scrutineers, to ease your cares,
    Away with slight objections;
Say what ye will, 'tis female skill,
    That conquers at elections;
In warm disputes the case is plain,
    And he who's much concern'd, Sir,
His fav'rite object to obtain,
    Must leave no stone unturn'd, Sir.

[In a later version of this song, first published in *The Political Songster*, 1784 (see No. 17n.), the first four lines of the third stanza read:

A May-day frolic to embrace,
    'Mongst other projects (told of)
In canvassing it seems her Grace
    A *sooty knight* laid hold of;]

THE NEW WINDOW TAX
Tune: *Master Pol, &c. in Midas*
[1783]

I'LL block up lights ere Christmas Day,
    For windows I have plenty,
And dear for daylight he must pay,
    Whose number's more than twenty;
In spite of debate — the rudder of state
    Too long has been misguided,
And mischiefs great upon us wait,
    That can't be well avoided.

I fear I soon must emigrate,
    My burdens are so heavy,
There's not a week can pass, but what
    I'm plagu'd for some fresh levy;
But wither to go, I'm puzzled to know,
    To better my situation,
For England's sake — I'll courage take,
    And wait a reformation.

Yet when that happy time will come,
    I'll not pretend to mention,
To crown the work, we must at home
    Away with all dissension;
For long as the State can furnish a bait,
    On which there's wealth depending,
The prize to gain — mankind 'tis plain,
    Will always be contending.

But hark what news from o'er the main,
    Where ELLIOT wing'd his stingers,
The Spaniards will be meddling seen,
    Yet always burn their fingers;
And once more, egad — their drubbings they've had,
    A curious tale to tell-o,
A pirate's nest — make war a jest,
    And laugh at Don Barcelo.

It cannot sure the Fair affront,
    For where's the degradation?
Tea drinking will, depend upon't,
    Come more and more in fashion;
The Window Bill — with joy will fill
    The deaf, the blind, the cripple,
When rum and tea no duty pay,
    How will the paupers tipple.

To man, tho' nature's gifts are great,
    Her laws by not observing,
The staff of life is hard to get,
    Industrious poor are starving;
Provisions to sell — tho' shameful to tell,
    For pelf howe'er ill-gotten,
Ship loads advance — and o'er to France
    They carry our beef and mutton.

I wish the State of wranglers quit,
    And moderation taught 'em,
And GEORGE, I hope, has found a PITT
    Of sound and honest bottom;
But if, in the man, deception I ken,
    Whatever ground I stand on,
I'll give him o'er, and never more
    A statesman's word depend on.

A SELECTION OF SONGS

WHIPCORD
Or, the walking stationers
Tune: *Have you not read a book call'd Tristram Shandy*
[1784]

REUBEN and Moses, two poor Walking Stationers,
  Bitter complaints to each other laid down;
Few better clad of the wide world's parishioners,
  Ever on ten toes went trudging to town;
    REUBEN says, 'MOSES,
    He's wrong who supposes,
That worse men than Israelites never wore shoes;
  Survey the affairs of mankind,
    Accounts of their actions peruse,
  And CHRISTIANS in knavery you'll find,
    More expert than the keenest of JEWS'.

MOSES says, 'REU. I'm in trade a mere novice,
  These three days I've travelled and not sold a quill;
And public report says, some men in high office,
  Have robb'd our PROFESSION, their pockets to fill;
    That those in high station,
    Have plunder'd the nation,
To prove, a man need not much logic to use;
  For if we look up at the great,
    A recent affair clearly shews,
  That amongst the grandees of the State,
    Are many worse fellows than JEWS.

'Twelve hundred good guineas for pens, ink, and paper,
  In twelve months, you'll say, is a round sum to spare;
To reap such an order, how would my heart caper,
  JEWS cannot, alas! such emoluments share;
    And then, in the rattle,
    Observe how they prattle,
About a three hundred and fifty pound bill;
  I'd turn hempen-merchant, I swear,
    Lord NORTH to supply at my will;
  For more WHIPCORD he buys in one year,
    Than would any SYNOGOGUE fill.

'WHIPCORD', says MOSES, 'is one of those articles,
   Useful that's counted, if rightly apply'd;
I've seen of the kindest sort, nine knotted particles,
   Blister the back of a Black-a-moor's hide;
      To see a good flogging,
      I long to be jogging,
For that, I'm persuaded, would well serve the land;
    At the POST was the BLUE-RIBBON'D LORD,
    Or the MAN OF THE PEOPLE to stand,
   Though flogg'd with his Lordship's own cord,
      What creature would cry — "Stop your hand"?

'In St Stephen's no doubt, since a famous intrigue, Sir,
   Their speeches must laughable be to attend;
CHARLES FOX calls his Lordship his noble Colleague, Sir,
   His Lordship calls Charles his Right Hon'rable friend;
      FOXITES and BURKITES
      And other arch hypocrites
Long seem'd to make REFORMATION their pride;
   What strange alteration time makes,
      When a fav'rable prospect they spy'd,
   They snatch'd at the gilded crown cakes,
      And the general reform threw aside'.

'Of life', ere says REUBEN, 'I reach the meridian,
   In trade, as I live, will I alter my plan;
I'll go for instructions to good SAMPSON GIDEON,
   And get myself nat'raliz'd soon as I can;
      No BAILIFF'S grim dunner,
      No LAWYER'S lank runner,
But holds a poor JEW in the rankest of scorn;
   For matters are got to that pitch,
      Half the kingdom at honesty spurn;
   And, depend on't, we ne'er shall get rich,
      Unless our RELIGION we turn'.

'My son ELEAZAR, his own recantation',
   Says MOSES 'shall read, if he'll listen to me;
I'll send him to Oxford for fresh education;
   He one day or other may CHANCELLOR be.
      For when subtle REYNARD,
      Broke into the VINEYARD,

And snatch'd at the grapes as in clusters they grew;
I found from a very slight glance,
At the maxims which statesmen pursue;
That he stands for court favour no chance,
Who is not too sharp for a JEW'.

[When this song was published in *New Ballads*, 1805, the following rubric was added:
This Song, appropriate to the present Times, was written about twenty years ago, on the *famous* Coalition, and is now printed by particular request.]

ON BLANCHARD'S AERIAL VOYAGE TO THE CONTINENT
A balloon song
Tune: *The lilies of France*
[1785?]

THE world to amaze, and keep Fancy alive,
How nobly commences the year 'eighty-five;
In *Ether's* wide field, amongst those who ascend,
To fetch news from the *Clouds*, and for glory contend;
Eclips'd the fair fame of *Lunardi* must be
For *Blanchard* and *Jefferies* fly over the sea.

From *Dover's* high cliffs how majestic the sight,
For, sure, such a scene would to *Gods* give delight!
How wond'rous to see, of bold Mortals a pair,
Ride over the *Waves* in a *Chariot of Air!*
Then tell me what heart can amazement refrain,
When men start from *Earth* and fly over the *Main!*

What can't they perform, who to work boldly set,
Invention is but in its infancy yet;
And, when with new *Worlds* we acquainted become,
Abroad as our *Aerial Travellers* roam,
To their safety we'll drink, not forgetting the *Two*,
Who first o'er the *Ocean* undauntedly flew.

To Commerce, my boys, since we all wish success,
Invention encourage, and Science caress;
As free-hearted Britons make Genius their boast,
With Lovers of *Trade*, then, let this be the toast:

Chorus
Store of wealth to the man, in an *English Balloon*,
Who carries the first *Pattern-Card* to the *Moon*.

BILLY'S QUITE TOO YOUNG
Tune: *There's na luck about the house*
[1786]

'TWAS when the odious shop-tax had
    To murmurs given vent,
And through the kingdom want of trade,
    Increas'd the discontent;
Of worthy citizens a band,
    Who found themselves oppress'd,
To G[renvill]e their thoughts would recommend,
    And thus their minds express'd.

'The servant who his country's love,
    So rapidly has lost,
Whose conduct reason must reprove,
    No longer deign to trust;
The man may wear an honest heart,
    Nor does he lack of tongue;
And doubtless may his best impart,
    But still he's quite too young.

'Your ministry once more disband,
    Nor think it bad advice;
The trading int'rest of the land,
    Will at the cause rejoice:
And may not those to public woes
    Who patiently submit,
As well be worried by a FOX,
    As swallow'd in a PITT'.

On certain PROPOSITIONS think!
    What difficulties start,
When commerce stands on danger's brink,
    It must alarm the heart!
The sturdy lads of Lancashire,
    Full six score thousand strong,
The helm to manage, all declare,
    That BILLY'S quite too young.

We grant the youthful financier,
    In industry excels,
But in his breast, too great, 'tis clear,
    An obstinancy dwells;
A paltry tax on servant maids,
    Of foes creates an host,
And may when levied — from the shades,
    Bring up Wat Tyler's GHOST.

The friends to commerce, justice says,
    Have bitter cause to frown,
With them no fav'rite ever was,
    More suddenly let down;
Then let us beg since in the case,
    The KING can do no wrong,
The reins in other hands you'll place,
    For BILLY'S quite too young.

A STROLLING BALLAD-SINGER'S RAMBLE TO LONDON

Tune: *Last week in Lent I came to town*

[1790]

THE first of April 'SIXTY-THREE,
    To London I went *budging*,
For know you all of my degree,
    Go on their Ten toes trudging;
At COVENTRY, I stopp'd to see
    If anything was wanting,
From pocket lodge — pull'd out my *fodge*,
    And straight'way fell to chanting.

And as I pass'd the Streets along,
   The people round me gazing!
Some cry'd out ''tis nobly sung,
   And worthy of our praising';
My Voice was clear, my Heart was stout,
   Then why should I repent it,
A decent penny soon I got,
   And in the Evening spent it.

Next Morning by the break of Day,
   Oh think of my good luck, Sir,
A-tramping on the broad highway,
   A TINKER I o'ertook, Sir,
Who told me that — Trade was so flat,
   That he was almost undone,
Yet on the road — with Spirits good,
   He was ganging away to LONDON.

I pleased was with Company,
   And lik'd his occupation,
Two better suited could not be,
   To travel o'er the Nation;
Where'er we come — I and my *Chum*,
   Some business have to settle,
I tramp each Town — whilst he sits down
   To mending of his KETTLE.

From DAVENTRY up to TOWCESTER,
   Together we went *jogging*,
Stop frequently, and cry 'good Sir,
   Of Gin bring us a Noggin';
But as to *prog* — where'er we jog,
   So little is our swallow,
A crust of bread — serves us for food,
   When pockets are grown shallow.

But now observe an odd affair,
   Just entering into STONY,
We met a sturdy jovial Tar,
   And seeming fraught with money;
Who cry'd 'my lad — can'st tip's a quid,
   Of nice and choice Virginia',
Quoth I 'my Blue — and welcome too,
   Without one single penny'.

He serv'd himself, then cry'd 'my boy,
   Let's tipple whilst we've leisure',
So *Tinking* TOM, the TAR, and I,
   Sat down to take our pleasure,
In flowing bowls — we soak'd our souls
   Till morning light was peeping,
When Sailor Jack — lay on his back
   Upon the ground a-sleeping.

We left the Tar to pay the *shot*,
   Then budg'd away to FENNY,
Rejoicing at our happy lot,
   As bold and bluff as any;
Through BRICKHILL past — and came at last,
   To HOCKLEY in the hole, Sir,
Where in delight — we spent the night,
   No further then would stroll, Sir.

Each house was full of company,
   Not one you'd empty find, Sir,
Upon a bed of straw we lay,
   But this we did not mind, Sir;
For 'mongst the throng — by downright song,
   So flush'd was I with treasure,
Tho' small the town — I earn'd a crown,
   By singing *The Jovial Grazier.*

Here having got a decent fill,
   Of what is call'd good liquor,
We cap the summit of CHALKHILL,
   But few could mount it quicker;
At DUNSTABLE — pick'd up a *Cull*,
   With whom we beat a parley,
Pursu'd the rig — and danc'd a jig,
   From thence in the morning early.

In MARKET STREET we make no stop,
   Nor call at Mother Dolben's;
Not tasting either bit or drop,
   Until we reach St ALBANS;
Where Brother BRASS — and I might pass,
   An hour in conversation,
Pay down our *shot* — then off we trot,
   Ne'er dwell long in one station.

JOHN FREETH

By twelve o'clock we came in sight,
 And plainly could discern it,
A place, which if my judgment's right,
 The learned call it BARNET;
Necessity press'd on me still,
 To make another rally;
For let the back go how it will,
 We must not starve the belly.

To LONDON we came safe and sound,
 But sworn at HIGHGATE both were,
Tom was for the BOROUGH bound,
 To part we very loth were;
The mind tho' nothing here controls,
 'Tis more than twelve to ten, Sir,
That such a pair of merry souls,
 Ne'er tramp the ground again, Sir.

Next morn resolv'd the town to range
 (About I must be steering)
A step I took across the 'Change,
 But nothing found worth hearing;
Of BULLS and BEARS — and lott'ry snares,
 Regardless of what fame says,
I fled from SCRIP — and took a trip,
 With speed towards St JAMES'S.

The KING was going to Parliament,
 A numerous crowd was round him,
Some huzza'd him as he went,
 And others cry'd — 'confound him!'
At length a shout — came thundering out!
 Which made the air to ring, Sir,
All in one voice — cry'd 'no excise,
 No BUTE, no Cyder KING, Sir'.

'Mongst every company I got,
 Of BARBERS, SMITHS, and BAKERS;
Chiefest tone was 'd—n the SCOT,
 And all such vile PEACE MAKERS';
Resolv'd no more — the streets to scour,
 Or here for bread to scramble,
I hasted down — to this good Town,
 So ended my London ramble.

[In an earlier version of this song, 'A ballad-singer's ramble to London', first published in *The Political Songster*, 1771, lines 5–7 of the tenth stanza have 'Trull, ... Then bilk'd her Crib' for '*Cull*, ... Pursu'd the rig'.]

BLOOD ROYAL
Tune: *Caesar and Pompey*
[1790]

A TOAST if I offer, pray do not be cruel,
I never with pistols wish'd fighting a duel;
With weapons of steel — over ducks, geese and turkeys,
Engage if I must, much the pleasantest work is;
No soul for free speaking would wish to confine me,
And thousands I know will in sentiment join me.

The blood which some boast of, from this or that quarter,
A Knight of the Thistle, or Knight of the Garter,
Was ne'er any better, or is at time present,
Than what freely flows in the veins of a PEASANT;
'Twixt that of a MONARCH and that of a BEGGAR,
When shed to distinguish a DOCTOR 'twould stagger.

When LENNOX'S courage was put to the trial,
He levell'd his pistol, and shot at Blood Royal;
And sanguine the world would have thought his desire,
A BISHOP and DUKE had he kill'd at one fire;
I mean not to question His HIGHNESS'S spirit,
But why not a LENNOX as good blood inherit.

'Tis not at all times that birds meet of a feather,
The high and the low will by chance mix together;
NELL GWYNN who cry'd 'oysters' — and often apply'd to,
The blood of a STUART was closely ally'd to;
Nay ENGLAND'S first KING who was famous in action,
If hist'ry speaks truth was of spurious extraction.

Whatever their birth, or whate'er their employment,
The lovers of friendship, and social enjoyment,
Who order and decency pay due respect to,
To what I here offer will never object to,
'May the heart that is honest live always in clover,
And freedom of sentiment spread the world over'.

BOTANY BAY
Tune: *A cobbler there was*
[1790]

AWAY with all whimsical bubbles of air,
Which only excite a momentary stare;
Attention to plans of utility pay,
Weigh anchor and steer towards BOTANY BAY.

Let no one think much of a trifling expense,
Who knows what may happen a hundred years hence;
The loss of America what can repay?
New colonies seek for at BOTANY BAY.

O'er Neptune's domain how extensive the scope!
Of quickly returning how distant the hope!
The CAPE must be doubled, and then bear away,
Two thousand good leagues to reach BOTANY BAY.

Of those *precious* souls which for nobody care,
It seems a large cargo the kingdom can spare;
To ship a few hundreds off make no delay,
They cannot too soon go to BOTANY BAY.

They go of an island to take special charge,
Much warmer than Britain, and ten times as large;
No Custom-house duty, no freightage to pay,
And tax free they'll live when at BOTANY BAY.

This garden of Eden, this new promis'd land,
The time to set sail for is almost at hand;
Ye worst of land-lubbers, make ready for sea,
There's room for all about BOTANY BAY.

As scores of each sex to this place must proceed,
In twenty years time — only think of the breed;
Major Semple, should Fortune much kindess display,
May live to be king over BOTANY BAY.

For a general good, make a general sweep,
The beauty of life is good order to keep;
With night-prowling hateful disturbers away,
And send the whole tribe into BOTANY BAY.

Ye chiefs who go out on this naval exploit,
The work to accomplish, and set matters right;
To IRELAND be kind, call at CORK on your way,
And take a few WHITE BOYS to BOTANY BAY.

Commercial arrangements given prospect of joy,
Fair and firm may be kept ev'ry national tie;
And mutual confidence those who betray,
Be sent to the bottom of BOTANY BAY.

JOHN WESLEY'S PROPHESY
Tune: *St David's Day*
[1790]

THAT sage Divine, JOHN WESLEY, says,
(I'll not the point contend)
In eighteen hundred, thirty-six,
The World will have an end.

Of those uncommon lengths that go,
Who gospel truths peruse;
I ask no more than just to know
From whence he gets his News.

The confirmation may wait,
And some to ease their fears,
Say no such News from Heaven yet,
Has reach'd the Bishop's ears.

JOHN FREETH

Few Priests which must from hence be hurl'd,
    But longer time would crave,
And many say, a better World
    They never wish to have.

Change Brokers, whether young or old,
    Religion never shocks,
Or this foreknowledge greatly would
    Have tumbled down the Stocks.

When England's Lords and Commons have,
    With Warren Hastings done;
For want of time 'tis thought no more
    State Trials will come on.

What strange confusion will be seen,
    What fear the mind betray,
When men to save their souls begin,
    Estates to give away.

The Lawyers of their fees bereft,
    Will all look wond'rous thin,
Of parchment, when no time is left
    To fill another skin.

The plough will rest, the arts be dead,
    Each author drop his quill;
And not a creature stand in need,
    Of Esculapian skill.

To banking houses, sweep-soots then,
    Will all go uncontroll'd;
Neglected throw their black flour by,
    And fill their bags with gold.

The buskin heroes to a man,
    The world whilst Atlas props;
Will live as gaily as they can,
    Until the curtain drops.

Since Father Time so very soon,
    His bottom must wind up;
With dry lips rather than lie down,
    Replenish every cup.

Then let to crown our evening's mirth,
 A toast to those go round;
Of every sect throughout the earth,
 Whose hearts are true and sound.

[In a later version of this song, published in *A Touch of the Times*, 1803, stanzas six and nine have been omitted, and in stanza five 'Jew' has been substituted for 'Change'.]

SONG ON THE REGENCY BILL
Tune: *As I was driving my waggon one day*
[1790]

THE huntsman who goes to the fields with his hounds,
Though healthy at all times can't keep them in bounds,
And should his pursuit a misfortune o'ertake,
The yelpers are sure strange confusion to make.

Just so at the helm, when affairs are not right,
For treasury trumps, men are ready to fight,
And PITT I'm afraid who has earn'd honest fame,
Must throw down his cards and retire from the game.

In the popular days of JOHN WILKES, 'tis well known,
When the rights of election were trampled upon;
On politic ground, FOX a champion stepp'd forth,
And the people he then call'd 'the scum of the earth'.

In them, say what trust can the kingdom repose,
Who merely from envy just measures oppose?
As clear it appears as the sun at noonday,
For places — they'd all become Vicars of Bray.

The Regency Bill sorely hurts, but alas!
Necessity pleads, the restrictions must pass;
For mark to his Highness what SHERIDAN said,
''Tis better to have half a loaf than no bread'.

JOHN FREETH

'Twould be wrong not to mention LLANDAFF'S grave divine,
The subject he treated, and twisted so fine;
In earnest the House would have thought he appear'd,
At Lambeth had he not so wishfully leer'd.

Ye wranglers five years who've been laid on your backs,
By chance of the spoil when you come in for snacks;
The loaves divide nicely, and give if you can,
The Northumberland greyhound a sop in the pan.

When BURKE pays the troops, and his friends give him joy,
Of the King's goodness speak, and he'll make a sham cry,
For EDMUND a Jesuit's part plays as true,
As every old MACKLIN play'd Shylock the Jew.

No son for his sire that retains real love,
Confidential old servants would wish to remove,
A brimmer then fill — and with freedom give round,
'The man true and firm to his trust that is found'.

THE BIRMINGHAM OVERSEERS
Tune: *How happy a state*
[1790]

WHILST friendship I boast of, and truth is my guide;
Of Birmingham's welfare to sing is my pride;
Nor is there a town if we search the land o'er,
That pays a more decent regard to the poor.

OVERSEERS the good things of the world love to taste,
Of the present to speak — not forgetting the last;
Unanimity through the whole business appears,
For why — they were all in the cause VOLUNTEERS.

Years ago vestry-meetings unpleasant were found,
But now the proceedings with pleasure are crown'd;
Alteration took place in the year 'eighty-five,
And the spirit of office is still kept alive.

A SELECTION OF SONGS

Tune: *St David's Day*
Some years ago, the case was such,
And such the seeming fear;
The Tradesmen then was anger'd much,
When chosen OVERSEER.

The Scene is changed — no matter how,
No fear the mind besets;
And he much favour'd must be now,
That into office gets.

So free a spirit is gone forth,
I will be bold to say;
CERTIFICATES in real worth,
Are sinking every day.

For Volunteers their zeal to shew,
So cheerfully advance;
That twice this office to go through,
There is no kind of chance.

And social mirth and harmony,
Have taught us to believe;
The next that wish O'erseers to be,
Must handsome premiums give.

Tune: *Welcome, welcome*
From the sumptuous living met with,
From the joys that freely flow;
Think what grief our bosoms beat with,
Out of the place when forc'd to go;
Pity any fond connexion,
Should distress of mind bring on;
When convinc'd on cool reflexion,
That our duty we have done.

Come then every social brother,
Give our drooping spirits ease;
Lasting friendship for each other,
Shall the troubl'd mind appease;
Hard as some may think our case is,
'Ere twelve months upon us steal,
Those good souls who fill our places,
Grief as great as ours may feel.

185

JOHN FREETH

Tune: *'Twas at a place call'd Dover in Kent*
Trace all the towns the Kingdom round,
  One, only one, stands fair to view;
Where sixty thousand souls are found,
    Govern'd by only CONSTABLES two;
      Whilst levies eight,
      The work complete,
Who of the management can complain;
      To serve the community,
      Let love and unity,
Through the whole troubles of office reign.

Fill the balloon bowl to the brim,
  Every one his glass supply;
Hearts that have gain'd our warm esteem,
    Must not be pass'd unnotic'd by;
      Good friends to toast,
      Is freedom's boast;
Let tribute of true respect be shewn,
      To MAGISTRATES duly,
      Who act, and act truly,
From motives of friendship to serve the TOWN.

BIRMINGHAM must — (whose fame shall ring)
  Second in size to LONDON be;
Every month fresh houses spring,
    Every year new streets we see;
      Whilst health remains,
      And plenty reigns,
We'll drink in a bumper of hearty cheer,
      'Of friendship the lover,
      And all the world over,
To every worthy OVERSEER'.

THE COACH DRIVERS
Or, Billy's not too young

Tune: *The dusky night*

[1790]

THE good old coach, BRITANNIA, still
    Jogs merrily along,
And manag'd well will always fill,
    Tho' BILLY is *but Young*.

Right heart of Oak's the axle-tree,
    And what much makes it fam'd,
The BASKET and the BOOT we see
    With precious budgets cramm'd.

In sixteen hundred eighty-eight,
    'Ere gamblers dealt in stocks;
The COACH broke down — the DRIVER dropp'd
    Dead weight from off the BOX.

A DUTCHMAN lent a lifting hand,
    The wheels again went round,
And have not Dutchman from this land
    The like assistance found?

The second GEORGE his steeds to drive,
    Much us'd the PELHAM bit;
But passengers in general prize
    No name like that of PITT.

Lord NORTH, who too far westward ran,
    In mist and mire long beat,
A WHEEL dropp'd off, and he was then
    Oblig'd to quit his seat.

Old CHATHAM'S fame in high degree,
    On record long shall stand,
A COACHMAN good and true was he,
    As e'er took whip in hand.

JOHN FREETH

The arduous task his son befell,
    A YOUTH who, like a SAGE,
Holds tight the reins — and drives as well
    As those of twice his age.

Three years ago, when burdens cloy'd,
    Through Britain all the Song,
(With judgment nice the reins to guide)
    Was 'Billy's quite too young'.

For when on trade he laid his strokes,
    The land with clamour rung!
And wealthy CITS, with angry looks,
    Cry'd 'Billy's quite too young'.

'Tis clear from last St STEPHEN'S wake,
    In spite of all the din,
GEORGE will not with his COACHMAN part,
    Nor change his WHIPPER-IN.

For wear and tear, tho' dear we pay,
    The SPRINGS continue strong,
And now to drive us, thousands say,
    That 'BILLY'S not too young'.

Drive on, *Old Boy*, thy skill is known,
    Still whirl the WHEELS along,
Till OPPOSITION fairly own,
    That BILLY'S not too young.

THE DIVERSION OF QUOITS PLAYING
Tune: *The hounds are all out*
[1790]

MANKIND will their favourite pleasures pursue,
    The Mind must be ever employ'd;
The Fancy to please is the Motive in view,
    And each will his Hobby Horse ride — my brave Boys.

A SELECTION OF SONGS

Some take up their Bats, and the Cricket ball bang,
　　Some brisk in the Fives Court are seen;
Of the Sports of the Field many fondly harangue,
　　And some boast the Sports of the Green.

Amusements are fashion'd for every age,
　　And Novelty pleasure excites;
But we in that old rustic pastime engage,
　　The manly Diversion of Quoits.

The Britons of old by this practice we know,
　　The Brave to the Field did invite;
The same nervous Arm that could twang the long Bow,
　　Was accustom'd to throw the broad Quoit.

　　　Tune: *Hark, hark away*

　Come, come my Boys to sport away,
　With pleasing Games we'll crown the Day;
　Follow your Sire[1] ye Social Throng,
　See how alert he trips it along;
　　　　The wisest Man,
　　　　From Nature's plan,
　Who pictur'd Life was pleas'd to say, Sir,
　　　　For every Class,
　　　　There always was,
　A Time to work, and a Time to play, Sir.

　The Clock's struck four, the Game begin,
　Longer to dally 'twere a Sin;
　Off with your Hat, for Partners throw,
　Off with your Coats, your best to do;
　　　　Equally match'd,
　　　　That's widely pitch'd;
　Strive with more edge to ground your Pieces;
　　　　Room enough yet,
　　　　One lucky hit,
　Makes full amends for twenty Misses.

　Cheer up my Boy, exert your strength,
　Study to find a proper length;
　Mind your next piece, be sure be straight,
　The best by chance are sometimes beat;

189

JOHN FREETH

Good, good again,
That makes us ten;
Who at such play can ever grumble;
Fortune forbear,
What luck is there!
See how those Trinkets[2] roll and tumble.

Now to the Contest close attend,
And this will be a glorious end;
Seven good Quoits the Hob surround,
Not one three inches from it found;
A Toucher here,
Another there,
Drops within the breadth of a Finger,
Who more can do,
That noble throw,
Crowns the Game with a double Ringer.

Lucre our object cannot be,
For Pence a piece we only play;
Tho' but a trifle still the Game,
From all can strict attention claim;
The Feather's fled,
The Hob lies hid,
Close to the Ground the Pieces pin it;
Drawing so near,
Many would swear
The virtue of the Loadstone's in it.

Finding by chance the Weather wet,
Why then we under cover get,
Handing the friendly Cup about,
Until we've drunk the Jorum out;
Cheerful and gay,
Drink down the Day,
Joining in pleasant Conversation;
Hearty and true,
All Summer through,
This is our weekly Recreation.

1.   The Father of the Society, a worthy Character, who plays with alertness though in the eightieth Year of his age.

2.   Very small Quoits.

A SELECTION OF SONGS

LORD MACARTNEY'S EMBASSY TO CHINA
A Warwickshire ballad
[1793]

WHILST busy minds are o'er and o'er,
  The Rights of Man declaring;
The Eastern regions to explore,
  MACARTNEY is preparing;
A *fête* so grand the heart would sting
  Of Russia's proud Czarina,
To see a British General greet
  The Emperor of China.

The noble hero to escort,
  Such pride the mind bewitches,
The favourite cry, is — 'that's your sort';
  And when he Pekin reaches,
Like Solomon — so fame relates,
  He'll seem (if true the story)
When rushing from his temple gates,
  In all his pomp and glory.

From sordid views, however warm,
  Are modern speculators,
And tho' the kingdom seems to swarm
  With inland navigators;
Not one of these will dare to brave,
  The ocean wide and briny,
Lest they should find a watery grave,
  Before they get to China.

What pleasure here must tradesmen feel,
  For toil how 'twill requite 'em,
When calls for goods of brass and steel,
  Are brought — *ad infinitum*;
With fancy buttons, soft or hard,
  Gilt, silvered, or platina,
'Twill take an age to pattern-card
  The vast empire of China.

JOHN FREETH

Should building ten more centuries,
    Keep rapidly increasing,
The land be blest with tranquil joys,
    And commerce never ceasing;
The town of Birmingham will reach
    The banks of fair Sabrina,
And larger then than Pekin be,
    The capital of China.

As fancy o'er the world will roam,
    In martial scenes delighting,
Should Asia half as fond become,
    As Europe is of fighting;
The Poles with more than common joy,
    Would cross the river *Dvina*,
To see old Kate well basted by
    The Emperor of China.

That Britain has her summit gain'd
    Is all an idle notion;
Her wealth will more and more extend,
    Whilst mistress of the ocean;
Then let us sing in Freedom's land,
    Vivant Rex et Regina,
The British Tars, Macartney, and
    The Emperor of China.

PATENTEE PADS
Tune: *An old woman clothed in grey*
[1793]

FALSE emblems which *Actresses* wear,
    (Whatever the fancy bewitches)
To many as awkward appear,
    As Frenchmen would seem in Dutch breeches;
Our good English matrons with glee,
    Would chat about lasses and lads,
But anger'd would much be to see,
    Or hear any talk of *Twin pads*.

However eccentric the mind,
　　'Tis hop'd all such farcical scenes,
Will be to their province confin'd
　　Us'd only by tragical Queens;
For what great delight can be found,
　　In striving to seem plump and jolly;
Sure fashion in life's giddy round
　　Has now reach'd the summit of folly.

In Fleet Street the London prints say,
　　A scene of high humour occurr'd;
A lady stopp'd short on the way,
　　And help — speedy help was the word;
An *Accoucheur* was sent for in haste,
　　That proper relief might be had,
When just as her stays were unlac'd
　　On the floor dropp'd a fine chopping *Pad*.

So truly prepost'rous of late,
　　Theatrical ladies have been!
The *Pads* so much gazing create,
　　There's not a *Cork rump* to be seen;
Some say *Women's rights* 'tis invading,
　　Such sham swelling garb to put on,
For how about false bills of lading,
　　Can ships by their rigging be known.

Ye fair who adorn Britain's Isle,
　　Disdain to fall into the rage;
Such whims of the brain a short while,
　　May tend to make sport on the stage;
Let truth be the grand regulator,
　　Keep close to the bosom — what glads,
The sound honest dictates of nature,
　　A blaze make of *patentee pads*.

JOHN FREETH

ALARMS OF WAR IN THE SPRING OF 1794
Tune: *All of them Kings in their turn*
[1798]

THE Spring is commencing with dire alarms!
A million of people are now in arms;
For Gallican stubbornness still defies,
The power and skill of the brave Allies.

Chorus
Instead of its ceasing — the rage is increasing,
And who can tell when it will end.

In Flanders, when fighting in former days,
For Slaughter what were they compar'd to these?
With MARLBOROUGH, TALLARD, and
PRINCE EUGENE,
One general action clos'd each campaign.

Chorus
But good luck, or bad luck — where one blow was then struck,
There now has been more than ten.

Last Season betwixt the *Loire* and the *Rhine*,
By Bayonet, Gun, and the Guillotine,
More blood has been spilt, I presume, by far,
Than in all the Battles of QUEEN ANNE'S war.

Chorus
Yet 'stead of its ceasing, &c.

To Kingdoms' partition, despotic game,
With Russia and Prussia has been the aim;
At *Pilnitz* in Council a plot was laid,
Poor *Poland* 'twas thought no crime to invade.

Chorus
But all Mischief Aiders — and daring Invaders,
'Tis hop'd their deserts will receive.

194

A SELECTION OF SONGS

The Dutch have been plaguily tarr'd and teas'd,
The Danes and the Swedes cannot rest well pleas'd,
For fear the Colossus of Female Souls,
Should serve them the same as she serv'd the Poles.

Chorus
But spite of their scheming — harangues, and exclaiming,
    Old Kate was too deep for them all.

The World is a Theatre — War's a Trade,
And 'All in the Wrong' is frequently play'd;
What's Life but a dance — and in reason's spite,
Not one in a million steps always right.

Chorus
Great Prussia's Commanders — who once danc'd to Flanders,
    A turn-about Jig have commenc'd.

The OUTS will perpetually make a rout,
Till overtures start for a turn about;
They cry up Reform, and warmly exclaim,
PITT, RICHMOND, and PORTLAND, have done the same.

Chorus
But getting snug places — they put on new Faces,
    And left their old Friends in the lurch.

All Europe is now in a strange uproar!
And much I'm afraid we shall all be poor;
As many declare their ALL is at stake,
The ALLS as they stand, in the lump to take.

Chorus
There's SAVEALL and SLAYALL — Old England is PAYALL,
    And ALL is a comical scene.

JOHN FREETH

MORE GUINEAS, AND LESS PAPER CREDIT
Tune: *Mrs Casey*
[1798]

THROUGH serious doubts, and sad distrust,
    Have many minds been troubled,
The Merchants feel a sore disgust,
    And Tradesmen's fears are doubled;
However fam'd, however great,
    The Bank of England's power,
For Trade no current cash can beat,
    What's issued from the Tower.

Chorus
Then let good Guineas more abound,
   The Land at large has said it,
And true it is, the Kingdom round,
   There's too much paper credit.

Since Germany has drain'd the Land,
    Of Guineas so much wanted,
The Traveller from hand to hand,
    Finds various Notes presented;
He looks at that, he looks at this,
    Perhaps not one in ten, Sir,
Will suit him — then the language is,
    'I beg you'd call again, Sir'.
        Chorus — *Then let good Guineas, &c.*

Bank Bills 'twill be confess'd by all,
    Are useful, light, and pretty;
But counterfeits where'er they fall,
    The consequence is weighty;
Since paper has such havoc made,
    From so much overflowing,
Sure Government, for sake of Trade,
    Will set the Mint a-going.
        Chorus — *Then let good Guineas, &c.*

New pictures of his Majesty,
    So beautifully shine-o,
There's nothing captivates the eye,
    Like full-weight ready rhino;

The Silver coin is mostly base,
    (Each Knave the public fleeces)
Of Copper little good we trace,
    Save BOULTON'S penny pieces.
        Chorus — *Then let good Guineas, &c.*

Old Sages who but little drink,
    And are at all times heedful,
Will tell you he who holds the chink,
    Enjoys the one thing needful;
From what the best of laws decree,
    However some have wander'd,
That pure and solid coin give me,
    The true old Tower Standard.
        Chorus —*Then let good Guineas, &c.*

Till now was ABRAHAM NEWLAND'S name,
    Throughout the Land respected,
And long had London's City Dame,
    With strictest prudence acted;
But when the amorous MINISTER,
    The good old Lady ravish'd,
To keep alive the German war,
    Uncommon Sums were lavish'd.

    Chorus
And thus the wheel of Life goes round,
  As year on year advances;
And trade by all, 'tis clearly found,
  Too much a game of chance is.

ON ADMIRAL NELSON'S VICTORY
BRITANNIA TRIUMPHANT
Tune: *All shall yield to the mulberry tree*
[1798]

FROM the MOUTH of the NILE, flush'd with glory, behold!
What tidings are brought, and how pleasingly told;
The darling of Neptune, of Britain the pride,
Strikes terror to France, and her schemes has annoy'd.

JOHN FREETH

Chorus
All shall yield to thy sovereignty,
Bless'd BRITANNIA *bend to thee;*
Gallia's proud sons shall trembling own,
The glorious deeds by Britons done.

Of Russell's achievements traditions may boast,
And tell at La Hogue how his fleet swept the coast;
But the conquest which Nelson so nobly has won,
All the deeds of the fam'd 'Ninety-two has outdone.
    Chorus — *All shall yield, &c.*

The Sun never witness'd till this happy year,
A contest so lasting, so close and severe;
The stoutest built ships, Egypt ever beheld,
To strike to the brave British flag were compell'd.
    Chorus — *All shall yield, &c.*

Unpitied, her folly shall Gallia mourn,
Her *tri-colour'd streamers* are terribly torn!
Her FAVOURITE is lost, the grand scheme's overthrown,
And her much boasted fleet to destruction is gone.

Chorus
All shall yield to thy sovereignty,
Bless'd BRITANNIA *bend to thee;*
Matchless and free, thou still shalt be,
And mistress reign of every sea.

ON THE UNCOMMON DEARNESS OF CORN
Tune: *Merry sons of freedom push about the pitcher*
[1798]

THE year 'Ninety-five of all others to mention,
Will long be recorded for rage and dissension;
All States are convuls'd — 'tis the age of delusion,
And Europe was never in greater confusion.

Chorus
Is it not alarming! Can it stand to reason?
That people should starve in a plentiful season.

198

Royal Debts and Rioting cause much consternation!
Fighting for we scarce know what, brings on desolation;
Commotions will spring up, from hunger — for truly,
When robb'd of the Staff of Life, Men will be unruly.
  Chorus — *Is it not alarming, &c.*

A scarcity was sounded, the crisis was trying,
And dearer Corn became from the eagerness in buying;
But they who the cause impartially examine,
Now tell us 'twas all an artifical Famine.
  Chorus — *Is it not alarming, &c.*

At more than one Guinea per strike, some retail'd it,
The oldest men living, with wonder beheld it!
Yet still from dark holes, where many had consign'd it,
A deal might been had — but Money was to find it.
  Chorus — *Is it not alarming, &c.*

It Providence has pleas'd a good harvest to send us,
Yet Bread still is dear, tho' the Seasons befriend us;
Some broach the word CONSCIENCE, by way of digestion,
But Conscience it seems is kick'd out of the question.
  Chorus — *It is not alarming, &c.*

Our *Prelates* say but little — our *Prophets* much are slighted,
The people more with plays than preaching are delighted;
And *Christians* there are, who for Interest will rush at —
Those things which a TURK or a PAGAN would blush at.
  Chorus — *Is it not alarming, &c.*

At the helm of the State, let who will have direction,
I trust to my Toast there will be no objection;
For Peace a desire, may the Great be possess'd with,
And a LARGE LOAF for Sixpence, the people be bless'd with.

  Chorus
Ever may the Friends to good order live quiet,
And never may the poor any cause have to riot.

JOHN FREETH

THE TARS OF OLD ENGLAND
(Written on the day the news came of Lord Howe's victory)
Tune: *Heart of Oak*
[1798]

TO Old England's glory, behold from the West,
What tidings are brought, and how fondly express'd;
Fair Fame sounds her Trumpet, again to make known,
What deeds on the waves have by Britons been done.
Chorus
Peace and Plenty's our wish, but as Lords of the Main,
On every commotion,
When call'd to the Ocean,
Our Wrongs we'll revenge, and our Rights we'll maintain.

Our Leader, whose skill and whose courage is good,
Years ago with brave Hawke, found to vict'ry the road;
The land rings with general plaudits of joy,
His merit shall rise and malignity die.
Chorus — *Peace and Plenty, &c.*

The French by our thunder were quickly struck dumb,
The conflict was rapid — and ages to come,
Will tell what a caper they cut to the tune,
Of BRITONS STRIKE HOME! on the first day of JUNE.
Chorus — *Peace and Plenty, &c.*

Of the Line, Six were captur'd — how glorious the day,
Two went to the bottom, not one wish'd to stay;
The *tri-colour'd Streamers* compell'd were to bow,
They soundly were drubb'd, and paid dear to know HOWE.
Chorus — *Peace and Plenty, &c.*

That Bugbear Invasion is now done away,
For Britons are Masters, and will be at Sea;
Push the goblet about, and we'll toast as we sing,
Our Fleet and our Armies, our Country and King.
Chorus
When the Lion is rous'd and to Arms Britain calls,
At France when at variance,
'Tis known by experience,
Our surest defence is our stout Wooden Walls.

BULL-BAITING
Tune: *Jolly mortals fill your glasses*
[1803]

BY the poor — hard times forgetting —
   Hours of gladness will be spent,
Being well assur'd bull-baiting
   Sanction'd is by Parliament.

Old athletic games pursuing,
   Which the rights of nature crave,
Keeps the vital spirits glowing,
   And fresh vigour gives the brave.

Yielding due subordination
   To the laws the State which guard,
Why of rustic recreation
   Should a poor man be debarr'd?

Coal-pit lads in every station,
   Of your pastime make the most,
Windham shall, on this occasion,
   Be the colliers' favourite toast.

Turn the Shropshire brindled bull out,
   Tie him strongly to the stake,
They shall see who stop the whole out,
   Noble sport next Madeley wake.

Severn-bred fresh-water sailors,
   O'er their cups who cheerly sing,
Leap for joy, like sturdy nailors,
   At the sound 'a ring, a ring'.

Bull-dogs now shall gain high credit;
   They who prize them for their blood,
Say the very best are bred at
   Wyrley Bank and Dudley Wood.

For the choicest puppies send off,
   (Justice winks at trivial crimes)
When the war is made an end of,
   Then there will be ranting times.

JOHN FREETH

When to sport the bull-dog hastens,
　Him you'll find — as truly told —
Like a placeman when he fastens,
　Plaguy loath to quit his hold.

Though grave senators may soften
　Blunders which they sometimes make,
No bull-baiting beats what often
　Happens at St STEPHEN'S wake.

PEACE AND PLENTY
Tune: *As I was driving my waggon*
[1803]

THE tables are turning — there's cause to rejoice,
Better times, never fear, we shall have in a trice;
From a happy event which has just taken place,
Joy sparkles in every true honest face.

Of seasons for more than a century seen,
Eighteen hundred and one the most fruitful has been;
No eye ever witness'd more beautiful crops,
Of wheat, oats, and barley, pears, apples, and hops.

With acorns and nuts, oak and hazels abound,
Of potatoes abundance are ev'rywhere found;
And a roasted potato, when butter is plenty,
If good of the kind may be counted a dainty.

But tho' through the kingdom all people allow,
Nature's blessings did never more bountiful flow;
Of but little avail is a plentiful crop,
If monopoly every blessing locks up.

In both town and city — nay, everywhere,
Our markets too much like 'Change Alley appear;
Corn-brokers become of fair traders the scoff,
And no matter how many lame ducks *waddle* off.

Navy contracts no longer the country can glean,
Twenty thousand fat hogs countermanded have been;
To lovers of pork joyful news this must be,
For a spare-rib has long been a rare-rib to see.

Speculators in grain surly faces may make,
Sudden death may await those who've made a deep stake;
But humanity pleads — bloody conflicts are o'er,
And strangers to war may we be evermore.

BONAPARTE'S CORONATION
Tune: *Religion's a politic law*
[1805]

HASTE, haste to the grand RAREE-SHOW,
   And join the magnificent train,
Perhaps the whole century through
   The like may not happen again;
Old and young, rich and poor, trip away,
   Ambition will not be restrain'd,
NOTRE DAME until this present day
   Such a motley tribe never contain'd.

So uncommonly great was that splendour,
   If true what the Paris prints tell,
King SOLOMON'S Temple for grandeur
   The TUILERIES could not excel.
Crowning monarchs of old, howe'er grand,
   To this were but faint imitations,
Which long upon record will stand,
   The most *holy* of all coronations.

At the scene let who would be allur'd,
   From laughter some could not refrain,
When the unction his HOLINESS pour'd,
   On the head of the new CHARLEMAGNE;
At the mummery Gravity smil'd,
   Whoever might feel disappointed,
He's sure the most *promising* child
   His HOLINESS ever anointed.

JOHN FREETH

Let who will call it high Popish fun,
  Or term it a fulsome *humbug*,
There never 'twixt father and son
  Was witness'd a more loving hug.
In Rome, ages past, 'twas the fashion,
  The Pontiff's great toe to embrace,
Such a farce would degrade the great nation,
  And therefore it did not take place.

Years back, go no further than ten,
  Expiring when monarchy lay,
That word INDIVISIBLE then
  Through France had republican sway;
This news, which resounds far and near,
  Will quickly get over the main,
And I should not much wonder to hear
  The death if it were of TOM PAINE.

THE PIEBALD COALITION
Tune: *As I was driving my waggon*
[1805]

ON political ground, let who will rule the roost,
Of Patriots 'twere but a folly to boast;
A subject so stale let who will go upon,
At the shadow may catch, but the substance is gone.

Whate'er in the Senate great minds may declare,
That Treasury sweets the grand aim is to share,
Or say why parties this strange coalition,
The *piebald* connection, this odd composition.

An alliance is formed — wonders never will cease,
And the Wolves, and the Sheep, the Fox, and the Geese,
Crowd round an old Lion, much troubled in mind,
In the scramble for pow'r, wishing favour to find.

P[i]tt and F[o]x, to give Add[in]gt[o]n's party a sweat,
And two greater opposites sure never met,
Consulting, 'tis rumour'd, at midnight were got,
And the man of St MAWE'S made a third of the plot.

A SELECTION OF SONGS

'The Premier', says Charles, 'soon his quarters shall shift,
You the motion bring on, and I'll give it a lift,
'Tis not for our int'rest that wrangling should cease,
I the war always d—d, and I'll now d—n the peace'.

'Your language', says Billy, 'is certainly right,
To rout him our standards we'll freely unite;
The people may wonder, and laughter begin,
But mark the old saying — *let those laugh that win.*

'When my country was bleeding at every pore,
The Cinque Ports I took special care to secure;
The Crown my great services honour has done,
But the Cinque Ports my purpose will not serve alone.

'Matters all must allow, have been strangely arrang'd,
Since T[ie]rn[e]y and I situations have chang'd;
When we shot at each other, what soul would have thought
On this side of the House I should ever been brought'.

But in them say what trust can the kingdom confide,
Who from int'rested motives just measures deride;
As clear it appears as the sun at noonday,
For places they'd act the old VICAR of BRAY.

From Invasion tho' England has nothing to dread,
Stability's wanted, rank envy is spread,
INDEPENDENCY weeps at INTEGRITY'S fall,
And FAME justly sings *Tantarara R[ogue]s all.*

The PLAN of BIRMING

Smallbrook Street

Cold Bath

The Parsonage

Dudly Street

Worcester Street

Lea Lane

Mercer or Spicer Street

High Town

Corn Cheapen

Moor Street

Cock or Well Street

Park Street

Lloyds Square Record Mills

Over Mill Lane

The River Rea

Scale of ten perch or 55 Yards

Digbeth

Deretend

Moor Lane

In the Year 1700 Birmingham Contained 30 Streets, 180 Courts and Alleys, 2,504 Houses, 15,032 Inhabitants, one Church dedicated to St Martin & a Chappel to St John & a School founded by Edward 6th also a Dissenting Meeting Houses.

the
Edwd Digb
Member
for the Co
this Plate is hu
by their most obed
The Plate in the Possession of Dugb

Westley's **1731** *Plan of Birmingham* showing the site of Freeth's C

I/xxx. 7. 304ʰ

AM, Survey'd in the Year 1731.

To Wolverhampton & Walsall

New Hall Lane

Great Pool

To Stafford

Staford Street

Whole Hall or Steel Hause Lane

Newton Street

Hill Street or Chappell Street

Broad Street

Priory

Moor Street or Mole

Cole Hill Row

Thomas Street

Alms Houses

Land for Building

Land for Buildings

The Butts or Stafford Street

To Coles Hill

To Sutton & Lichfield

To Sutton Coldfield

rable
Peyto Esq.
liament
Warwick
Dedicated
Serv.t W. Westley

the Increase of this Town from 1700 to y.e Year 1731.
is as follows. 25. Streets. 50 Courts & Alleys. 1415. Houses.
8254. Inhabitants. together with a new Church, Charity
School. Market Crofs. & 2 Meeting Houses. for a farther account see y.e 1700